The USS ESSEX

and the Birth of the American Navy

FRANCES DIANE ROBOTTI
JAMES VESCOVI

Adams Media
Avon, Massachusetts

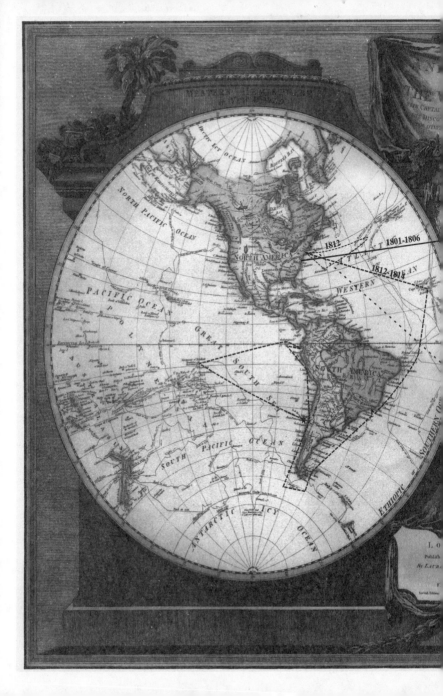

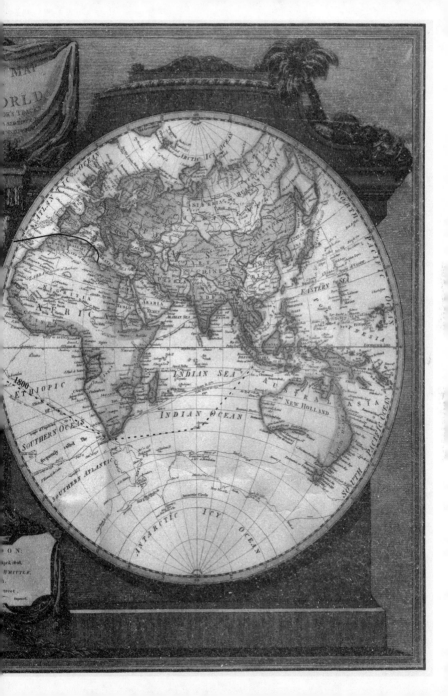

Published by
Adams Media, an F+W Publications Company
57 Littlefield Street, Avon, MA 02322. U.S.A.
www.adamsmedia.com

ISBN: 1-59337-192-6

Printed in the United States of America.

J I H G F E D C B A

Library of Congress Cataloging-in-Publication Data
Robotti, Frances Diane
The USS Essex : and the birth of the American Navy /
by Frances Diane Robotti and James Vescovi.
p.   cm.
Includes bibliographical references and index.
ISBN 1-59337-192-6 (pbk)
(Paperback originally printed with ISBN 1-58062-282-8)
1. Essex (Frigate)—History. 2. United States—History, Naval.
I. Vescovi, James. II. Title.
VA65.E7R63   1999
359.8'32'0973—dc21   98-52334
                                       CIP

This publication is designed to provide accurate and authoritative information with regard to the subject matter covered. It is sold with the understand-
ing that the publisher is not engaged in rendering legal, accounting, or other
professional advice. If legal advice or other expert assistance is required, the
services of a competent professional person should be sought.
— From a *Declaration of Principles* jointly adopted by a Committee of the
American Bar Association and a Committee of Publishers and Associations

This book is available at quantity discounts for bulk purchases.
For information, call 1-800-872-5627.

To the late Harry Hamilton,
a founder of the Nautical Research Guild
and first editor of the *Nautical Research Journal*

Contents

Cast of Characters

Enos Briggs

Shipbuilder of 850-ton man-of-war *Essex*, the finest creation of his thirty-year career. The majority of Briggs's vessels were not warships, but merchantmen sold to Salem shippers plying the lucrative East India and European trades. Among his most famous was the 342-ton *Friendship*, which traveled to such far flung places as Java, China, London, Hamburg, and Archangel.

Elias Haskett Derby

An enterprising shipping magnate, he played a leading role behind construction of the Salem frigate "to oppose French insolence and piracy." Derby became a millionaire by directing his fleet of vessels toward new and highly-profitable markets in the Far East. Among the crew on Derby's ships was Supercargo (business manager) Nathaniel Bowditch, a mathematician and astronomer, whose *Practical Navigator* (1802) has been the bible of navigation for two centuries.

Benjamin Stoddert

America's first naval secretary, he dispatched ships to fight France and the Barbary States. Stoddert, a successful Georgetown shipper, was an energetic and competent secretary, quickly getting ships to sea, establishing navy yards, and placing naval agents in important cities. He eventually resigned the office because he was disgusted with the country's vacillation toward its navy.

Captain Edward Preble

First captain of *Essex*, he was tough but fair, perfectly suited for the ship's maiden voyage around the Cape of Good Hope to Jakarta. Preble had a reputation for training young men to become competent officers, and a good many who passed under his command went on to their own notoriety. They include Stephen Decatur, Isaac Hull, and William Bainbridge (all of whom won momentous victories over British frigates during the War of 1812), Thomas Macdonough, who led the victorious U.S. fleet on Lake Champlain in 1814, and David Porter, the last captain of *Essex*.

Captain William Bainbridge

Essex's second captain, Bainbridge had a knack for resurrecting himself from blunders and went down in history as captain of *Constitution* when she defeated HMS *Java* in 1812. With her superior speed, *Java* tried twice to cross *Constitution*'s bow and rake her with cannon fire. Each time Bainbridge countered the enemy's moves, keeping the ships side-by-side. The firing soon came fast and hard.

Constitution's superior cannons eventually downed *Java*'s masts, and the British struck their flag. After sailing back to the United States, Bainbridge and his crew were decorated with medals and feted at banquets in a host of cities.

Captain Richard Dale

Commander of the first successful American squadron to the Mediterranean to protect America's interests in 1801. A Revolutionary War hero, Dale had escaped from England's Dartmoor Prison by walking out through the gates disguised as a British soldier. He fled to France and fell in with Captain John Paul Jones, who made him first lieutenant aboard *Bon Homme Richard*. That vessel fought perhaps the most famous naval battle of the war, a horrible two-hour combat against HMS *Serapis* in 1779. With the two vessels locked together, and *Bon Homme Richard* sinking, Dale led a boarding party that secured the victory.

Yusuf Qaramanli

The Bashaw of Tripoli, his seizure of merchant vessels brought American naval squadrons to the Mediterranean. Yusuf would reign for nearly forty years, all the while trying to build up Tripoli as a maritime power by expanding the navy, maximizing exports, and quelling internal revolts. His rule ended in 1835, amidst economic and political turmoil.

Captain David Porter

The bold and reckless captain of *Essex*, he led her through her glory years raiding British commerce before confronting an enemy with cannons he despised. Porter had many ups and downs in his naval career, but no one can fault him for lack of initiative and foresight. In 1815, he proposed opening relations with Japan, an idea that would not be realized until the 1850s. Porter wrote to President James Madison: "Let us visit those parts [of the world] that have been perfectly explored; search out those of which we have only traditional accounts, and traverse those parts of the ocean over which a ship has never passed." The intrepid Porter, of course, offered his services for such a mission.

Captain James Hillyar

Veteran captain of HMS *Phoebe*, he waited for David Porter to make a mistake at Valparaiso, then attacked, possibly in neutral waters. Hillyar was a modest man with a solid reputation and a daring feat to his name. In 1800, while with HMS *Niger*, he led a boarding party that swiftly captured a 20-gun Spanish corvette off Barcelona. The tale eventually found its way to Horatio Nelson. Three years later, when the two men crossed paths, the famous Admiral invited Hillyar to dine with him. "Send your boat on board, and come to me," he wrote, "for I want to have a long story from you."

Joel Poinsett

American diplomat sent to Chile to expand U.S. influence, his assistance to Chilean Rebels would earn him the moniker "the arch enemy of England." Poinsett served at various times as a congressman, secretary of war, and ambassador to Mexico and did not hesitate to use his influence to sway local politics. In 1830, when the government called him home from Mexico, he brought with him a native wild flower with brilliant red leaves, which became known as the poinsettia.

David Glasgow Farragut

The informally-adopted son of David Porter, he served aboard *Essex* as a midshipman before climbing through the ranks and becoming the Navy's first rear admiral in 1862. During the Civil War, Farragut and his stepbrother, David Dixon Porter, combined forces to capture New Orleans. The two men also went on to other victories—Porter at Vicksburg, Farragut at Mobile Bay, where he issued the famous cry, "Damn the torpedoes, full speed ahead!"

Foreword

"God and Navy, we adore in times of danger, not before. The danger past, all is requited: God is forgotten, and the Navy slighted." Once again we are hearing this lamentation from naval persons, as the American navy shrinks radically from the 600-ship navy of the Reagan years, to a number soon to be under 300. The robust military and foreign policy of the eighties of which the policy of "maritime superiority" and naval buildup was a cornerstone, was a major contributor to cold war victory. But as in every other war, victory was followed by immediate and precipitous disarmament, which very often, of itself, sowed the seeds for the next war.

Nowhere is this pattern more evident than in naval history. On V-J Day in 1945, the U.S. Navy had 105 aircraft carriers, 5000 ships and submarines and 82,000 vessels and landing craft deployed around the world, manned by experienced citizen-sailors and led by aggressive and seasoned admirals. They and their allies had conquered

Japan, delivered the liberation of Europe, and sunk the entire navies of Germany, Japan, and Italy. Yet only three years before, they had been a small force of mediocre quality, repeatedly humiliated and nearly driven from the Pacific by a superb Japanese navy, while failing to stop German submarine devastation of the Atlantic bridge. Many historians believe that "a major cause for World War II was the almost mindless quest for naval disarmament" after World War I. This indeed is the pattern of American naval history.

A uniquely effective approach to naval history is through studying the life of great capital ships. Some of the best works have used this method, focusing on such great warriors as H.M.S. *Victory*, U.S.S. *Constitution*, H.M.S. and later U.S.S. *Macedonian*. It works so well because capital ships often serve a half-century or more, spanning war and peace, readiness, and neglect, success and failure. But always they are shapers of history. In the hands of qualified writers, there is no better way to tell an important story of men and events.

Frances Robotti and James Vescovi are not naval historians, and that is a distinct advantage in this excellent new classic history of the frigate *Essex*. They bring a sense of adventure to the story, all too often missing from writers who have spent a lifetime in the field. As important, they do not presuppose a knowledge of naval jargon and lore, and, unlike Patrick O'Brian, for instance, they don't hesitate to explain in simple terms what "langradge" or "slops" are.

The *Essex* saga is not only a great tale of the sea, but it is an important source of many insights on the origins of our nation and the role of seapower in our own and the modern world's history.

After the Revolution, George Washington had said, "Without a decisive naval force we can do nothing definitive, and with it everything honorable and glorious." But the nation was very slow to follow his advice, preferring instead John Adams' warnings about going abroad in search of dragons to destroy. It was not until the Yankee traders found themselves preyed upon by the Barbary states on the one hand, and severely bullied by the French and British navies during the Napoleonic war, that an American navy was reborn. Even John Adams was converted, declaring that America must ". . . apply all our resources to build frigates, some in every principal seaport. These frigates ought not to be assembled in any one port to become an object of a hostile expedition to destroy them. They should be separated and scattered as much as possible from New Orleans to Passamaquoddy." It was from that resurgence that *Essex* was built by the citizens of Salem, of the finest white oak (far superior to the Baltic oak of the Royal Navy), and from a design tradition now well recognized as having produced the finest sailing combatants every produced.

From its commissioning, *Essex* was in the thick of making history, from the Barbary coast through the undeclared war with France, and the War of 1812 with Britain, until her capture in 1814, and subsequent recommissioning in the Royal Navy. Many of our great naval heroes served aboard her, including Preble, Bainbridge, Porter, Farragut, and the authors profile them in full color. They have done a truly masterful job in writing insightful and accurate history as great adventure. Let us hope it is the first in a series.

— JOHN LEHMAN
February 1999

John Lehman served for six years as Secretary of the Navy during both Reagan administrations and served twenty-five years in the naval reserve. He has served as staff member to Dr. Henry Kissinger on the National Security Council, as delegate to the Force Reductions Negotiations in Vienna and as Deputy Director of the U.S. Arms Control and Disarmament Agency. Dr. Lehman has written numerous books, including *Command of the Seas* and *Making War*.

CHAPTER ONE

Essex and the Young American Navy

Although we recommend taking good care of your vessel and people, yet we should deem it more praiseworthy in an officer to lose his vessel in a bold enterprise than to lose a good prize by too timid a conduct.

— CONTINENTAL CONGRESS, LETTER TO CAPTAIN
ELISHA WARREN OF THE SLOOP *FLY.*

*T*he USS *Essex*, a thirty-two-gun frigate built in Salem, Massachusetts, in 1799, was not the most glorious vessel in the history of the American navy, yet she was unique. Sailors throughout the world remarked on her speed and beauty of line, and the list of men who commanded her— Edward Preble, William Bainbridge, James Barron, and David Porter—reads like a who's who of the early American navy. She was the first U.S. warship to round the Cape of Good Hope into the Indian Ocean. Thirteen years later, she became the first American man-of-war to round the Horn into the Pacific, where her crew fought and lost one of the bloodiest sea battles in U.S. history.

Yet, *Essex* was also typical of many warships of her era. She did not go down in history as the victor in any momentous combat, like the more famous frigates *Constellation* and *Constitution*. Many of her fifteen years in the U.S. Navy were spent in ordinary, during periods when the United States faced no war and had downsized its navy. When she was at sea, *Essex* spent much of her time performing the mundane but necessary task of protecting American merchant vessels from the Barbary States of North Africa and other enemies. And like a fair share of U.S. men-of-war, she was captured and ended up in the British navy. *Essex* was an integral part of the young U.S. Navy, and her singular and ordinary qualities make her a worthy subject of study.

The U.S. Navy, now the world's most powerful and advanced, began with jumps and starts, interspersed with extraordinary milestones. The exact origin is difficult to pinpoint, but the *Gaspee* incident is a good place to start. The year was 1772, when the white oaks used to build *Essex* were growing along the Merrimac River, outside Salem. In June of that year, an armed British schooner, *Gaspee*, patrolling for colonial vessels that were violating England's Navigation Acts, was boarded from whaleboats by a group of colonial seamen led by Abraham Whipple and burned in Narragansett Bay off of Providence, R.I. Three years later, as Britain's relations with her North American colonies worsened by the day, British frigate commander Sir James Wallace discovered Whipple's role in the destruction of

Gaspee and wrote to the rebel seaman, "You, Abraham Whipple, on the 17th of June, 1772 burnt his Majesty's vessel the *Gaspee*, and I will hang you to the yardarm." Whipple wrote back: "To Sir James Wallace: Sir—always catch a man before you hang him."

Such was the spirit of the nascent American navy. From its beginnings, its officers and crew did not hesitate to thumb their noses at countries with superior firepower. The irreverent impulse seemed natural for a nation of thirteen fractured colonies who declared their independence from the strongest naval power on earth. Boldness—absolutely essential in a navy that was often short on gunpowder, cordage, and provisions—was nurtured by the country's first captains, among them John Paul Jones, Stephen Decatur Jr., Isaac Hull, and Oliver Hazard Perry. These men and their crews brought honor to a host of ships—*Bon Homme Richard*, *Constitution*, and *Niagara*—whose names are carved into American history books.

As the prospect of war heated up with Great Britain, the United States did not possess a unified navy. Rather, individual colonies were scrambling to put a few fighting ships onto the seas and rivers. The first colony to act was Rhode Island, whose legislature, after the attack on *Gaspee*, fitted out two vessels under the command of Whipple.

The first step in creating a national navy came when General George Washington—though Congress had given him command of the army only—commissioned the schooner *Hannah*, on 5 September 1775, into national service. Washington's foray into naval affairs was triggered by his army's desperate need for ammunition and other

(THE MARINERS' MUSEUM)

THE SIX-GUN AMERICAN WARSHIP *LEE* (LEFT) TAKES THE BRITISH ORDNANCE VESSEL *NANCY* IN NOVEMBER 1775. THE CAPTURE PROVIDED GEORGE WASHINGTON'S ARMY WITH MUCH NEEDED MUSKETS AND SHOT.

supplies. He had no intention of dispatching *Hannah* to take on ships of the all-powerful British navy. Rather, her mission was to capture British store ships and make haste back to port with much needed materiel.

Two months later, Washington had six vessels operating under his command, and this minuscule navy, whose crews were recruited from the ranks of the army, surprisingly met with early success. One of the richest hauls came with the capture of *Nancy* by the American warship *Lee*, under John Manly, in November 1775, accomplishing exactly what

Washington had hoped for. The *Lee*'s flag had a green pine tree on it (a common symbol on colonists' flags) and the motto "Appeal to Heaven!" Certainly, the haul from *Nancy*, which struck her flag without resistance, was a blessed one. It consisted of 2,000 muskets, 30 tons of musket shot, 30,000 round shot, 100,000 flints, and many barrels of powder. It was a quantity of munitions that would have taken the colonies a year and a half to manufacture.

A messenger bringing news of *Nancy*'s capture arrived in Philadelphia when the Continental Congress was deciding, ironically, how to round up materiel and other supplies to fight the British. The messenger knocked on the meeting room door but was ordered to wait. He persisted until he was admitted. He delivered his news. So moved was John Adams that he rose to his feet and proclaimed, "We must succeed—Providence is with us—we must succeed!"

The enthusiasm was contagious. The Marine Committee was established by the Congress and, in a milestone act, was ordered to "devise ways and means for furnishing these colonies with naval armament, *and report with all convenient speed.*" The committee consisted of seven men, John Adams among them, and soon recommended fitting out thirteen ships, ranging from twenty-four to thirty-two guns, at a cost not to exceed $67,000 each and to be ready by March 1776. Congress voted half a million dollars to foot the bill, and with that, an embryonic American navy was officially born.

The new navy was viewed by General Washington with mixed emotions. Despite the success of *Lee* and other vessels, the ragtag fleet was giving him headaches. "The plague, trouble, and vexation I have had with the crews of the armed vessels, are inexpressible," he wrote to Congress in December 1775. "Every time they come into port, we hear nothing but mutinous complaints . . . . The crews of the *Washington* and *Harrison* have actually deserted them." Washington worried that the navy would follow its own priorities and would not support his military initiatives, a fear that came to pass.

Dissension was so prevalent that the navy's first commander in chief, Esek Hopkins, was sacked soon after his appointment. Hopkins, who was being paid an annual salary of $1,500, set off in the winter of 1776 to the Bahamas—a British colony—where he seized one hundred cannons and a goodly number of supplies. It was a victory of which he could be proud. Unfortunately, Hopkins had not followed the more urgent instructions given him—to cruise off and protect the coast of Virginia. He was censured, removed from his post, and not replaced.

Despite the lack of naval cohesion, the Marine Committee strongly believed its officers should look like a unified body; so it established a code of dress. Officers cut dashing figures. Captains wore blue coats with red lapels, a slash cuff, stand-up collar, yellow buttons, blue britches, and a red waistcoat. Midshipmen were similarly attired, though not quite so colorful or elegant. As for salaries, it was established that captains commanding ships of twenty or more guns would make $60 per month, while those of ships carrying between ten and nineteen guns would take home $48. Lieutenants earned between $24 and $30, while surgeons made $25. A midshipman's salary was $12, while seamen got $8.

The navy was not America's only fighting force on the seas during the Revolutionary War. There were also privateers, defined as private armed vessels allowed by the government to cruise against merchant ships of an enemy power. Privateering—first recorded in Great Britain in 1295 during the reign of Edward I—was an important part of the American war effort because the nation had such a small navy. The advantage of privateering was that it kept merchant vessels and sailors employed during wartime, when trade lagged because shipowners were wary of sending vessels out to seas patrolled by an enemy. Even landlubbers signed up to take a berth aboard a privateer, whose commanders promised rich rewards. Handbills that circulated during the Revolutionary War asked for "seamen or landmen who desired to make their fortunes in a few months." Crewmen received a percentage of whatever they captured after the booty was sold at public auction. Anything from almonds to wine to tea to the captured vessel itself went on the block, but success was never guaranteed. Privateers sometimes cruised for months without a successful capture, and they themselves were fair game to enemy ships.

However, there were success stories. For example, Salem, one of the country's bustling ports, sent to sea over 150 privateers that made close to 450 captures. But many crews of privateers returned home with little to show for their efforts. Because they were lightly armed, privateers avoided combat at all costs. They aided a war effort but were no substitute for an experienced and well-financed navy.

America's navy, unfortunately, was neither experienced nor well financed. There were a handful of victories, many of them scored by John Paul Jones in his eighteen-gun *Ranger*. The colonists were also successful in raiding merchant shipping around the British Isles, subsequently causing a rise in insurance rates. However, in the end, America's navy was drastically outgunned and outmanned by the Royal Navy.

Of the thirteen vessels authorized by Congress in 1775, all were eventually captured or destroyed. The thirty-two-gun *Randolph* had been blown to smithereens after taking a hit in her magazine, in March 1778, during a fierce battle with the sixty-four-gun *Yarmouth*. Only four of *Randolph*'s 315-man crew survived. The thirty-two-gun *Washington* and twenty-eight-gun *Effingham* suffered more ignoble defeats. They were burned to keep them from falling into British hands. Even the battle for which John Paul Jones is most famous—his defeat of the fifty-gun *Serapis* by the forty-gun *Bon Homme Richard*—was a pyrrhic victory. Both ships were heavily damaged, and Jones's vessel soon sank. America's victory in the Revolutionary War was not secured by her own men-of-war but by French Admiral de Grasse, whose fleet appeared at the mouth of the Chesapeake Bay in October 1781 to drive away the British fleet and thus assist General Washington in the final showdown at Yorktown.

Nevertheless, victory went to the colonists, and it was time for them to move ahead with their experiment in democracy. One of the first orders of business was to reduce the armed forces. Having so recently unyoked themselves from the British, the colonists were suspicious of large armies and navies, which in times of peace were looked upon as engines for establishing despotism. To that end,

Washington's victorious army was reduced to seven hundred men. The navy, or what was left of it, was totally disbanded. The newly completed ship-of-the-line *America*, with seventy-four guns, was given to France as a thank-you gift. Another surviving vessel, the thirty-two-gun *Alliance*, was sold to a private shipper (and subsequently converted to a China trade ship) to save the cash-stricken government the money needed to repair her. A few colonies kept a handful of ships to act as a kind of coast guard, but the United States was too poor and too divided under the Articles of Confederation to contemplate maintaining a national navy.

The choice was shortsighted. As one British official observed soon after peace had been made with the United States:

> *It is not probable that the American States will have a very free trade in the Mediterranean; it will not be in the interest of any of the great maritime powers to protect them from the Barbary States. They cannot protect themselves from the latter; they cannot pretend to a navy.*

The words proved prophetic. In July 1785, two American merchant vessels, *Dolphin* and *Maria*, were captured in the Mediterranean by ships from Algiers, one of several kingdoms along the North African coast comprising the Barbary States. The rulers of these states, who reported to the Ottoman sultan of Turkey, had been blackmailing world shipping for centuries, even though they did not possess large navies. Algiers, for example, had nine ships, the largest wielding thirty-two guns, and fifty gunboats—

nothing compared to the fleets of France and Great Britain. Nevertheless, the Barbary States could demand tribute payments for a couple of reasons. For one, many countries, such as Holland and Denmark, had large and active merchant fleets but relatively small navies. It was easier for these countries to pay off Barbary rulers than to send their navies, sometimes needed to protect local interests, deep into the Mediterranean. As for larger powers, like Great Britain and France, it was less trouble to pay tribute money than expend their energy—often needed to fight each other—laying waste to Barbary cities, some of which had well-protected and well-armed harbors.

Moreover, the European states used the North African potentates to harass the shipping of their enemies. Britain employed that strategy against the United States as a form of revenge after the Revolutionary War; British diplomats stationed along the Barbary Coast let it be known that merchantmen flying the Stars and Stripes were ripe for the picking. Ships from America had no navy and were no longer protected by the British Empire, they said.

The twenty-one crewmen of the *Dolphin* and *Maria* were stripped of their clothing and valuables, taken to Algiers, and paraded past crowds of heckling citizens to prison. They were then sold into slavery and ransom was set at a phenomenal $3,000 per head. The seamen wasted away while negotiations ensued; the United States had no choice but to buy peace with the Barbary nations through annual payments. America had no navy and, in addition, was too consumed with its own domestic survival to spend much energy protecting interests thirty-five hundred miles away.

Luckily for the Americans, a subsequent war between Portugal and Algiers lessened the depredations against U.S. shipping, for a while. American vessels often sailed under the protection of Portugal, but this situation did not last long. A peace was brokered between Algiers and Portugal and, by the 1790s, captures resumed. In July of 1793, eight American merchantmen were taken during a three-week period. By November, eleven American vessels with over one hundred seamen (seven of whom would die in captivity) were in Algerian prisons. Colonel David Humphreys, American minister at Portugal, wrote to Secretary of State Thomas Jefferson, "If we are to have a commerce we must have a naval force (to a certain extent) to defend it." Humphreys's qualifying phrase "to a certain extent" is extremely telling. It shows that, despite the attacks on U.S. shipping, many government officials were still averse to the notion of creating a full-fledged navy.

Nonetheless, some congressmen had had their fill of bullying and blackmailing. In the early months of 1794, the House of Representatives passed a resolution "that a naval force . . . ought to be provided for the protection of the commerce of the United States against Algerian cruisers." The resolution, which passed by the slimmest of margins, 43 to 41, eventually led to the construction of six frigates. Three would carry forty-four guns, and three would wield thirty-six. Secretary of War Henry Knox took charge of the building project because the nation had no secretary of the navy. The six frigates (and their host cities) were *Constitution* (Boston), *President* (New York), *United States* (Philadelphia), *Congress* (Portsmouth, New Hampshire),

Chesapeake (Portsmouth, Virginia), and *Constellation* (Baltimore). To captain these vessels, the United States reached into its past and selected Revolutionary War naval figures like Samuel Nicholson, Silas Talbot, Joshua Barney, and Richard Dale.

Resistance to raising a navy continued. Americans—particularly Jeffersonian Democrats—dragged their feet on any initiatives designed to resurrect a fighting sea force. They encouraged negotiations with Algiers even while the six warships were being built. Paying tribute, they reasoned, was cheaper than raising a navy from scratch. Their logic also was fueled by a continuing wariness of militias and navies. They argued that Louis XVI, the French monarch whose head had fallen to the guillotine the previous year, had brought on revolt of the people because of his nation's costly expenses—"the king, nobility, the priesthood, the army and, above all, the navy." James Madison, who led opposition to the frigates, went so far as to suggest paying Portugal to protect U.S. shipping.

The ruling Federalist party won the shipbuilding vote but not without the compromise that work on the six frigates would cease if peace were made with the Barbary States. The dey of Algiers, after catching wind of American resolve, hastened to broker a treaty. Though he agreed to stop his nation's attacks, he made out very well under the accord, signed in July 1794. The United States agreed to pay Algiers a hefty sum of $800,000, plus annual tributes. Ironically, the treaty cost the young nation about as much as six good frigates. At the insistence of President Washington, however, three of the vessels were completed because they were nearly finished anyway. They were *Constitution*, *United States*, and *Constellation*.

There were other sound reasons for completing the frigates. Other Barbary States were now preying on U.S. shipping. Second, there was a foreboding sense among Americans that the dey himself was not wholly satisfied with his arrangement, and his future actions would eat further into the U.S. Treasury. Finally, and most significantly, American shipping was being increasingly harassed by far more threatening powers: the British and French.

As of 1793, Great Britain and France were again at war and were using American shipping as a pawn in their struggle. Each side wanted American trade but would not countenance it with the other. American merchant vessels were forced to submit to lengthy searches by the warships of both nations. Many captains were forced to stand trial and, as if to rub salt into the wound, saw their perishable cargo spoil while awaiting judicial proceedings. When their vessels were intercepted by British warships, some American sailors were pressed into the Royal Navy. U.S. Minister to France Governeur Morris hit the nail on the head when he said, "One thing I am thoroughly convinced of, that if we do not render ourselves respectable we shall continue to be insulted."

The seizures hit the port of Salem hard. The *Salem Gazette* carried account after account of depredations. For example, on 5 November 1793, the *Gazette* reported, "Captain Joshua Webb of the schooner *Polly* was robbed of $200 by a privateer flying French colors but manned by British sailors, obviously a ruse." And on 17 February 1794, it stated that "at the Port of St. Kitts, 26 Americans are libeled" (libeled meant held prisoner for transporting contraband). Other accounts reported American seamen being beaten and deprived of food. Some died in prison.

American merchant skippers attempted to adapt to wartime conditions, taking advantage of French convoys (which often sailed under the protection of French warships) when shipping goods to France and British convoys when moving goods to Britain and its colonial ports. Seizures, however, still occurred, cut profits, and threw many people out of work. In Salem, the town's sailors held demonstrations and petitioned Congress for action. It is easy to understand why towns like Salem, which relied so heavily on sea trade, would rally to support and build *Essex*.

But, that was five years away. For now, President Washington and his government tried to address problems with the English and French through negotiation. He dispatched Supreme Court Chief Justice John Jay to Great Britain to settle the seizure question, as well as other thorny issues left over from the Revolutionary War. Jay returned home with a treaty that granted many concessions to Britain, including most-favored-nation trading status. Jay also promised that America would not allow French privateers access to its ports. Thirdly, naval stores, which France needed in its war against Great Britain, were deemed contraband. The one-sided agreement, which brought temporary peace, angered so many Americans that Jay once said he could ride across the nation by light given off from his burning effigies.

If the treaty angered Americans, it enraged the French, who deemed it a slap in the face from an ungrateful nation with a short memory. Had not Lafayette helped assure the victory at Yorktown? Had not the treaty of friendship signed in 1778 made France and the United States allies in practically all matters?

The United States, however, took a pragmatic view towards its French brethren. Americans wanted no part of foreign entanglements. Having ratified a new constitution in 1787, the nation was anxious to get down to the business of commerce. Also, Americans—while feeling some solidarity with a nation that also had unyoked itself from a monarchy—were troubled by the excesses of the French Revolution, which had terrorized that nation.

American aloofness made the French resentful; they took out their revenge by issuing a broad decree on what was considered neutral trade. It stated that "every vessel found at sea, laden in whole or in part with merchandise coming from England or her possessions, shall be declared prize goods, whoever may be the proprietor of these productions or merchandise." The decree made official and government-sanctioned a policy that was already being carried out.

Future decrees got tougher. In March 1797, France declared that "every American vessel shall be a good prize which has not on board a list of the crew in proper form, such as is presented by the model annexed to the treaty of the 6th of February 1778." No American captain had followed this "model" since the end of the Revolutionary War, and the French knew it. Their intent was to harass American skippers or frighten them from taking to the seas at all.

A typical example of French harassment was recorded in the *Philadelphia Gazette* on 6 April 1797, reporting the action involving the American merchantmen *Two Sisters* and a French privateer. The American captain, whose name was Worth, was ordered aboard and asked to sign a paper written in French. Worth refused, and the captain of the privateer drew his cutlass and threatened to cleave the American skipper in two. Worth still would not budge, arguing that it was absurd for him to sign a paper written in a language he did not understand. The French captain, with his weapon still drawn, ordered two American seamen to put their names to the paper, and they complied. The seamen had signed a confession that their ship was bound for Jamaica, a British port, and the French claimed *Two Sisters* as a prize.

While such incidents heightened tensions between the United States and France, the so-called XYZ affair set the two nations on an inevitable course for war. The incident, in October 1797, came during a last-ditch effort to address problems with France. Three U.S. diplomats—John Marshall, Elbridge Gerry, and Charles Pinckney—were dispatched to Paris, where they were met by three French agents (known as X, Y, and Z) who demanded a $250,000 bribe before negotiations proceeded. The Americans refused and returned home. The newspapers reported the incident, which triggered the famous quote: "Millions for defense, but not one cent for tribute!" Depredations by France, as well as Great Britain, continued. By 1797,

Secretary of State Thomas Pickering reported to Congress that over two hundred American ships had been plundered.

In April of the following year, Congress re-established its official navy—disbanded fourteen years earlier after the Revolutionary War—by a vote of 42 to 27. The legislative act was a key turning point in the development of the U.S. Navy and the nation as a whole. America would downsize its navy in future years, but never again would the nation find itself caught without some type of national force to protect its interests on the seas.

(COURTESY: US NAVY)

A SUCCESSFUL SHIPPER FROM GEORGETOWN, MARYLAND, BENJAMIN STODDERT RELUCTANTLY BECAME SECRETARY OF THE NAVY IN 1798. HE LEFT AFTER THREE YEARS, DISGUSTED WITH THE NATION'S WAVERING ATTITUDE TOWARD ITS NAVY.

The position of the secretary of the navy was also established. The first incumbent was Benjamin Stoddert, a successful and well-connected shipper from Georgetown, Maryland. As a young man, he had joined Washington's army, despite that his father had been a captain in the British army. Benjamin was so severely wounded in the Battle of Brandywine that his injuries plagued him for the rest of his life. In 1779, he was appointed secretary to the Board of War, where he made the acquaintance of future U.S. President John Adams and other leaders. When the

American capital was being moved from Philadelphia to the outskirts of Georgetown, President Washington asked Stoddert to buy up tracts around the proposed government site to prevent speculators from doing the same and selling the land at exorbitant prices to the cash-starved U.S. government.

Despite his patriotism, Stoddert thought long and hard about taking the position as naval secretary when it was offered in May, 1798. He wrote:

> *I hate office—have no desire for fancied or real importance and wish to spend my life in retirement and ease without bustle of any kind. Yet it seems cowardly at such a time as this to refuse an important and highly responsible position . . . . You know I have managed Peaceable ships very well. Why should I not be able to direct as well those of War? After all this preface I think there is about thirty to one I shall not accept.*

Stoddert defied his own odds. The position paid $3,000 a year, not a trivial sum, but Stoddert really needed to devote time to his personal affairs, which were suffering from poor investments, rather than directing the nation's small navy. But in the end, he could not refuse President Adams. On 19 June 1798, the President administered the oath of office for a position marked by very humble beginnings. The staff, numbering less than ten, included Stoddert, an accountant, some clerks, and a messenger. Repair and equipping of ships was done through naval agents located in the country's major seaports. The agents were paid $750 per year and a 2 percent commission.

Humble beginnings aside, Stoddert's first directive to his captains proved the American navy meant business:

> *You are, hereby, authorized, instructed and directed to subdue, seize and take any armed French vessel, or vessels sailing under authority or pretense of authority from the French Republic, which shall be found within the jurisdictional limits of the United States, or elsewhere on the high seas; and such captured vessel with her apparel, guns, and appurtenances, and the goods and effects which shall be found on board the same . . . to bring her within some port of the United States.*

To put punch into Stoddert's words, Congress supplied him with more warships, authorizing President Adams to hire or purchase twelve more vessels, with none to exceed twenty-two guns. This was in addition to the six frigates authorized earlier. By 1798, the American navy possessed twenty warships. A year later there were thirty.

No formal declaration of war was made in what historians have called "The Quasi-War with France." (In fact, French Foreign Minister Charles Talleyrand, who was behind the XYZ affair, was making peace overtures before much of the fighting began.) Nevertheless, the firing commenced, with America's first naval victory coming in June 1798, when the twenty-gun *Delaware* captured a fourteen-gun privateer by the name of *Croyable*. The American captain, Stephen Decatur Sr., sent his prize back to America, where she was aptly rechristened *Retaliation*. Command of her was given to Lieutenant William Bainbridge, who would become the second captain of *Essex* in 1801. Bainbridge would have a checkered career, often redeeming himself from blunders, a pattern that began as commander of *Retaliation*.

In November 1798, while cruising off the coast of Guadeloupe, Bainbridge and his crew mistook two French frigates for British warships they had seen a day earlier. Finding himself suddenly facing the forty-four-gun *Volontaire* and the thirty-six-gun *Insurgente*, Bainbridge ordered the flag struck without firing a shot. Any action on his part would have meant utter destruction for his ship and crew. *Retaliation* was now back in French hands.

Bainbridge was taken aboard *Volontaire*, where he watched *Insurgente* pursue two smaller American warships that had been sailing with him. The French man-of-war quickly gained on the American vessels, which were no match in speed and firepower. The French captain turned to Bainbridge and asked him how many guns the American ships wielded. One ship has twelve twelve-pounders, and the other carries twenty nine-pounders, lied Bainbridge, doubling the power of the American weaponry.

The captain of *Volontaire* was stunned, never expecting such force, and called *Insurgente* off the chase. Such ruses were not uncommon. Men-of-war sometimes flew the flag of a different—usually neutral—nation in order to catch an enemy vessel by surprise. The only hard-and-fast rule of that cat and mouse game was that a ship had to be flying her true colors when her men opened fire. At fault was the French captain, who had been foolish enough to believe Bainbridge.

A few months later, in February 1799, *Insurgente* was captured by the USS *Constellation*. It was not only the first major engagement of the war but also a battle in which a future *Essex* captain, David Porter, exhibited heroism and a coolness under fire. As the battle raged, the nineteen-year-old Midshipman Porter climbed into the rigging of the foretop and, while French cannonballs whizzed past him, cut down a damaged fore-topsail yard, which was in danger of pulling down the entire mast. Had *Constellation* lost the mast, it would have greatly hindered her maneuverability and speed, vitally needed under the intense battle conditions. Shortly thereafter, the French frigate, riddled by American fire and her decks strewn with seventy dead and wounded, surrendered.

After the fighting, Porter had a chance to show his mettle again. As French prisoners were being removed to *Constellation*, a storm erupted. Porter, First Lieutenant John Rodgers, and eleven American seamen were caught aboard *Insurgente*, surrounded by defeated French sailors. The enemy was quickly herded into the lower hold, and for three tense days, the "prison" ship made its way to St. Kitts to join *Constellation*. Not a single prisoner escaped.

Americans, so hesitant to raise a navy, grandly celebrated the capture of *Insurgente*. The captain of *Constellation*, Thomas Truxton, was awarded a gold medal by Congress. Toasting the navy was suddenly in vogue. Shop owners sold pitchers emblazoned with the words "Success to our infant navy," and people were singing a popular ballad called "Truxton's Victory."

The call went out for more warships, but the young nation was short on cash. Given the enthusiasm for the new navy and the news that the Barbary States were rattling their sabers again it is not surprising that money for several ships was raised by private subscription. America's largest cities— New York (population: 60,000), Philadelphia (41,000), and Boston (28,000)—responded by building frigates. The town of Salem, which had a population of less than 10,000 but which possessed a seafaring reputation second to none, came through with *Essex*. She would serve faithfully during the Quasi-War, and the Barbary Wars and famously during the War of 1812. The thirty-two-gun ship embodied America's spirit during the first two decades of the nineteenth century, when the navy—like the nation—was brimming with the attributes of youth: righteousness, cockiness, and speed.

CHAPTER TWO

Salem Builds a Frigate

This city will be better known hereafter for its commerce more than its witch tragedy. These enterprising merchants of Salem . . . speak of Fayal and the Azores as if they were close at hand. The fruits of the Mediterranean are on every table. They have large acquaintance at Cairo. . . . Anybody will give you anecdotes from Canton and descriptions of the Society and Sandwich Islands. They often slip up the western coast of their two continents, bring furs from the back regions of their own wide land, glance up at the Andes on their return, double Cape Horn, touch at the ports of Brazil and Guiana, look about them in the West Indies, feeling almost at home there, and land some fair morning in Salem and walk home as if they had done nothing remarkable.

— HARRIET MARTINEAU, *SOCIETY IN AMERICA*

O n 23 November 1798, the following announcement appeared in the *Salem Gazette*, from shipbuilder Enos Briggs:

ENOS BRIGGS, BUILDER OF *ESSEX*, PLACED THIS ADVERTISEMENT IN THE *SALEM GAZETTE* IN 1798 AND LET IT RUN FOR SIX WEEKS. ONE NAVAL CONSTRUCTOR IN 1807 COMMENTED: "THE WHITE OAK TIMBER AND PLANK WITH WHICH THIS SHIP WAS BUILT IS SUPERIOR IN QUALITY TO ANY WHITE OAK I HAVE SEEN MADE USE OF IN THE NAVY."

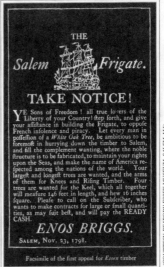

Facsimile of the first appeal for *Essex* timber

True lovers of the liberty of your country, step forth and give your assistance in building the frigate to oppose French insolence and piracy. Let every man in possession of a White Oak Tree be ambitious to be foremost in hurrying down the timber to Salem, and fill the complement wanting, where the noble structure is to be fabricated, to maintain your rights upon the Seas and make the name of America respected among the nations of the world. Your largest and longest trees are wanted, and arms of them for knees and rising timber. Four trees wanted for keel which will measure 146 feet and hew 16 inches square. Please call on subscriber who wants to make contracts for large and small quantities as may best suit, and will pay READY CASH.

Briggs's advertisement met with great success. On 11 January 1799, he placed another announcement in the newspaper to acknowledge

> the good people of the county of Essex [in which Salem is located] for their spirited exertions in bringing down trees of the forest for the building of the frigate. In the short space of four weeks the complement of timber has been furnished. Those who have contributed to their country's defence are invited to come forward and receive the reward of their patriotism.

Briggs concluded with this ditty:

> Next September is the time
> When we shall launch her from the stand
> And our cannon load and prime
> With Tribute due to Talleyrand.

Briggs had good reason to be excited. He would build fifty ships during his thirty-year career (which ended in 1818), but *Essex*, the Salem Frigate, was his finest.

At the end of the eighteenth century, it was hard to best the port of Salem, Massachusetts, in matters relating to ocean commerce. The town's residents were among America's most cosmopolitan because they had seen, touched, and tasted many of the world's exotic goods and treasures, which passed through their port on a daily basis. Residents had responded to Briggs's call not only out of a love of liberty but also out of self-interest. Salem was dependent on the sea. When American shipping was harassed, the town suffered. Deliveries of cargo were delayed; sometimes the cargo was plundered; insurance rates rose; and in the case of the Barbary States, crews were enslaved and ransomed. Building *Essex* was a way of safeguarding the town's livelihood.

Salem's shipping boom began in the years directly after the Revolutionary War. With the war over, merchantmen, some formerly privateers, could ply the seas without fear of capture from the English. Soon enough, however, American captains discovered that there were too many vessels chasing too little business, a situation aggravated by Britain's revengeful act of closing off trade with the West Indies, traditionally a huge market for U.S. shippers.

Salem's enterprising citizens had to look elsewhere for new markets. Owners of merchant fleets dispatched their captains toward little-known and distant ports, where their vessels would compete against maritime powerhouses like Holland and France. Elias Haskett Derby, the king of Salem shippers, sent his *Grand Turk* to the Far East, while his vessel *Light Horse* sailed to St. Petersburg to open up trade with Russia.

Derby was among the town's most prosperous and clever shipowners, who knew how to motivate his employees and crews. For example, he allowed his countinghouse personnel to invest in his ventures, and his sailors were each given the equivalent of eight hundred pounds of freight room, which they used to bring home goods to sell for their own profit. Consequently, Derby's vessels attracted young, ambitious men, hungry for profit and adventure.

A sense of enterprise ran in the Derby family. Elias Jr., at the age of twenty-two, was given command of one of his father's vessels and sailed off to Canton with a cargo of tobacco, fish, butter, and rum. Upon reaching the Isle-de-France (modern-day Mauritius), he discovered he could sell his wares at a greater profit. He also sold his ship to a Frenchman in need for $13,000, twice its value. With his monetary windfall, he bought two more vessels and sailed both to Bombay, where he traded for cotton and sent it home to Salem. He sailed the second

(COURTESY: PEABODY ESSEX MUSEUM, SALEM, MA)

SALEM'S MERCHANT PRINCE ELIAS HASKET DERBY, ONE OF THE TWO LARGEST CONTRIBUTORS TO THE *ESSEX* SUBSCRIPTION, DIED THREE WEEKS BEFORE THE VESSEL WAS LAUNCHED. HIS ESTATE WAS VALUED AT OVER $1 MILLION.

vessel to Isle-de-France with another cargo, which he successfully sold. He ventured on to Calcutta, where he found a buyer for his vessel and returned home by hitching a ride on one of his father's ships. And thus Salem's shipping families did business.

Salem's fashionable Federal Street was lined with the mansions of successful shippers. Elias Derby Sr., the town's first millionaire, built a home that cost $80,000. Derby was displeased with the plans of his first architect, Charles Bulfinch, who designed the U.S. Capitol, and he eventually

The harbor of Salem, Massachusetts, a town with a seafaring reputation
second to none. In 1797, Captain Jacob Crowninshield returned from
a voyage to India with the first elephant ever to be exhibited in the
United States (Admission: $.25).

turned to the talents of a local boy, Samuel McIntire, who
would carve the woodwork on *Essex*.

Derby Street, down by the wharves, was a hive of
activity. Tanned and bearded sailors walked the streets or
lounged in tavern doorways. Pet parrots roosted on shoulders, and a monkey scampered next to its owner. Nearby
shops sold exotic wares: carved ivory, scrimshaw, knives
made from sharks teeth, Hawaiian idols, boomerangs,
mummies, grass belts, gongs, headdresses adorned with
ostrich feathers, and engraved pipes carved from walrus
tusks.

In 1799, the year *Essex* was launched, a group of captains thought it a wise idea to house their curios under one roof for the purpose of collecting and exhibiting them. The result was the East India Marine Society. Captain Jonathan Carnes, who in 1796 had discovered the source of the pepper trade in Sumatra, for centuries the sole domain and secret of the Dutch, was the first man to make a donation to the society. Over the years, the collection grew. In 1867, the society, in gratitude for a $140,000 gift from London merchant George Peabody, changed its name to the Peabody Museum.

The *Essex* subscription began in July 1798, before the call for white oak went out. At its conclusion, 101 people had pledged nearly $75,000. Amounts were as large as $10,000 each from Elias Derby Sr. and William Gray, another successful shipper, and as small as $10 from a man named Edmund Gale. Conspicuously absent from the subscription roll was George Crowninshield, another Salem shipping heavyweight. In lieu of pledging money, George had offered to sell his ships *America* (654 tons) and *Belisarius* (261 tons) to the navy, with the intent that they would be converted into war vessels. Many citizens considered the gesture disingenuous; the Crowninshields, it was said, were only offering their ships because they would be of no use during the Quasi-War, when they were at great risk at sea. In the end, the offer was declined by the government because the congressional act allowing for subscription did not permit the outright purchase of vessels, and George Crowninshield's name never appeared on the subscription roll.

The Crowninshields notwithstanding, the subscription went embarrassingly slow for some time, and Secretary Stoddert had to ask U.S. Secretary of State Timothy Pickering, who hailed from Salem, to give his fellow townsmen a prod. By pressure and patriotism, the sum reached $74,700. This amount was loaned to the government at 6 percent instead of the usual 8 percent, a significant savings to the American government, which at this time was still paying off debts incurred during the Revolutionary War. Building a man-of-war by subscription, not uncommon during this time, was a win-win situation. The government, at the time reticent about spending money on its military, added a ship to its fleet at reduced cost, while the townspeople got a ship to protect their interests, not to mention a vessel they had named and could expect to take pride in.

Salem's subscribers met at the town's courthouse to decide what type of vessel to build. American naval strategy of the era was influenced by Philadelphian Joshua Humphreys, considered one of the finest shipbuilders in the nation and the man chiefly responsible for the six frigates approved by Congress in 1794. His designs of men-of-war with heavier batteries, longer spars, and finer lines were so innovative that they were emulated by the British.

Warships of the day were divided into rates, according to their size and firepower. A first rate vessel carried 100 guns on four tiers. Horatio Nelson's ship at Trafalgar, the 102-gun *Victory*, was such a vessel. Second-, third-, and fourth-rate vessels carried between 90 and 50 guns. Along with first rates, they were designed mostly for major fleet battles and, as such, were referred to as "ships of the line."

(COURTESY: PEABODY ESSEX MUSEUM, SALEM, MA)

THE COURTHOUSE IN SALEM WHERE SUBSCRIBERS CONVENED IN AUGUST 1798 AND
UNANIMOUSLY VOTED TO BUILD A 32-GUN FRIGATE.

America had no ships of the line until after the War of
1812 because her navy was not large enough to engage enemies in massive sea warfare. U.S. naval strategy, rather,
focused on seeking out and destroying smaller warships and
on harassing enemy merchant shipping. This was accomplished with fifth rates, or frigates, which comprised the
heart of the early American navy. Frigates brandished
between 30 and 49 guns and were known for their speed
and finesse. The Royal Navy often used its frigates to scout
for the battle fleet, convoy merchantmen, and harass the

vessels of its enemies. Put another way, frigates, in their day, performed the role now carried out by destroyers.

Humphrey's innovations were quite simple. He prescribed building *fortified* frigates—that is, vessels that had a slight edge on standard British and French frigates. For example, the 44-gun frigate *Constitution* was 175 feet long and weighed 1,576 tons, while a British frigate carried 38 guns, measured 145 feet, and weighed far less. *Constitution's* size enabled her to have a larger crew, wield more powerful weaponry, and exhibit more speed. The latter quality

(COURTESY OF THE MARINER'S MUSEUM)

THE 102-GUN HMS *VICTORY* ON A VOYAGE IN 1778. SHIPS OF THE LINE WERE USED BY THE NAVIES OF POWERFUL EUROPEAN NATIONS FOR MAJOR FLEET ENGAGEMENTS, SUCH AS THE BATTLE OF TRAFALGAR, WHEN HORATIO NELSON, IN COMMAND OF THIS MAMMOTH VESSEL, LED ENGLAND'S VICTORY OVER THE COMBINED FLEETS OF FRANCE AND SPAIN.

enabled Humphrey's fast frigates not only to chase down enemy fifth rates but also to outrun ships of the line, against which there was no contest.

The U.S. government had given Salem the choice of building a 32-gun frigate or an 18-gun sloop. The *Gazette* of 28 August 1798 reported, "At a meeting in the Court House in this town on Tuesday evening last of those gentlemen who have subscribed to build a ship for the service of the United States, it was voted unanimously to build a frigate of thirty-two guns." And so *Essex* was conceived.

Now the ship needed a midwife, someone who would make sure she came into the world in a fit and timely fashion. That job fell to Captain Joseph Waters, a Salem resident who had helped protect the port during the Revolutionary War. Waters's official title was agent—a general contractor of sorts who would work with the navy to put the shipbuilding plan into effect. Waters proved to be a bookkeeper's dream. The total construction costs of the basic ship with one suit of sails (not including provisioning) came in at $74,000, which was $700 below Salem's pledge.

Construction began in the spring of 1799, though the woodsmen of nearby communities such as Andover, Boxford, and Danvers went to work during the winter, hauling their best wood to Salem. The choice timber was white oak, cut specifically for the purpose of shipbuilding. A very snowy winter facilitated the transport of the logs from forests to a timber rendezvous point at the corner of Summer and Essex Streets.

The building site was Winter Island, a thirty-six-acre tract connected to the mainland by a causeway. For a century, the island had been used for fishing and, with its strategic location, had been the site of several forts. Winter Island was the only choice for the large 850-ton *Essex*, the likes of which had never been built in Salem. There was plenty of room for lumber, shacks for the blacksmiths and draftsmen, and a sloping beach on which to construct a building way that would guide the completed ship into the water.

The model, or plan, for *Essex* was prepared by Captain William Hackett, who hailed from a shipbuilding family in Salisbury, Massachusetts. The fifty-nine-year-old Hackett, who had recently completed *Merrimack*, another vessel built by subscription, had made a good name for himself in the business, having designed John Paul Jones's sloop *Ranger* and the seventy-four-gun *America*, given to France at the end of the Revolutionary War. Salem paid Hackett $100 per month for his services.

Building a ship during the last years of the eighteenth century required a combination of experience and exacting craftsmanship. The process started in a mold loft. (The exact location of the loft for *Essex* is unknown, but it had to have been a large, unobstructed, covered floor space, for it acted as the shipwright's studio.) Here plans for the ship were drawn out in small size on paper. The shape of the frames and other key parts were then chalked in full size on the floor. The goal of this exercise, known as lofting, was to cut out full-size molds or patterns that were used to shape pieces of timber for the various parts of the ship. Lofting was not a strict science, and accomplished shipwrights did not adhere rigidly to formulas. Experience and rules of

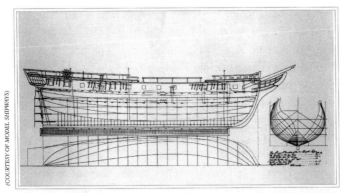

(COURTESY OF MODEL SHIPWAYS)

A FACSIMILE OF SHIPWRIGHT PLANS FOR *ESSEX*. SHIPWRIGHT WILLIAM HACKETT,
WHO WAS SIXTY WHEN HE DESIGNED *ESSEX*, HAD PLAYED A ROLE IN THE DESIGN AND
CONSTRUCTION OF A NUMBER OF IMPORTANT WAR VESSELS, INCLUDING THE
ENORMOUS 74-GUN SHIP-OF-THE-LINE *AMERICA* AND 20-GUN SLOOP *RANGER*. IN
1777, CAPTAIN JOHN PAUL JONES USED THE LATTER VESSEL TO RAID COASTAL
TOWNS IN GREAT BRITAIN. WHILE HIS CRUISE WAS NOT ENTIRELY SUCCESSFUL, IT
SHOCKED THE BRITISH PUBLIC FOR ITS AUDACITY.

thumb, passed down from generation to generation, were
liberally employed. A ship was a living work of art, and
shipwrights had to know how to adjust designs and bend
the rules, as in any act of creation.

After the design work, the first order of business was to
lay the keel. This was accomplished for *Essex* on 13 April
1799. Ships were built around their keels, akin to a back-
bone in a human body. Stem and stern posts were attached
to the ends of the keel. After the ship's frames, or ribs, were
attached, a skeleton was achieved. A scaffolding was thrown
up, and workmen began hammering on planks.

A variety of craftsmen was needed in the construction,
among them sawyers, carpenters, and joiners for the

woodwork; caulkers to pack the ship's seams with oakum (strands of old rope treated with pitch); lead men to line the scuppers (the ship's gutters); and glaziers to prepare the glass.

Many of the names of craftsmen who worked on *Essex* deserve mention. The sails were made by Samuel Buffum and John Howard; duck cloth for the sails was woven at the factory of Daniel Rust. Jonathan Haraden, a privateering captain in the Revolutionary War, made rigging for the frigate at his rope walk on Brown Street. The ship's copper work, which included sheathing for the bottom, fastening pieces, and lightning rods, was manufactured by Paul Revere, who was sixty-four and living in Boston. Alden Briggs, the brother of the shipbuilder Enos, worked as a blacksmith. Finally, Anjier McIntire worked as a joiner, and his brother, Samuel, the architect, did much of the ship's wood carving, including the all-important figurehead.

Figureheads have graced the bows of vessels since ancient times. Though decorative, their purpose was also spiritual in that they served as a set of ever-vigilant eyes guiding the vessel (some cultures even painted eyes on each side of the bow). Figureheads on American colonial vessels were often carved in the image of the ship's namesake, such as *Hancock*, named after the most famous signer of the Declaration of Independence. Other vessels sported figureheads of a symbolic nature. John Paul Jones, for example, chose the goddess of liberty for *America*.

Whatever type of figurehead adorned the vessel, its presence was as indispensable as cannonballs or rum. Sailors were never happy when a shipowner dispensed with a figurehead on a new vessel to cut expenses. Just how

THE INDIAN FIGUREHEAD, ALONG WITH ALL THE DECORATIVE WOODWORK ON
ESSEX, WAS CARVED BY SAMUEL MCINTIRE, AN ARCHITECT WHO ALSO DESIGNED
HOMES OF MANY OF SALEM'S WEALTHY MERCHANTS, SHIPOWNERS, AND CAPTAINS.

passionate sailors were and are about figureheads is related
in the following tale.

While *Constitution* was being overhauled in Boston
Navy Yard in 1834, the yard commandant, Captain Elliot,
decided to replace the existing figurehead—a scroll, repre-
senting the Constitution, guarded on both sides by dragons—with a figure of Andrew Jackson, the nation's current
president. The citizens of Boston, who loved their famous
ship and despised Old Hickory, said they would tar and
feather Elliot if he executed his plan. Unfazed by the threat,

Elliot changed the figurehead. While the ship lay at anchor, however, a young man named Dewey rowed out and beheaded Jackson. Dewey became an instant hero and, in an act more audacious than the first, brought the head to Washington, D.C., to show the secretary of the navy.

McIntire's figurehead for *Essex* was an Indian, a common symbol that represented strength and independence. One painting of *Essex* shows the Indian actually astride, a staff in one hand and a tomahawk over his shoulder, suggesting a confident fighting spirit.

Work on *Essex* proceeded through the summer. There were many tasks, including plumbing; stowing kentledge (ballast); ordering cannons, muskets, and gunpowder; and acquiring pumps. The wooden bottom had to be covered in Paul Revere's copper sheathing, which protected the vessel from the teredo (its name derived from the Greek word *teredon*, to bore). These wormlike boring clams feasted on oak and were the ruin of many a fine ship. Sheathing also hindered the formation of barnacles, which when layered thickly, slowed down a vessel by several knots. That could make all the difference when trying to catch or fly from an enemy.

Agent Joseph Waters, the man chiefly responsible for orchestrating the flow of supplies needed to build the ship, earned every penny of his commission. Like all agents, he had to deal with tardy shipments, shady contractors, and shoddy goods. One of his biggest headaches was shotmaker Benjamin Seymour. The well-meaning Seymour had no skill for judging his limits. No warship—or merchantman, for that matter—could sail without shot for her cannons.

Shot for *Essex* was months late and caused the ship's first captain, Edward Preble, and Navy Secretary Stoddert, both of whom were anxious to get the vessel to sea, many sleepless nights. Seymour's correspondence to Waters is a litany of apologies, false promises, and excuses. "I hope no material inconvenience has been hitherto suffered, and will forward them [the shot] to you directly," he wrote in October 1799 to Waters, who had heard nothing from him for two months. Seymour was never short on providing alibis for his overdue shot. He wrote again: "The tedious delay has been occasioned by the want of water, for the furnace has been twice obliged to stop. . . . I am well aware that the Publick service supersedes every private consideration, and however I might personally suffer, would not impede the sailing of the Ship one hour." In the meantime, correspondence makes clear that Seymour was casting shot for other vessels. He had spread himself too thinly and, in the end, never came through for *Essex*.

The building of *Essex* was not all hard work and frustration. There was time for levity and symbolic celebration. When the ship's hemp cables were completed, for example, they were conveyed to Winter Island on the workers' shoulders and led by a fife and drum procession, *a la* the Spirit of 1776.

The big celebration occurred on 30 September 1799, when *Essex* was launched amid great fanfare. Ship launchings, then as now, were dramatic and patriotic events. Only the ship's hull had been completed; the masts, spars, and rigging would be erected after the vessel was afloat. Salem's citizens, perched on the hills of the mainland or ensconced in front-row seats costing $1 each on Winter Island, had been looking forward to the event since the keel had been laid five and a half months earlier.

The act of ship launching is bound in ritual and superstition. In ancient times, ships were decked with flowers and leaves. After the pouring of a libation, they were sent on their way. In the Middle Ages, vessels were blessed by priests.

Launching was done on a wooden structure, aptly named a "cradle," that bore the vessel along greased tracks, called ways, into the water. The launch atmosphere was tense, as the crowd awaited the possible appearance of a bad omen that would curse the vessel. For example, if the bottle of wine used in the christening did not break, that was a bad sign. The same was true for a launch accompanied by fatalities. The ship was said to be "launched in blood," although Norsemen held a different view of that expression—they actually tied victims to rollers upon which the ship rode down on its way to the sea, thereby making a blood sacrifice. USS *Chesapeake,* one of the navy's ill-fated frigates, not only got stuck during her launch (the tallow had grown cold) but also killed a man when she finally did go. However, superstition only goes so far. *Constitution* also got stuck on her way to the sea. Three more attempts were needed to get her into the water, yet she was one of the navy's greatest warships and remains moored in Boston Harbor today.

The launch of *Essex*, in front of twelve thousand spectators, proceeded without a hitch. Enos Briggs gave the order to remove the blocks and drive the wedges; the Salem

Frigate, its oak creaking and moaning, slid into the water, according to the *Gazette,* "with the most easy and graceful motion amidst the acclamation of thousands." (Like all new wooden ships, *Essex* leaked until her planks expanded, and a small crew was assigned to pump her out.) The launching was followed by the customary dinner for workmen and special guests and included beef, cheese, cider, rum, and puddings.

Upon her completion, the length of the Salem Frigate measured 141 feet on the gun deck, 118 feet on the keel, and 37 feet at the beam. Her depth of hold was 12 feet 3 inches and her displacement was 850 tons. Her major expenses broke down roughly as follows: carpentry, $26,616; spars, bolts, and blocks, $12,719; cordage, $10,075; blacksmith, $8,372; copper bolts, $4,339; sails, $3,732; painting and plumbing, $2,256; and anchors, $1,082. Joseph Waters's commission came to about $1,500. All these costs were covered by Salem's subscription.

The government was responsible for provisioning the ship. Such provisions amounted to another $80,000 and included the following: military stores, $31,992; an extra suit of sails and anchors, $16,812; ships stores, $12,709; twelve months' worth of provisions (which included pork, beef, salt fish, bread, rice, molasses, and three thousand gallons of rum), $12,304; clothing, $3,867; and hospital stores (which included mustard, tea, pepper, ginger, and French brandy), $1,527. The total cost to build and outfit *Essex* takes on more meaning when compared with other ships of the era. *Constitution*, for example, whose 1,576-ton displacement was nearly twice that of *Essex*, cost a little over

$300,000 in 1794; and the thirty-six-gun *Congress*, completed about the same time as *Essex*, came in at $198,000. (Shot for *Congress* had been provided by Benjamin Seymour!)

Out of civic pride and self-interest, Salem had built the biggest ship it could afford: a thirty-two-gun frigate. She was a respectable vessel, though there was a problem inherent in her size. The British had not sent to sea a frigate of less than thirty-eight guns since 1784. This put

(COURTESY OF MODEL SHIPWAYS)

MODEL OF *ESSEX*. THE RECORD OF *ESSEX* IS PERHAPS THE MOST THOROUGH OF ANY VESSEL OF ITS DAY, THANKS TO THE "FRIGATE ESSEX PAPERS," WHICH CONTAIN ACCOUNT BOOKS, BANK RECORDS, AND HUNDREDS OF RECEIPTS PERTAINING TO THE VESSEL'S CONSTRUCTION. THE PAPERS SURFACED IN 1940 WHEN WILLIAM CROWNINSHIELD WATERS, JR., THE GREAT GRANDSON OF JOSEPH WATERS, WHO OVERSAW BUILDING OF THE SALEM FRIGATE, SHOWED UP AT THE PEABODY MUSEUM WITH TWELVE CARTONS OF PAPERS HE'D FOUND AT HIS HOME. ONE CONTAINED THE *ESSEX* DOCUMENTATION.

Essex, too small to be considered one of Humphrey's fortified frigates, at a tactical disadvantage. Her captains would think twice about going up against a forty-four-gun Royal Navy frigate. At the same time, *Essex* was too large to be considered a sloop or brig, which carried about twenty guns and generally were faster than frigates and certainly more agile and maneuverable inshore. *Essex,* in summation, was a bit of an orphan, but the U.S. Navy was pleased to get her and, through the years, made good use of her in a variety of roles.

As the citizens of Salem watched their frigate slide into the water, they had a right to feel proud. After all, the town had provided America with its third largest vessel (by subscription), and she was off to protect the country's interests around the world. As the *Gazette* reported the day after launching:

> *The Committee acting for the subscribers, Colonel Hackett, the superintendent, and Mr. Briggs, the master builder, have thus the satisfaction of producing for their country as fine a ship of her size as graces the American Navy. It is not yet known who will command her but all hands agreed that she is well calculated to do essential service for her country.*

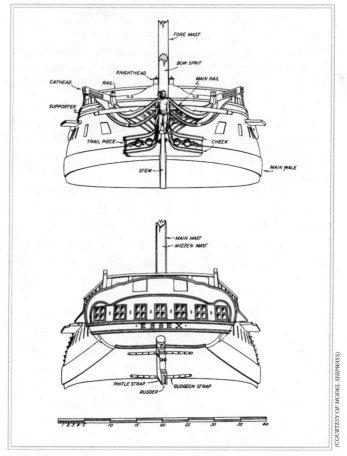

(COURTESY OF MODEL SHIPWAYS)

THE BOWS AND STERNS OF NAVAL VESSELS CHANGED MARKEDLY THROUGHOUT THE CENTURIES. THE STERNS OF SEVENTEENTH CENTURY WARSHIPS, FOR EXAMPLE, WERE OFTEN ORNATELY CARVED WITH COATS OF ARMS, RICH FLORA, AND EAGLES. IN MAN-OF-WAR SHIPS FROM LATER CENTURIES, STERNS WERE LESS ELABORATE, REFLECTING A MORE SIMPLE CLASSICAL SPIRIT AS WELL AS AN EFFORT BY NAVIES TO CUT COSTS. LITTLE IS KNOWN ABOUT THE STERN OF *ESSEX*, AS IT IS NEITHER DESCRIBED IN DOCUMENTS OR WELL-REPRESENTED IN ARTWORK FROM THE ERA.

CHAPTER THREE

The Shakedown Cruise

I have the honor to acquaint you that *Essex* in coming out of
the Harbor sailed much faster than Congress & is I think in
every respect a fine frigate.

— CAPTAIN PREBLE, LETTER TO SECRETARY OF THE
NAVY STODDERT

*E*ssex, though a spanking new creation of a respected
shipwright, was about to embark on a shakedown
cruise that would test both vessel and crew. A new ship was
like a newly broken horse; she possessed her share of idio-
syncrasies, which had to be harnessed by a rider who exhibited control—one who could make the individual attributes
of the vessel serve his purposes. Mastery would also have to
be exhibited over the new and untried crew. How would
the men work together? Who would emerge as the crew's
leaders? Troublemakers? Would the ship be filled with a
spirit of cooperation, or turpitude?

Much of the success of any cruise boiled down to one
factor: the captain. A man-of-war, no matter how fine her

(COURTESY OF U.S. NAVY)

EDWARD PREBLE, FIRST CAPTAIN OF
ESSEX. HIS TOUGH, NO-NONSENSE
STYLE MADE HIM A FITTING
COMMANDER FOR THE VESSEL'S
MAIDEN VOYAGE IN 1800.

lines or how fast her gun crews, was often only as effective as her commander.

Essex could not have possessed a more suitable captain for her maiden cruise than Edward Preble. Among sailors, Preble had a reputation as a disciplinarian, though he earned their respect because he lived under the same rules he imposed. His strictness was no show of machismo; it was a tool to whip the crew and ship into top-fighting shape. A cruise with Edward Preble kept each sailor on his toes. He inspected his vessels from stem to stern every day. The decks were washed down twice daily. The guns were exercised regularly. His men were to be shaved and wearing clean clothes twice a week. Unlike some captains, Preble gave his crews Sundays off and did not skimp on their grog (rum cut with water). He was not afraid to flog men who were derelict in their duty or caught stealing or fomenting trouble. Indeed, during *Essex*'s first cruise, a seaman named William Ash was put into irons for inciting the crew to mutiny.

In addition to his crews, Preble gained the respect of sailors from other nations for his boldness. A prime example came on a night in September 1803, while he was in command of *Constitution*, off the coast of Spain. The air was murky with haze when a mysterious vessel appeared. The area was frequented by ships from the Barbary States, which had been seizing American merchant vessels, and Preble ordered the decks cleared for action. He hailed the vessel, whose commander refused to identify her.

"I now hail for the last time," stated Preble. "If you do not answer, I will fire a shot."

An English voice shot back: "If you do, I'll return a broadside."

"I should like to catch you at that!" barked Preble. "I now hail for an answer. What ship is that?"

"This is His Britannic Majesty's eighty-four gun ship of the line, *Donnegal*, Sir Richard Strachen commanding. Heave to and send a boat."

The air went silent. The speaker aboard *Donnegal* was issuing Preble a challenge. If you do not believe me, fire away, and take your chances. If you do believe me, submit to the humiliation of sending your boat across.

Preble did not budge: "This is the *Constitution*, forty-four guns, Captain Edward Preble commanding! I'll be damned if I'll send a boat to any ship!"

It was a gutsy move. An eighty-four-gun ship could have crushed *Constitution* in minutes.

Preble then added, "Blow your matches, boys!"—a signal to his gun crews to prepare to fire.

The captain aboard the mystery ship backed down and, a short while later, sent a boat across to *Constitution*. The vessel turned out to be the Royal Navy's thirty-two-gun

Maidstone, no match for one of Humphrey's fortified frigates.

Like most of America's early captains, Edward Preble had saltwater in his blood. He was born in Portland, Maine, on 15 August 1761, the son of Brigadier General Jedidiah Preble and Mehitable Bangs, and he shipped aboard a privateer at sixteen without his father's knowledge. During the Revolutionary War, in 1779, he became a midshipman aboard the frigate *Protector*, which was captured two years later.

Preble was confined aboard the infamous prison hulk *Jersey* in New York Harbor, in whose wretched confines thousands of American prisoners of war died. He was fortunate enough to be exchanged for a British officer, though not before he came down with typhoid. He was made a lieutenant in 1782 aboard the twelve-gun *Winthrop*, which captured a fair share of prizes before the end of the war.

Like many fellow officers, Preble entered the calmer milieu of merchant service during the postwar years (though his vessel was captured once by pirates). In the 1790s, as tension mounted with France, America recalled its best naval lieutenants to its ranks, and Preble was among them. By 1798, he was given command of the fourteen-gun brig *Pickering*.

Despite Preble's solid reputation, he was not the Salem committee's first choice to captain *Essex*. That honor fell to a native son, Captain Richard Derby, a nephew of shipping prince Elias (who, unfortunately, had died three weeks before the vessel was launched). The only problem with the committee's call to service was that the thirty-four-year-old

Richard Derby was not around to answer it. He was at sea with the merchantman *Juno*.

This put Stoddert in an awkward position. He had to get his frigate to sea. How long should he wait for Derby? He did not want to offend the committee by barging ahead with his own candidate. But winter was setting in, and the secretary feared that the newly outfitted *Essex* would be locked into Salem's harbor, which had a reputation for freezing over early in the season. In the end, Stoddert found a solution. He gave Preble *tentative* command of *Essex*, as the following letter, dated 21 October 1799, reveals:

> *Sir:*
>
> *Having heard nothing of Captain Derby and the Frigate* Essex *being now ready for the attention of a Commander, I have the honor to direct that as soon after the receipt of this as you conveniently can, you repair to Salem and assist in preparing that ship for sea, to command her in the event of her being ready before Captain Derby's return. It may possibly be a favorite object with the Committee that Capt. Derby should have command of the* Essex, *and I have therefore informed them that he might command her if he should chose to do so upon your return from a cruise.*

Preble arrived in Salem a week after receiving the letter, though not before taking care of some important business—that is, his marriage to Mary Deering of Portland. He took command of *Essex* on 7 November, when the ship was ready and completely rigged, but with only a skeletal crew on board. He immediately ordered more sailors aboard the vessel to hold it in the event of a storm. Richard Derby returned in mid-December, too late to take command of *Essex*. While he may have been disappointed, he was probably relieved not to have to face the myriad frustrations in preparing a man-of-war for her first voyage.

Foremost was recruitment. Unlike their British counterparts, American captains could not dispatch press gangs—groups of sailors who rounded up recruits by force—to fill their ship's complement of men. They had to ferret out willing and decent recruits. Any captain could round up enough landlubbers to fill a vessel, but often these men were of questionable character, running from debt or bad marriages. The best candidate was an able seaman already in possession of the skills to hand, reef and steer, as well as to handle a vessel's armament. No commander wanted to face a howling storm or hostile enemy with a "green" crew.

Preble also had to find his commissioned, warrant, and petty officers, who included master (who was responsible for navigation), boatswain (the working of the sails and rigging), gunner (cannons and ammunition), coxswain (the ship's boats), master-at-arms (policing the sailors), carpenter, and sailmaker, as well as the midshipmen, who were young men in training to be officers. Secretary Stoddert assisted with the recruitment at high levels, appointing, among others, the surgeon and purser (responsible for provisions, stores, and funds). Some recruitment was done in Boston by Third Lieutenant George Lee, who had less than satisfying success because he was competing against recruiters from other warships and privateers.

Also recruited for service aboard *Essex* were marines, a new fighting force created by President Adams on 11 July 1798. The presidential act provided for 881 men between the ages of eighteen and forty, five-feet six-inches in height or better, "healthy and robust," and possessing "unequivocal characters for sobriety and fidelity." On shipboard, marines, adorned in short blue coats, red vests, and blue pantaloons, acted as the captain's security force, guarding whatever on the vessel needed protection and breaking up fights among sailors. Marines did not perform sail handling duties and did not go aloft, except in the lower rigging during battle to fire their muskets at enemy sailors. Although marines reported to a commandant, they were under the final authority of the captain once aboard ship.

Essex recruits signed up for one year, and monthly salaries of crewmen varied widely. At the bottom of the ladder were boys and ordinary seamen, who were paid between $5 and $12, while the armorer (who was responsible for maintaining small arms and other metal work) and cook got $18. Midshipmen earned a dollar more per month, while the captain's clerk received $25. Near the top of the pyramid, at $40, were lieutenants, the purser, and the master. Captains received $75.

Naval pay was augmented by the captures a crew made, though this was an unreliable source of income. A captured (prize) vessel and its contents, if successfully brought into a port of the victor's nation, was condemned (judged a fair prize) by a federal court and sold. Proceeds were divided up among the officers and crew, with the latter receiving the smallest slice of the pie. It is important to note that the amount of pie divided up was dependent on the size and strength of the prize vessel. If the prize was of equal or superior strength to the ship that captured it, then the full value of the prize was doled out to the victors. In the case of a forty-four-gun frigate capturing an eighteen-gun brig, however, only half the value of the brig went to the officers and crew. The other half went into a navy pension fund.

The prize system was established to foster initiative and enterprise, though it rarely made captains into rich men. For some, the system was a source of temptation because it presented a captain with a hard choice: to burn a captured vessel, which hurt the enemy but netted officers and crew no prize money, or to attempt to bring the vessel home, which netted prize money *only if* the vessel was not recaptured. Such temptation dogged David Porter throughout his second cruise on *Essex*, an issue that will be taken up later.

Recruiting was only one of Preble's problems. Poor weather was delaying shipments of needed supplies. Preble saw that he was going to miss his 15 December sailing date and wrote to Stoddert:

> *I find it impossible to get Essex ready for sea in less than 10 days after time I first expected, owing to weather & many disappointments. Yesterday was a violent snow storm and today rain. Our Canister & Grape shot has not arrived yet from Plymouth although shipped several days ago. Our coals, Butter, Rice, Medicine Chest, Chains for our chain pumps, hospital stores, part of our lanterns & many other articles are yet to come from Boston, present*

state of weather & wind will not admit of packet [a small cargo vessel] reaching here for several days.

According to Preble, the weather was so bad that many shippers were reluctant to let their vessels sail with *Essex* on her first mission, in which she was ordered to sail to the port of Batavia (today known as Jakarta) and back. Shippers were more worried about losing their vessels to poor weather than to French privateers.

As if Preble did not have enough to worry about, he was now short one officer. Lieutenant David Phipps was ill and confined to his bunk. As his condition worsened, Preble took aboard a replacement, George Washington Tew, a senior midshipman.

It is perhaps a miracle that *Essex* departed on 22 December 1799, only one week late, weighing anchor from Salem, a port she would never see again. Flags flew at half-mast to honor ex-President George Washington, who had died eight days earlier. As *Essex* slid passed Winter Island, where her keel had been laid nine months earlier, a sixteen-gun salute was fired from Fort Pickering.

Essex sailed to Newport, Rhode Island, where Preble was forced to land some of his marines, who he told Stoddert were "unfit for service." In all, he was short twenty-five men, but he did not consider it important enough to further detain his cruise, which began on 7 January 1800, alongside the thirty-six-gun *Congress*, captained by James Sever, and three merchantmen. (A merchantman was a privately-owned ship, not as well armed as a government warship, used for transporting cargo or passengers.) It was a

JOSEPH HOWARD'S WATERCOLOR OF *ESSEX*, THE FIRST AMERICAN
AMONG THE TRADESMEN WHO WORKED ON THE VESSEL AS A

WARSHIP TO ROUND BOTH THE CAPE OF GOOD HOPE AND CAPE HORN.
SAILMAKER WAS JOHN HOWARD, FATHER OF THE ARTIST.

simple convoying mission, nothing glorious but certainly necessary, with the ever-present possibility of engaging an enemy ship.

The first leg of the voyage tested the mettle of both man-of-war crews. Winter storms raged with ferocity, and after a few days, the ships were separated. In such a case, Preble and Sever had planned to rendezvous at the island of St. Helena, six hundred miles northwest of the Cape of Good Hope, but *Congress* never appeared there. Gales had wreaked havoc on her mizzenmast, foremast, and bowsprit, and she had been forced to limp back to America, arriving at Norfolk on 24 February 1800. The crew did not fare well, either. Eight men suspected of plotting mutiny were arrested by Sever, who was considered an incompetent and capricious captain. Still, several suspects were eventually punished and dismissed from the service.

Essex, too, had her share of problems. After arriving at the Cape of Good Hope, Preble wrote on 13 March to Stoddert:

> *On my passage out much of iron work has given way; fore & main trestle trees & fore & main crosstrees broken, owing to bad quality of wood & their not having been properly secured at first. Nearly all main shrouds & all topmast stays have been carried away, they were too small & their quality infamously bad. These disasters lengthened my passage & will detain me here at least ten days, as considerable wood and iron work is to be done to masts, a complete gang of shrouds to be fitted & water to fill.*

Whether the ship's deficiencies were due to the defects that are part of any new vessel or to shoddy workmanship is not clear. Whatever the reason, Preble was hardly ready to scuttle the ship. He told the secretary that "*Essex* is much admired for beauty of her construction, by officers of the British Navy."

Preble found that his shrouds and stays weren't the only deficient element on his ship. Some crew members weren't performing well, having exaggerated their sea experience to get higher pay. He wrote:

> *After a fair trial of my ship's company at sea, I found many impositions had been practiced on recruiting officers at the time of their engagements, and on 9th of Feb I had a muster on board for purpose of rating them according to merit & reduced pay of a considerable number, a list of whose names I have enclosed.*

Life aboard a warship required strict discipline. If a captain could not command the respect of his men on calm days, he certainly could not expect it during battle. The best captains used force only when necessary, and the implement of choice was the cat-o'-nine-tails, or "cat," a short wooden stick covered with baize and usually holding nine tails of tough, knotted cord two feet in length. Sailors who were flogged with this horrible device were tied to a grating pulled from one of the ship's hatches and set upright. In the company of the crew, the captain read the article of war that the seaman had supposedly violated. The boatswain's mates

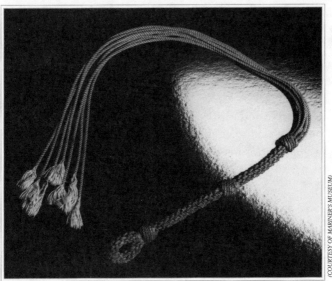

(COURTESY OF MARINER'S MUSEUM)

THE CAT-O-NINE TAILS MOST OFTEN HELD NINE TAILS OF TOUGH, KNOTTED
CORD. A BRITISH SEAMAN FLOGGED WITH THE DEVICE COMMENTED:
"I PUT MY TONGUE BETWEEN MY TEETH, HELD IT THERE, AND BIT IT ALMOST
IN TWO PIECES."

often gave the whipping, bringing the cat down with full force. One blow was sufficient to break the skin. After a number of lashes, another mate took over to give the first a rest. When the deed was accomplished, the sailor was removed to the sick bay, where he was attended by the surgeon. The beaten body healed up after several weeks.

Generally speaking, the American navy was more humane in dolling out punishment than its British counterpart. U.S. commanders could not give out more than twelve lashes, according to naval regulation. "If the fault shall deserve a greater punishment, he [the captain] is to apply to the Commander-in-Chief of the Navy in order to the trying of him [the guilty party] by a Court-Martial, and in the meantime, he may be put under confinement." In the Royal Navy, thirty-six lashes with a cat were not uncommon. In all fairness, it must be stated that American captains sometimes got around their twelve-lash limit by breaking down the sailor's misbehavior into two or three offenses and handing down twelve lashes per offense.

What was it like to be flogged with a cat? In 1832, one poor seaman recorded his impressions:

> *I felt an astounding sensation between the shoulders under my neck, which went to my toe-nails in one direction, and my fingernails in another, and stung me to the heart, as if a knife had gone through my body . . . . He [the boatswain's mate] came on a second time a few inches lower, and then I thought the former stroke was sweet and agreeable compared to that one . . . . I put my tongue between my teeth, held it there, and bit it almost in two pieces.*

When used overzealously, the cat-o'-nine-tails made sailors bitter, whether they felt its lash or not. In the Royal Navy, it lowered morale and contributed to a high desertion rate. Between 1776 and 1780, in fact, the British Navy lost twenty thousand men to battle and disease and forty-two thousand to desertion (though certainly not all due to the cat). Moreover, the cat did not produce a better fighting force. As one Englishman later put it, "In the days we had the cat we had no discipline; now we have the discipline and no cat." While lore and modern-day attitude contribute to the myth that the cat was an everyday occurrence, records indicate the opposite. In the American navy, only a handful of men aboard any vessel was punished with the device, and such punishment was outlawed in 1852.

Despite the bumpy start, Preble had confidence in his crew and ship, which soon reached Capetown. At the port were several British warships, including the seventy-four-gun *Tremendous* and three American merchant vessels, two heading for Batavia, one returning to the United States. Preble stayed at the port for two weeks, repairing his ship and taking time out to socialize with English naval officers and the local governor. *Essex* weighed anchor on 28 March, leaving a spare mainyard on shore (presumably for *Congress*), and soon had the honor of being the first American man-of-war to show her colors beyond the Cape of Good Hope. By May 1800, the Salem Frigate had sailed across the Indian Ocean and reached Batavia, a bustling port near the Straits of Sunda, which separates the Indonesian islands of Java and Sumatra.

Batavia and its environs, with their rich trade in coffee, sugar, and spices, had for two hundred years been under the control of the Dutch East India Company (known by the Dutch acronym of VOC). In the latter part of the eighteenth century, however, Holland's colonial interests were in turmoil, due to VOC corruption and the fact that European wars were spilling over into this corner of the world. Holland's military setbacks with England in 1784 and France in 1795 had further weakened the Dutch monopoly and opened the area to outside traders, including

Americans. By 1800, when *Essex* arrived, the VOC had been officially dissolved, and the area's rich resources, though ostensibly controlled by a Dutch government dominated by France, were up for grabs. There was much opportunity, but the climate in Batavia, in addition to being hot and muggy, must have been tense.

Preble quickly got down to business. As he wrote to Stoddert: "I cruised in entrance of straits for a fortnight, in which time I boarded 13 Sail of American Merchant Ships richly loaded, whole of which would have been captured had a single French Privateer been cruising in my stead." There were rumors of French vessels in the area, and Preble cruised the port, looking for a confrontation: "They have privateers about Straits of Sunda & I hope *Essex* can pick up some of them."

On 9 June, he posted a notice announcing the formation of his convoy:

> *The Frigate* Essex *will sail from Batavia Roads on the 18th & will take under convoy merchant ships of U.S. bound to westward . . . . Commanders who wish to benefit by this convoy are requested to receive their distinguishing vanes, & on Sat. morning they are requested to deliver a manifest of their cargoes on board* Essex *& at the same time receive signals and instructions.*

These signal vanes were small flags, each different, that allowed for identification at long distances. For example, the vane of the merchant ship *China* was a red flag at the main mast, while *John Buckley* had a white flag at the mizzenmast. These were needed to keep track of vessels, most (if not all) of which Preble and his crew had never seen before. Communication among the ships was done through day and night signals known only to the convoy. The vanes and signals helped identify the presence of an enemy privateer that might attempt to slip in and capture one of the merchantmen.

Two of Preble's diary entries provide a look at the day-to-day routines of a navy captain charged with convoy duty. Preble divided his time between logistics, cruising for French vessels, and shipboard discipline.

Tues. June 24, 1800. Detained a prow that we had reason to think was employed by French privateer to give them Intelligence. Dutchman on board confessed he had received money for above purpose. At 6 PM saw ship to Windward standing in Pepper Bay under her 3 topsails. Anchored at night. . . . At 7 saw a sail in offing. Gave chase at meridian to ship we supposed to be French Cruiser. We have 11 sick men on board.

Sunday June 29, 1800. Delivered to Capt. Benners ship one Cask Beer. Also to ship John Buckley a large barrel of vinegar. Employed preparing ship for sea. Whipped at gangway Amos Wheaton for neglect of duty, also Jos. Davenport for gross neglect of duty. Both Marines. At 1/2 2 saw sail come into Straits, called boats from shore and gave chase. Spoke ship, she called Columbia 109 days from Capes of Delaware.

Preble and his crew would capture no French privateers, but that did not make their cruise unsuccessful. The convoy, which sailed on 1 July, consisted of fourteen vessels with $1 million worth of cargo now under protection of *Essex*. The ships ranged in size from the brig *Sally* (113 tons, 8 men, 6 guns) to a vessel that was bigger than *Essex* herself, the ship *China* (1,055 tons, 151 men, 36 guns). It is important to note that *China* would have been no match for *Essex* or any other man-of-war that, in addition to being more strongly built, carried a highly trained gun crew and a detachment of marines. The convoy vessels were bound for Baltimore, New York, Salem, and other ports, and their cargoes included coffee, tea, sugar, pepper, and camphor.

Upon his departure, Preble left behind a good supply of beef, pork, butter, bread, beans, and rum for *Congress*; he did not yet know the ship had returned to the United States. In the event these supplies were not needed by *Congress* or any other American man-of-war at Batavia, Preble left instructions that they be auctioned off, with the proceeds returning to the navy.

Keeping a convoy together, even under calm weather, can be compared to sheepherding. Merchant vessels came in all sizes and conditions. Some were swift sailers; others should have been broken up for scrap on the spot. In addition to protection, the escorting naval vessel assisted merchantmen with everything from food to cordage to medical aid. Ships that were especially slow were towed, or even left behind. After all, merchant captains, paid by weight to carry cargo from one port to another, had profits to make. The sooner they completed a voyage, the sooner they could embark on another. A slow voyage also cut into a merchant captain's profit because he had to feed his crew for a longer period. By the time Preble had anchored at the island of St. Helena, halfway through the trip, only six of fourteen ships were still with him. (Ships in a convoy were also separated because, at a given point, a vessel would turn off to follow its own course. At that time, a captain would turn over to Preble his signal book, which listed the secret flag signals used by a convoy to coordinate its movements.)

One minor event on the return trip bears telling. On 16 October, Jason Howard, the ship's schoolmaster, died at the age of twenty-seven of an unknown cause. Schoolmasters acted as teachers to the midshipmen and, when needed, did the duties of chaplain. A day after Howard's body was committed to the deep, the contents of his trunks were sold to the crew, as was the official practice, and the $66 collected was forwarded to his family. About a dozen men would die during the first cruise of *Essex,* though Preble does not list cause of death in his log.

Essex took five months to return to America, arriving in New York on 19 November after a voyage plagued by storms. A letter from Secretary Stoddert congratulated Preble on his successful mission and ordered him to pay and discharge his crew so that the vessel could be refitted for another cruise. This was easier said than done, as Preble had discovered that his purser was terribly incompetent and had "caused more expense to the Govt. than 10 times amount of his pay & rations." Finally, the crew, except for thirty-five sailors kept aboard *Essex* to keep her safe at her anchors, was discharged, and Preble was given leave to return to Portland to see his new wife and attend to private affairs.

By the time *Essex* had returned from Batavia, the Quasi-War with France was coming to an end. Begun two years earlier, the conflict had forced America to re-establish her navy and raise a ten-thousand-man army (the country feared a French invasion). The young nation had made a good stand, with a particularly proud moment coming on 1 February 1800, when Thomas Truxton in *Constellation* faced off against *Vengeance* in the war's bloodiest engagement. The battle occurred off the island of Guadeloupe in the French West Indies, and when the smoke cleared, the crew of *Vengeance* did not know what had hit them. With 50 dead and 110 wounded, the ship was barely able to reach the nearby port of Curacao. Her captain, A. M. Pitot, reported that he had been attacked by a ship of the line, no small compliment for the crew of the frigate *Constellation*, who had suffered fewer casualties: 14 killed and 25 wounded.

By war's end, the United States had taken eighty-four ships, including two frigates, and recaptured another forty vessels. Most importantly, perhaps, was that the navy had shown the American public that it was not a drain on national coffers but an asset needed to defend the nation's multimillion-dollar shipping trade. The cost of re-establishing the navy was about $6 million, not a bad investment considering *Essex*, on a single voyage, was protecting $1 million in cargo. Negotiations with France, now headed by Napoleon Bonaparte, produced a treaty signed early in 1801, with neither side gaining anything except the cessation of hostilities.

In April of that year, Edward Preble learned that he had been assigned a second tour aboard *Essex*, this time to the Mediterranean, but he had to decline due to bad health. On 22 April he received a letter from Acting Secretary of the Navy Samuel Smith stating:

> *It is a subject of great regret that your indisposition should prevent your proceeding with squadron. I will write to Captain Bainbridge who I cannot doubt will accept command of Essex but being just arrived will require time to pay off his crew & remain with his family.*

Bainbridge, in fact, gladly accepted the commission. Given the nature of his previous assignment—delivering tribute money to the Barbary States—he could only hope that America, which had neutralized the aggressive policies of France, would now turn its guns on the Algerian dey and other potentates.

By April 1802, Preble's health prompted him to leave the service, though the navy refused to accept his resignation, instead placing him on furlough. It proved to be a wise move. By the following year, he had regained enough of his health to be selected as the commodore of a squadron sailing to the Mediterranean to confront the Barbary States. *Essex* would be included in that squadron, though not before she sailed under Captain Bainbridge on another mission.

CHAPTER FOUR

Mediterranean Duty

I hope I shall never again be sent to Algiers with a tribute
except it be from the mouth of a cannon.

— CAPTAIN WILLIAM BAINBRIDGE

When Dey Hassan of Algiers died and was replaced by
Dey Bobba Mustapha, the American consul at Tunis,
William Eaton, went to greet the new leader. These were his
observations:

> *We were shown to a huge, shaggy beast, sitting on his
> rump upon a low bench covered with a cushion of embroi-
> dered velvet, with his hind legs gathered up like a tailor, or
> a bear. On our approach to him, he reached out his
> forepaw as if to receive something to eat. Our guide
> exclaimed, 'Kiss the Dey's hand!' The consul general
> bowed very elegantly, and kissed it, and we followed his
> example in succession. The animal seemed at that moment
> to be in a harmless mood. He grinned several times but*

*made very little noise. . . . Can any man believe that this
elevated brute has seven kings of Europe, two republics,
and a continent tributary to him when his whole naval
force is not equal to two line-of-battle ships? It is so.*

While the Barbary States did not possess impressive
armies or navies, they had been preying on European shipping for centuries. Upon gaining her independence and no
longer being under the protection of the British Royal
Navy, the United States soon got a taste of North African
depredations. No American captain better knew the frustrations in dealing with the Barbary potentates than William
Bainbridge.

DURING MUCH OF HER EARLY LIFE, *ESSEX*, LIKE MANY VESSELS IN THE YOUNG U.S.
NAVY, WAS ASSIGNED TO THE MEDITERRANEAN SEA TO PROTECT AMERICAN
INTERESTS FROM THE BARBARY STATES LINING THE NORTH AFRICAN COAST.

Bainbridge had been a Barbary victim twice: first as captain of the twenty-four-gun *George Washington* bearing tribute to Algiers and then as commander of the ill-fated frigate *Philadelphia*. He once wrote Secretary Stoddert: "This Regency [Algiers] looks on the United States exactly like this: you pay me tribute, by that you become my slaves, and then I have a right to order as I please."

Sandwiched between command of *George Washington* and *Philadelphia* was Bainbridge's brief tour as captain of *Essex*, a successful but not entirely satisfying cruise. It began in late April 1801, when he received the following letter from Acting Secretary of the Navy Samuel Smith, who had replaced Benjamin Stoddert:

You have arrived at the moment when arrangements are making for retaining Officers in service designated by Peace Establishment. Nine Captains are to be kept in service. Your general good Character makes me anxious that you should be one of number. Captain Preble has written that his state of health will not permit him to proceed with Squadron. Ship Essex *under his command will proceed from N.Y. to Hampton Roads where you will join & take command.*

The "Peace Establishment" was bureaucratic jargon for saying that once again, now that peace had been achieved with an enemy, in this case France, the government had decided to downsize the navy, a sore point with Stoddert. His public reasons for stepping down were ill health and sagging personal finances, but it is clear that he had departed mainly due to his disgust with the nation's vacillating attitude toward its navy.

Why Bainbridge was among the select few retained in the shrinking navy is not entirely clear. He had no great achievements to his name and, in fact, had one serious blunder. As was mentioned in Chaper One, his vessel, *Retaliation,* was captured in 1798 by two French frigates he'd mistaken for those of Great Britain. Bainbridge had atoned for his mistake, though, saving two American vessels sailing with him from capture by lying about their strength to his French captors. And, while a prisoner, he successfully negotiated for the release of not only his own crew but also hundreds of other American merchant sailors in captivity. These two acts were more than face-saving and humanitarian gestures; they possibly saved him from censure for surrendering *Retaliation* without a shot, an act the navy did not look upon kindly, no matter what the odds.

After his release, Bainbridge was promoted to the rank of master commandant and given charge of the brig *Norfolk*, eighteen guns. Under his command, *Norfolk* captured the French lugger *Republican* (a lugger is a small, usually two-masted vessel with fore and aft sails) and destroyed several other vessels.

William Bainbridge was born in Princeton, New Jersey, on 7 May 1774, the fourth son of Dr. Absalom Bainbridge. Young William was given a good education but elected to enter the merchant marine at fifteen. At the impressive age of nineteen, he was in command of his own ship. Three years later, he showed his skill in battle when his vessel, *Hope*, was attacked by a British schooner during a voyage from Bordeaux. Though out-gunned (eight to four) and out manned (thirty to nine), Bainbridge and his men kept up their fire until the schooner struck her colors. The young captain did not have enough crew members to take the schooner as a prize. Instead, he told the vessel's skipper "to go about his business and report to his masters that if they wanted his ship they must send a greater force and a more skillful commander."

(COURTESY OF U.S. NAVY)

WILLIAM BAINBRIDGE, SECOND CAPTAIN OF *ESSEX*, MADE HIS SHARE OF NAVAL BLUNDERS, BUT WENT DOWN IN HISTORY AS CAPTAIN OF THE U.S.S. *CONSTITUTION* WHEN SHE SENT HMS *JAVA* TO THE BOTTOM OF THE SEA IN 1812.

Bainbridge was an impos-ing figure for his day, six feet tall, with a fair complexion and dark eyes. In 1798, returning from a cruise to Europe, he met and married Susan Heyliger on the island of St. Eustatius in the West Indies. They would have four children.

Bainbridge was ardent and impetuous, far more courte-ous with his officers than his sailors. He certainly took no guff from the British, especially during the post–Revolution-ary War years, when the Stars and Stripes garnered little respect throughout the world. A Royal Navy captain once overtook one of Bainbridge's vessels and impressed a sailor he suspected of being English. Bainbridge replaced his crew member by stopping a British merchantman and taking one of its sailors into his ranks. (Legend has it that he was careful to chose a bachelor—so as not to steal any man from his family—and that the man was happy with the transfer to the American vessel.)

Bainbridge was a strict captain who did things by the book and held a tight rein on his ship, as is evidenced by this notice posted on board *Essex* as she sailed in June 1801:

> *Should any person quit his station before he is regularly relieved or ordered to do so, he is to ride spanker boom three hours on succeeding watch & his grog stopped for three days, for second offence of similar nature he is to be put in irons & flogged as I may direct & lose his grog for 15 days.*

(A word about naval punishments: The spanker boom was a long spar about a foot in diameter, positioned about six feet above the quarter deck, that held down the lower edge of the spanker sail. A rider would have to hold onto the boom with his arms and legs wrapped around it as it shifted back and forth to catch the wind. Rough seas and inclement weather made the ride far more difficult. At the end of three hours, the guilty party would have sore muscles, chafed skin (if he were forced to ride it bare-chested) and a bruised ego, for the punishment was meant to humiliate. This penalty was good only for waisters and other sailors. Foretopmen and junior officers, who were used to going aloft, were chastened by "mast-heading," where the offender was sent aloft to the upper crosstrees to hold on tightly for a period of time.)

It could not have been easy for a captain as tough and proud as Bainbridge to command a ship appointed to take tribute to the Algerian dey in the fall of 1800. Yet, this ignoble task—to deliver a shipment of lumber, sugar, china, coffee, cloves, tin, and gunpowder—fell to the twenty-six-year-old captain of *George Washington*. The annual tribute, established by a treaty signed in 1795, was the price America paid for the dey's "friendship," shorthand for keeping Algerian cruisers from preying on American merchantmen. Bainbridge discovered the truth about the so-called friendship when, upon delivery of the goods, the dey ordered him to deliver *his* Algerian tribute (presents valued at $500,000) to the sultan in Constantinople, to whom *he* paid tribute and with whom he was of late on shaky terms. Worst of all, the dey demanded that Bainbridge make the delivery under the Algerian flag—an insult to the captain of any navy. The flag of another nation was flown for two reasons only: either to create a ruse to fool enemy ships or, after surrender, to show defeat.

Bainbridge refused to make the voyage. The dey threatened to scrap the friendship treaty, pointing out that it had been signed by his predecessor. Furthermore, he threatened war—the last thing America needed, now that she was locked into a skirmish with France. Of course, there was no time for Bainbridge to consult his superiors in Washington, and he finally agreed to make the voyage. The factor that perhaps turned the tables for him was the position of his ship. He had made the mistake of anchoring *George Washington* deep inside the harbor, within range of the dey's guns.

There also is some suggestion that self-interest influenced Bainbridge's decision. Having been allotted some space aboard his frigate, it is possible that the American captain saw an opportunity to make some money in a voyage to exotic Constantinople. At the time, a captain's salary amounted to a little over $1,900 per year. While that sum was generally sufficient to support a family in a respectable middle-class life, as well as allow the captain to do his share of required entertaining at sea, it was far from a bonanza. American captains looked for ways to augment their income, the most obvious being the capture of enemy merchantmen and men-of-war. As one would expect, however, these income producers could not be counted on and rarely amounted to a windfall. Captains also made money moving large amounts of specie from one port to another for American merchants. A man-of-war, like a floating armored car, provided a good deal more security than a merchant or packet vessel. This practice, regulated by the American government, allowed captains to take 0.5 percent on the first $10,000 and 0.25 percent on the remainder. The system was known as "carrying freight," and U.S. Navy captains could do it only for U.S. citizens. A captain who transported $20,000 from Rio de Janeiro to Baltimore made $75—about half a month's pay. Specie was simply money in coins, as opposed to paper currency. Coins were more valuable on the high seas since paper money could fluctuate more in value.

While nearly all captains were anxious to boost their incomes, it seems out of character that for the almighty dollar, Bainbridge would do the dey's bidding. For a self-respecting captain, no amount of money could compensate for the ignominy of carrying a cargo of tigers, ostriches, sheep, parrots, and antelopes, not to mention the Algerian ambassador and his entourage of one hundred, on a three-week voyage.

Bainbridge sailed under the Algerian colors, though he struck them and raised the Stars and Stripes when out at sea. He took great pleasure in tacking his ship, which confused the praying Muslims on board, who had a difficult time reckoning which direction was east. After tasting Barbary humiliations, Bainbridge would write to Secretary Stoddert

(COURTESY OF U.S. NAVY)

ALGIERS IN 1800. ITS LEADERS HAD BEEN DEMANDING TRIBUTE PAYMENTS FROM EUROPEAN STATES FOR CENTURIES. COUNTRIES THAT WOULD NOT PAY UP HAD THEIR MERCHANT VESSELS CAPTURED AND CREWS ENSLAVED.

these prophetic words: "Had we 10 or 12 frigates or sloops in these seas, I am well convinced in my own mind that we should not experience these mortifying degradations."

Bainbridge was politely received by the sultan, who had never before seen the Stars and Stripes. The Algerian emissary, however, was accorded a cool reception, and while he kowtowed to the sultan for six weeks, Bainbridge cruised the area. *George Washington* finally returned to Algiers in December 1800. The dey demanded that he make another voyage to Constantinople to further assuage the sultan, but the captain refused. On this occasion, Bainbridge anchored his ship well outside the range of Algerian cannons. Moreover, he held in his possession a firman, a decree from the Sultan that, in this case, permitted Bainbridge safe passage and good treatment. It was rare for a Westerner to possess such a paper; it turned the tables on the dey and even allowed Bainbridge to obtain release of French prisoners, including women and children, whom he delivered to Europe. (Though America technically was still at war with France, freeing Christians from Muslim captivity was considered a noble act above the cause of war.) Once again, Bainbridge exhibited his uncanny ability to reverse a bad situation.

Several days after Thomas Jefferson became president in 1801, he convened his cabinet to discuss the increasing belligerence of the Barbary States. The new president quickly learned that campaign promises—specifically one to cut government costs, including those of the navy—tied his hands. After the Quasi-War, the United States had reduced its victorious fleet, selling all but six ships and retaining only

9 of 28 captains and 36 of 110 lieutenants. It was a clear sign that Congress and the nation still chose to walk the risky road of appeasement rather than bear the cost of maintaining a respectable army and navy during peacetime. President Jefferson had to find a way to keep military spending to a minimum while defending national interests.

He soon hit upon a compromise familiar to all presidents who must uphold national pride but who are not prepared to ask Congress for a declaration of war: He would flex American military muscle on his own authority. To that end, he dispatched a squadron to the Mediterranean to protect U.S. shipping, create a show of force, and retaliate if provoked.

The squadron, dispatched on 20 May 1801, was lead by Commodore Richard Dale, who sailed aboard *President*, a ship captained by James Barron. (Often, commodores did not command their own ship; thus, they would not be distracted in their efforts to oversee an entire squadron. The title also allowed them to move to another vessel if the need arose.) Other vessels in the squadron included the thirty-eight-gun *Philadelphia*, under Barron's brother, Samuel; *Essex*, under Bainbridge; and the twelve-gun schooner *Enterprise*, under Lieutenant Andrew Sterret.

Richard Dale was one of the more seasoned veterans of the American navy. Born in Norfolk, Virginia, in 1756, the eldest of five children, he took a berth at the age of twelve aboard his uncle's ship, which was sailing for Liverpool. As the Revolutionary War drew near, he became a lieutenant aboard a warship belonging to the state of Virginia. After being captured and imprisoned, he met an old schoolmate who had decided not to join the American cause and who convinced Dale to change sides. While the two sailed up the Rappahannock River, they came under American gunfire, and Dale was wounded by a musket ball to the head. He was brought back to Norfolk and, during his convalescing, resolved "never again to put myself in the way of the balls of my country."

After recovering in July 1776, Dale became a midshipman aboard *Lexington*, commanded by John Barry, and took part in a number of successful voyages, including a cruise in the English Channel to capture English merchantmen. In September 1777, however, *Lexington* was captured. The crew were imprisoned not as prisoners of war but as men guilty of treason and, therefore, kept under harsher conditions. Dale escaped six months later but was recaptured and confined for forty days in a dungeon called the "black hole." He fled again in February 1779, made his way to France, and joined John Paul Jones aboard *Bon Homme Richard* as a master's mate. Impressed with the young sailor, Jones promoted Dale to first lieutenant. During *Richard*'s defeat of the British frigate *Serapis*, Dale, swinging from a rope, led the American boarding party to secure the victory in the closing moments of one of the most notable naval battles of the Revolutionary War.

At war's end, Dale joined the merchant service, commanding several ships in the East India trade. By 1794, however, with trouble heating up for the young democracy, he was soon appointed one of six captains in the newly resurrected American navy. By 1801, his fine record secured him the appointment as commodore, at which time he sailed, as was mentioned, with *President*, *Philadelphia*, *Essex*, and *Enterprise* to the Mediterranean.

No naval officer would have envied Dale. His instructions were a commander's nightmare. He had to go up against a crafty enemy, yet he could play only defense. He could not fire his guns unless attacked. If he took prisoners, he was ordered to land them as soon as possible. He was not allowed to take captured ships and their cargo as prizes—a fact not lost on American sailors looking to augment their meager pay. And, as if Dale did not have enough to handcuff him, he was allowed to blockade the harbors only of those nations who had declared war on America—yet the Barbary States often came to each other's aid.

One such declaration was made the day before Dale sailed, though he did not get word of it until he arrived in the Mediterranean. The bashaw of Tripoli had chopped down the flagpole at the American consulate, an act deemed a declaration of war.

The North Africa state of Tripoli had won its autonomy from the Ottoman sultan of Turkey in 1711. The first ruler, Ahmad Qaramanli, unified the country by strengthening the navy and putting down internal revolts. Political stability allowed economic life to prosper, and Tripoli increased its exports of wheat, barley, dates, and textiles. When Ahmad's reign ended in 1745, however, the nation deteriorated, due mostly to the weak leadership of his son and, after him, his grandson, Ali. Infighting among Qaramanli family members and outside groups worsened the situation until 1795, when Ali's youngest son, Yusuf, took power.

Yusuf's goal was to return Tripoli to the glory days of his great-grandfather. He set out to accomplish this by reinvigorating the dilapidated navy so that it could prey on foreign merchant ships and their crews, which could be ransomed at a high price. A stronger navy also enabled Tripoli to demand tribute money as a kind of insurance against seizures. Most European nations viewed paying tributes as the cost of doing business in the Mediterranean and signed treaties so that their merchantmen could sail unmolested. Treaties provided for an immediate lump sum, followed by annual payments in the form of cash, naval stores, and even ships themselves. Nations that did not sign on the dotted line were at risk. When Austria and Sweden refused to pay tribute money, their ships and men were captured and ransomed for over $100,000. They then signed on, like the rest of Europe. Both seizures and tributes were big moneymakers for the North African states.

The United States was particularly at risk in this situation because it had a small navy over three thousand miles away. After a series of captures and ransoms, America, too, signed a treaty with Tripoli. But now, Bashaw Yusuf Qaramanli had declared war. He believed the spirit of the treaty had been violated by America's more favorable treatment of the dey of Algiers, who had recently received a frigate from his friends in Washington, D.C. The bashaw now wanted one, too.

William Eaton, the American consul in Tunis, hearing of the bashaw's deed before learning of the U.S. decision to send an American squadron, sagely wrote: "It is now a fair question whether our treasury shall be opened to buy oil of roses to perfume that pirate's beard or our gun batteries to chastise his temerity." This time America had chosen the latter—though with hesitation. Jeffersonian foreign policy kept an extremely tight rein on naval officers, for fear that they would provoke a war that would drain U.S. coffers.

American captains, like those who sailed with Dale's squadron, had to prepare their crews for the Barbary sailors' mode of warfare. Barbary captains tried to close with an enemy ship as quickly as possible so that their men could board the vessel for hand-to-hand combat with their razor-sharp scimitars. This tactic made up for their general inferiority with cannons. Against this technique, the best defense was offense—raw firepower that would keep the enemy ship at a distance. American seamen aboard *Essex* and other ships spent much of their time perfecting the teamwork needed for effective and rapid broadsides. Gunnery practice was taken regularly and with real cannonballs (a practice Royal Navy captains deemed too expensive). American captains would set up a flag attached to a floating barrel a half mile away and let their gun crews perfect their aim.

Essex was equipped with twenty-six twelve-pounder cannons on her gun deck and ten six-pounders on her quarter deck. These designations indicated the weight of the ball fired by the individual guns. The diameters of twelve-pound and six-pound balls were four and a half and three and a half inches, respectively. (The ball from the thirty-two-pound carronade—known as a "smasher"—which would get *Essex* in trouble during her final battle, was six inches in diameter.) The guns were made of cast iron and weighed thirty-two hundred pounds (twelve-pounder) and sixteen-hundred pounds (six-pounder) and rested upon wooden carriages. When not in firing position, the guns were kept well secured inside the gunports. If one of these cannons came loose and rolled about as the ship heaved, it could cause tremendous damage to the vessel and any sailor that got in its way (hence the term *loose cannon*).

The ship's company, including the gun crews, were directed to their assigned battle stations by a long roll on the drums of the marine bandsmen and by the shouted orders and whistles of the boatswain's mates. The senior man at each gun, designated the gun captain, ordered his crew to remove the lines that held the gun fast and then to run the gun inboard for loading. The ship's gunner and his mates were stationed at the magazines (there were normally two, one forward and one aft), ready to distribute ammunition. To ensure safety, the magazines were located deep in the hold of the vessel, near the keel, where enemy shot could not strike them. The magazines were sheathed in lead or copper sheeting, which was fastened with copper nails to ensure that they were fireproof and waterproof and that no iron fastenings would be left exposed, where a brush from a shoe nail could cause a fatal spark. Anyone entering the magazine put felt slippers over his shoes, also to prevent sparks. The magazine was dark, except for a lantern in an adjacent compartment that shown its light through a window in the intervening bulkhead.

Well before the roll of the drums and the incessant action of battle, the gunner had measured out separate charges of powder and poured it into individual woolen serge bags called cartridges. There were different sizes for different guns. Before being filled and tied shut, the cartridge looked like a modern tube sock. Cartridges eliminated the time-consuming and dangerous handling of loose powder, especially important because powder used in the nineteenth century was far more volatile than modern, smokeless powder. When the gun was fired, the cartridge was completely consumed. As a safety precaution, the bore of the cannon was swabbed out with a wet piece of sheepskin attached to a ramrod to extinguish lingering sparks. Then the next cartridge was rammed down the barrel. The shot, which was made of iron and did not explode, was kept near the guns for quick use.

Since the magazine door had to be left open during battle, a woolen blanket with a vertical slit down the middle was hung over the entrance. Cartridges were handed out through the slit. The blanket was damp, again to keep out sparks. Boys from the crew, called "powder monkeys," carried cartridges to the guns in leather buckets with a removable cover called a passing box. The box also allowed the powder monkeys to get past marine sentries, who were stationed at each hatchway on the gun deck to keep sailors from fleeing to the hold when the fighting got too heavy.

When an enemy ship was closing fast, the captain's commands came fast and furiously:

"Cast loose your guns!"—The lashings holding the cannons against the bulwarks were removed.

"Level yours guns!"—The cannon barrel was lowered so that it could be pushed through the gunport.

"Take out your tompions!"—A wooden plug or canvas cover over the gun's bore to keep it dry was removed.

"Load with cartridge!"—The sack of gunpowder was shoved down the end of the bore with a rammer.

"Shot your guns!"—The gun was loaded with one of three kinds of shot. Round shot, a cannon ball, was used to "hull" the enemy ship—that is, to make a hole at the waterline or damage masts; chain shot, two hollow cannon ball halves attached by a chain, was employed to tear apart the enemy's sails and rigging; and grape shot, two-inch iron balls wrapped inside canvas bags, was used for the deadly purpose of disabling enemy sailors and marines. (Langradge, a devilish mixture of nails or sharp pieces of metal, was another method of taking out men.)

"Run out your guns!"—The muzzle of the cannon was shoved through the gunport.

"Aim!"—Each gun captain stood right behind the gun and directed his crew to position the gun barrel properly, using the handspikes and quoins. Guns were aimed by the use of primitive sights.

A U.S. MAN-OF-WAR TAKES TARGET PRACTICE IN THE MID-NINETEENTH CENTURY.
NOTE THE SMOKESTACKS: VESSELS IN THIS ERA WERE POWERED BY STEAM AND WIND,
THOUGH THE MODE OF TARGET PRACTICE HAD NOT CHANGED SINCE SAILING SHIP DAYS.

(Lord Nelson had once remarked: "As to the plan for pointing a gun truer than we do at present, I shall, of course, look at it, or be happy, if necessary, to use it; but I hope we shall be able, as usual, to get so close to our enemies that our shot cannot miss the object.")

"Prime!"—A small amount of fine gunpowder carried in a powder horn was sprinkled into the touchhole.

"Fire!"—At this order, precisely timed with the roll of the ship, the gun captain would pull on a lanyard, which triggered a flintlock mechanism that fired the gun. It was hoped that every cannon on the ship would fire in unison, shredding sails, knocking out masts, and killing the enemy. (It should be noted that the flintlock mechanism was coming into use at the start of the nineteenth century. The mechanism was very much like that used on a muzzle-loading musket. The locks were safer to use and ensured a more even broadside. In the event the lock malfunctioned, each gun captain had at the ready a specially treated rope, called a slow match, that could be used to fire the gun.)

The shot, fired at 1,150 feet per second, gave the cannons a tremendous recoil, which was controlled with heavy ropes called breeching lines that were secured to bolts fastened to the side of the ship. The lines literally kept the guns from careening backward across the deck. After a gun had been fired several times, it would heat up significantly, causing the size of the bore to contract slightly. This would add greatly to the violence of the recoil. A hot gun would literally leap off the deck as it fired. Breeching lines that gave way meant disaster; the gun could wipe out crew members and even damage guns on the opposite side of the ship.

If these broadsides did not work—and the Barbary ship closed in—American ships possessed a second line of defense: sharpshooting marines perched in the ship's rigging to kill any sailors that attempted to swing aboard. In addition, the crew itself, armed with pistols, swords, and pikes, would muster to repel any boarders.

Bainbridge's diary aboard *Essex* from 17 July 1801 states:

> *At 9 AM, cleared ship for action. Slung all yards, stoppered sheets & rove preventer braces. Musquets in Tops. Small arms on deck & every preparation as in battle, came to quarters. Exercised great guns . . . repelled boarders and boarded.*

This was not real battle but, as Bainbridge states, "a sham fight." Practice made perfect. Bainbridge's diary, in fact, is filled with entries of such drills.

In July the squadron arrived in Gibraltar, where the Americans learned of Tripoli's declaration of war. Anchored in the harbor was the twenty-eight-gun *Meshouda*, a brig under the command of Tripoli's Admiral Murad Reis. Formerly the merchant brig *Betsy*, out of Boston, *Meshouda* had been captured by Tripoli just after the United States had ransomed it from Morocco.

Betsy cum *Meshouda*, in fact, had seen almost as many transformations as Murad Reis himself. Born in Scotland as Peter Leslie, the blond-haired Reis went to sea as a young boy. However, he deserted to avoid court-martial for mutiny and theft aboard his vessel, *Hampden*. He eventually converted to the Muslim faith and joined the Tripolitan navy (though the chronology of these events is not clear), which had its share of European drifters. Reis did himself no harm when he married the bashaw's daughter. He soon was made admiral.

Consul Eaton fervently believed that capturing *Meshouda* would cripple the bashaw's navy and allow the United States to negotiate peace on very favorable terms. In a letter dated 2 September to Samuel Barron and William Bainbridge, he wrote:

> *If you get possession of Commodore [Admiral Reis], force him to surrender his ships. His own is a Boston-built vessel of 18 nine-pounders on the main deck, six fours on her quarter, two bow and two stern chasers. His other [vessel] is a Swedish brig of 14 four-pounders. When you have executed project proceed to Tunis without making yourself known and give me notice. I will board you and lay before you a scheme I have to decoy Bashaw of Tripoli into your ship. . . . Cannot but repeat if you get possession of English renegade Murad Reis, it will decide contest with Tripoli.*

Eaton was convinced that capture of the vessels, whose sailors came from Tripoli's "first families," would "excite an insurrection in the Bashaw's kingdom and give us entire command of terms." However, there was a problem with Eaton's plan. *Meshouda* had dropped anchor at Gibraltar, a neutral port. The U.S. Navy could not touch her.

The bashaw's declaration of war did give Commodore Dale leave to blockade Tripoli's harbor. He took *President* and *Enterprise* east, to stand guard over Tripoli, and posted *Philadelphia* off Gibraltar, to watch Reis. As for *Essex*, Dale ordered Bainbridge to proceed to Barcelona, where "I understand there are 25 or 30 American vessels . . . and more at other Spanish ports waiting convoy to see them safe out of Straits [of Gibraltar]." He advised Bainbridge to keep a "lookout & speak every vessel to see if they are American captured by corsairs." On a number of occasions, American navy captains hailed ships bearing the Stars and Stripes only to find the vessel had been captured by Barbary pirates, who had imprisoned the American crew below.

Bainbridge and the crew of *Essex* had not been sailing for long when they encountered a new problem—not the usual harassment from Barbary pirates or bullying from British warships but an insult from the officers of *San Sebastian*, a Spanish xebec anchored at Barcelona. (A xebec was a three-masted Mediterranean ship with a long, overhanging bow and of significantly inferior strength, compared to a frigate.) Captain Bainbridge was ordered aboard the xebec to identify himself, a terrible breach of naval etiquette. The captain of one warship could not order his counterpart aboard unless to demand his surrender or, in the case of the Spaniards, to bully him. The crew of the xebec was testing the mettle of the new American navy. Bainbridge refused, and several gunshots were fired at the Americans.

Bainbridge kept his cool and reported the incident to the American consul. After diplomats from both sides fired off several rounds of epistles, the Spanish king directed the captain of the xebec to formally apologize to Bainbridge and his officers. In addition, the king issued an order to all Spanish captains to treat all U.S. naval personnel with courtesy—especially those of *Essex*.

Bainbridge and his crew then settled into the routine but important mission of escorting American ships through the Strait of Gibraltar, where Admiral Reis had conveniently positioned himself to raid American commerce. The escort procedure was to enter a port, such as Alicante or Malaga, and fire three guns, a signal for interested vessels to join the convoy. On 31 August, alone, *Essex* sailed with twenty-six vessels under her protection. It is a testament to this ship—as well as to *Philadelphia*, which kept Admiral Reis bottled up at Gibraltar—that Tripoli captured no American merchantmen after the arrival of Dale's squadron.

In addition to convoying vessels through the Mediterranean, Bainbridge aggressively pursued ships he suspected might be involved in capturing merchantmen. On 16 August, the crew spotted a xebec bearing down on a convoy being escorted by *Essex*. The Salem frigate gave chase and fired several shots to bring the vessel to. Through his spyglass, Bainbridge saw sailors wearing turbans. He immediately fired two guns over the ship's bow, a signal for battle. The shots elicited no reaction, and with the wind dying down, Bainbridge figured he had better act decisively. He ordered his crew to fire a broadside, which cut away the enemy's rigging and sails and "obliged him to haul down his colors." The Americans boarded the ship, which hailed from Tangiers. Bainbridge had to exercise great caution. America already was at war with Tripoli and on shaky terms with Algiers. There was nothing to be gained by provoking the rulers of another Barbary state. Bainbridge sent Dr. Wells, the ship's surgeon, to dress the wounds of an injured sailor. Then, satisfied that the ship was not responsible for any mischief, he released it.

A XEBEC, A FAST, OFTEN THREE-MASTED VESSEL, WAS COMMONLY USED
BY MEDITERRANEAN NATIONS.

Meanwhile, twelve hundred miles to the east, *President* and *Enterprise* had been watching Tripoli, successfully bottling up the bashaw's larger warships but unable to take action against Tripolitan feluccas—small vessels with a shallow draft that allowed them to run the blockade by staying close to shore. The feluccas were bringing Tripoli needed foodstuffs while Dale and his men sat powerless. They did not dare to operate their men-of-war in the uncharted and dangerously shallow waters along the coast or to attack the well-defended harbor.

Lieutenant Sterrett, however, commanding *Enterprise*, soon brought the navy some satisfaction with his guns. After a month-long standoff, Dale dispatched *Enterprise* to the island of Malta for fresh water. The twelve-gun sloop had not sailed long before she spotted the fourteen-gun *Tripoli*. A battle erupted, and Sterrett's well-trained crew soon laid waste to the Barbary vessel. All went according to plan. When *Tripoli* attempted to close on *Enterprise* so that her crew could board, marines raked the enemy with gunfire. *Tripoli*'s commander, Admiral Rais Mahomet Rous, finally hauled down his flag. When the Americans closed in to take possession of the vessel, however, the admiral raised the Tripolitan flag and commenced firing. A furious Sterrett countered with another broadside. The admiral tried his surrender trick again, without success. Sterrett kept up the pressure. Rous finally surrendered for good by throwing his flag into the sea. Sterrett sent aboard Lieutenant David Porter, who found thirty dead and thirty wounded among a crew of eighty. The Americans had not lost a single man.

Sterrett was not allowed to take *Tripoli* as a prize, as per the watered-down instructions issued by the U.S. government. His only course of action was to disable her, which he did by chopping down her masts and shoving her cannons into the sea. Admiral Rous, upon arriving in Tripoli with his crippled ship and injured men, was disgraced by the bashaw.

Sterrett and his crew did not walk away from the battle entirely empty-handed. Because they were not allowed to take the vessel as a prize, Congress later awarded them an extra month's pay for their welcome victory.

Throughout the early months of 1802, Essex—cruising as far east as Tripoli—continued to shepherd convoys into the relative safety of the Atlantic Ocean. In his orders to Bainbridge, Dale stated:

> *Your station will be in and around Gibraltar, Algeciras, the Straits and the straits mouth as far as Malaga. . . . Give every protection to American vessels also Swedish vessels as Swedish ships of war will do same towards our merchant vessels. . . . In no case leave your station for any length of time without being certain that two Tripolitan corsairs now laying at Gibraltar with their yards and topmasts down are in such a situation that they cannot go to sea under much longer time than you will be from station.*

Meshouda did not escape from Gibraltar; unfortunately for the Americans, however, Admiral Reis and his 350 men did. Reis bribed local skippers to carry his crew across the Mediterranean to the African coast, where they made their way to Tripoli on foot. The ship sat in the harbor, with the Americans unable to touch it. Nevertheless, the vessel was no longer a threat to Mediterranean shipping.

Commodore Dale was ordered home in March 1802. Considering that his hands were tied and he could not mount a full-scale attack on Tripoli, his ten-month term was a notable success. His squadron had allowed American shipping to sail unmolested, kept Admiral Reis bottled up in Gibraltar, and—thanks to Sterrett—neutralized the bashaw's vessel *Tripoli*. It was a good start, though the end

(COURTESY OF U.S. NAVY)

An American naval captain in full dress, as he would have appeared during the Barbary Wars in 1802. The coat was made of blue cloth, with the collar, lapels, and edges of the coat trimmed in gold lace. The vest and breeches were white, the epaulets also gold.

for Commodore Dale. The navy again asked him to lead a squadron to the Mediterranean—but with one change. Unlike the previous cruise, he would have to command his own vessel, having no captain under him. For Dale, the request was a severe breach of protocol based on a desire to save money at any cost; it triggered his resignation from the navy.

Essex was also ordered back to the United States. After making temporary repairs, Bainbridge sailed to New York in thirty-five days, arriving on 22 July 1802. The ship was then ordered to proceed to the Washington Navy Yard for further repairs, which did not make Bainbridge's crew happy. Many men had signed on at New York and wanted to be discharged there. Bainbridge's diary entry from 25 July picks up the story:

> *Discovered symptoms of mutiny among the crew, owing to the information they had rec'd from the Newspapers of the ship being ordered to Washington. They informed me by letter of their determination not to proceed;*

I then informed them I was determined to carry the orders of the Secy of the Navy into effect. Having ordered the Officers and Marines, mustered & examined the crew individually, left them the choice of doing their duty, or to be carried in irons . . . eighteen chose the latter & were immediately confined.

The mutiny never occurred, and by 29 July, *Essex* was bound for Washington.

Bainbridge has been criticized for having a low view of sailors, considering them nothing more than beasts who needed the threat of the cat or chains to keep them in line. His prejudice is chalked up to the fact that he joined the navy as a lieutenant, rather than working his way up through the ranks. While Bainbridge might have possessed little empathy for the difficult life of an ordinary sailor, no captain could countenance the slightest hint of mutiny. Bainbridge was obligated to follow orders from his superiors, just as his men were obligated to follow *his*.

Commodore Dale's replacement was Captain Richard Morris. Morris arrived in Gibraltar aboard *Chesapeake* (thirty-six guns) in May 1802 with a fresh squadron: *Constellation* (thirty-six guns), *New York* (thirty-six guns), *Adams* (twenty-eight guns), and the *John Adams* (twenty-eight guns). *Essex*, meanwhile, was "in ordinary" (i.e., placed out of commission until her services would be needed again) and undergoing extensive and costly repairs on her hull. It seems that a good bit of pine was used in the construction of the ship, and its chemical reaction with the white oak caused much rot.

Bainbridge, after superintending construction of the brig *Syren* and the schooner *Vixen,* was assigned command of the thirty-six-gun *Philadelphia* in a squadron commanded by Edward Preble in 1803. Preble, who had regained his health, replaced Captain Morris, whose year in the Mediterranean had been a failure. Ordered to blockade Tripoli, he instead had spent time convoying ships and—because he'd brought his wife along—dropping anchor at various ports for fetes. When Morris returned to the United States in July 1803, he was censured for "inactive and dilatory conduct."

In addition to *Philadelphia,* Preble's squadron included his own vessel, *Constitution* (forty-four guns), and the brigs *Argus* (eighteen guns) and *Syren* (sixteen guns), as well as the schooners *Vixen*, *Enterprise*, and *Nautilus*, each with twelve guns. The navy had seen from earlier experience that its frigates were useless for inshore work. The latter four ships were of shallow enough draft to enter shoal waters along the coast but sufficiently armed to defeat any vessel they met there.

The U.S. government, exhausted with the stalemate in the Mediterranean, had now given its captains permission to patrol more aggressively, as is revealed in the navy secretary's orders to Captain Bainbridge, which gave him "authority to subdue, seize & make prizes of all vessels, goods & effects belonging to the Bashaw of Tripoli or his subjects." However, the United States in no way wanted to rankle other Barbary states, and Bainbridge's orders were qualified with this word of caution: "Your Commission extending only to capture of vessels, goods & effects belonging to Bashaw . . . rights of all other nations are to be respected."

The Barbary region, however, was always filled with surprises. Preble and his squadron would arrive in the Mediterranean to find that Morocco now had declared war on America. The nation's emperor was angry that the ship *Meshouda*—originally the American brig *Betsy;* then captured by and ransomed from Morocco; then captured by Tripoli, renamed *Meshouda*, and commanded by Admiral Reis; then abandoned in Gibraltar; and now being sailed under the Moroccan flag—had been captured by Captain John Rodgers of *John Adams*. Rodgers had stopped the vessel as it was trying to run the blockade of Tripoli with guns and other contraband. (It also was possible that the Moroccan crew was going to restore the ship to the bashaw.)

Morocco's declaration of war was no idle threat, as Captain Bainbridge soon discovered. Two days after entering the Mediterranean, flying England's Union Jack as a ruse to cover his American identity, he hailed two mysterious ships, one of which turned out to be the twenty-two-gun Moroccan *Mirboka*, out to raid American commerce. The other vessel—Bainbridge discovered after running up the Stars and Stripes, revealing his true identity as well as the *Philadelphia*'s thirty-six guns—was the American brig *Celia*, whose Yankee crew was imprisoned below decks. Both ships were captured.

Commodore Preble knew the last thing he needed was a war on two fronts: Morocco in the west and Tripoli in the east. In an attempt to resolve the situation, he immediately sailed into Tangiers, where he requested and received an audience with the emperor. The meeting was tense. Five thousand Moroccan soldiers lined the beaches. As Preble and his entourage approached, the emperor's men ordered him to remove his sword, as was the Moorish custom. Preble refused, making it perfectly clear that America had come to bargain on its own terms. Preble was then asked to kneel before the emperor. Again, Preble declined. When the emperor asked him if he was not afraid of being imprisoned, Preble pointed out that his ships lay inside the harbor with their decks cleared for action. Their crews had been ordered to level Tangiers should their captain not return.

The emperor backed down, disavowed the actions of any Moroccan ships that had raided American merchantmen, and canceled the declaration of war. Preble departed with a re-ratification of a 1786 treaty that the emperor's father had signed with the United States, as well as with a fresh letter of friendship and peace to President Jefferson. Still, the seasoned captain did not trust the emperor, and he left *Argus* off the coast as a reminder to Morocco that he meant business.

Preble ordered Bainbridge and the crew of *Philadelphia* to Tripoli to blockade the harbor. As Commodore Dale and Lieutenant Sterrett had discovered, it was a thankless assignment. Tripoli's waters were not only shallow but also uncharted and filled with shifting sandbars.

Exactly what inspired William Bainbridge to go after a Tripolitan corsair inside shoal waters is uncertain. Perhaps he was tired of waiting. Perhaps he was seeking revenge for the humiliating experience as the Algerian dey's messenger to Constantinople. Whatever the reason, 31 October 1803 was a day he would live to regret. While in pursuit of the corsair, *Philadelphia* struck Kaliusa Reef, a long sandbar that ran parallel to shore and was known only to local seamen. The American frigate became embedded in twelve feet of sand and rock.

On shore, five miles away, the Tripolitans watched as the American crew struggled valiantly to free their ship. Bainbridge's first order was to back the sails, in hopes of driving the ship off the reef with wind power. That remedy failed. He then ordered the guns to be thrown overboard in hopes of lightening the ship. The anchors went, too, as did the ship's store of fresh water. Still, the vessel would not budge. With the end near, Bainbridge had his sailors cut

(COURTESY OF MARINER'S MUSEUM)

USS *PHILADELPHIA* STRIKES KALIUSA REEF, A SANDBAR OFF THE COAST OF TRIPOLI. CAPTAIN BAINBRIDGE AND HIS CREW TRIED VALIANTLY TO FREE THE VESSEL, INCLUDING CHOPPING DOWN THE FOREMAST TO TAKE PRESSURE OFF THE BOW—ALL TO NO AVAIL.

down the foremast, which he hoped would loosen the ship by taking pressure off the bow. This attempt also failed.

The Tripolitans, smelling a dying beast, sent their gunboats to close in on *Philadelphia*. Bainbridge fired his stern cannons (which had not been pushed overboard), hoping to buy time while his crew tried to scuttle the ship to keep it from falling into Tripolitan possession. It was too late. Surrounded by Tripolitan gunboats, Bainbridge surrendered.

The Americans, numbering three hundred, were robbed of their personal possessions and marched through Tripoli under a spitting, jeering mob. The sailors were imprisoned in an old smokehouse and put to work building fortifications; the cook was sent to the bashaw's kitchen. Carpenters were ordered to repair the *Philadelphia*. The ship had been towed to port after a storm and high tide freed her, a few days after capture. To Preble's horror, Tripoli had added a very powerful thirty-six-gun frigate to her navy.

Life in Barbary prisons, called *bagnios*, belied the meaning of the word *bathhouse*. (Originally, Barbary slaves were held in bathhouses because of their high fortified walls.) Prisoners were given a blanket and clothing, which were replaced once a year. Rations were meager—hardly enough to sustain men for backbreaking labor that began at sunrise.

Philadelphia's officers were accorded better treatment, being housed in a castle overlooking the harbor. Occasionally, they even were given freedom to tour the city. Bainbridge made the best of it, instructing his first lieutenant, David Porter, to have the midshipmen use their time "to study navigation and read such books as we are in possession of that will improve their minds." Bainbridge himself fretted constantly about the loss of his ship, writing to his wife: "If I am censured, if it does not kill me, it would at least deprive me of the power of looking any of my race in the face."

He was allowed to write to Preble, and he did so often, presumably to plead for ransom. His epistles were delivered via the Danish consul. However, writing between the lines in lemon juice (which reveals itself when heated over a candle), Bainbridge called for destroying *Philadelphia*, which the enemy had prepared for battle by recovering her guns from the bottom of the harbor. Preble had been mulling over the same idea. By February 1804, he had made plans to send in a small group headed by Lieutenant Stephen Decatur to burn the ship.

The attack, which Admiral Nelson called "the most bold and daring act of this age," took place on 16 February. Using a captured ketch (a small, two-masted vessel named *Intrepid*), Decatur and eighty volunteers, disguised as Maltese sailors, slipped quietly alongside *Philadelphia*. They overpowered a small crew just as their plot was discovered. Swarming through the ship, the Americans set fires, and soon the timbers and rigging of *Philadelphia* were ablaze. There is some speculation that Decatur and his crew could have actually sailed the ship out of the harbor and returned it to the squadron. This would have been risky and possibly cost many lives. More importantly, Preble's order had been clear: Burn the ship and "make good your retreat." Decatur and his men made their retreat without a single man lost (and only one wounded) and were able to relish the fruit of their mission—that is, to watch loaded cannons on the

BARBARY CAPTAINS TRIED TO CLOSE WITH AN ENEMY VESSEL AS QUICKLY AS POSSIBLE SO THAT THEIR MEN, WELL-TRAINED IN THE USE OF SCIMITARS AND PIKES, COULD BOARD FOR HAND-TO-HAND COMBAT. HERE LIEUTENANT STEPHEN DECATUR IS ABOUT TO FIRE HIS PISTOL AT AN ENEMY CAPTAIN. THOUGH OUTNUMBERING THE AMERICANS BY TWO TO ONE, THE TRIPOLITANS SURRENDERED SOON AFTER THEIR CAPTAIN WAS KILLED.

burning *Philadelphia* fire shots into Tripoli. Bainbridge could sleep easier, even though he and his crew would remain in prison another sixteen months. For his heroism, Decatur was promoted to captain, at the tender age of twenty-four.

With *Philadelphia* destroyed, Captain Preble once again set his sights on Tripoli, which he planned to bombard into surrender. The first bombardment was launched on 3 August. To further press his point, Preble dispatched gun-boats provided by the Kingdom of Naples inside the outer harbor to attack Tripolitan vessels. A second bombardment was carried out four days later, but the standoff continued. Tripoli was heavily fortified and defended by twenty-five thousand soldiers.

A few hours after ending the second bombardment, Preble received word that the U.S. government, upon learning of the destruction of *Philadelphia*, was beefing up the Mediterranean squadron with four more frigates. Unfortunately for Preble, one of the vessels would be commanded by Samuel Barron, who was senior to him and would replace him as commodore.

Preble kept up the bombardments, hoping to wrest a settlement from the bashaw before Barron arrived. Preble even entertained a Tripolitan offer for peace—at a cost to America of $500 per man—but rejected it. Barron assumed command in mid-September.

Preble returned home disappointed, though perhaps consoled by sentiments expressed in letters like the one he received from an English diplomat at Malta:

> *If I were to offer my opinion, it would be that you have done well not to purchase peace with the enemy. A few brave men have indeed been sacrificed, but they could not have fallen in a better cause, and I even conceive it advisable to risk more lives rather than submit to terms which might encourage the Barbary States to add fresh demands and insult.*

Preble certainly was pleased by the hero's welcome he received in America. The nation was grateful for his

(COURTESY OF U.S. NAVY)

Edward Preble received a hero's welcome and a congressional gold medal for his work in standing firm against and weakening the resolve of the Bashaw of Tripoli. Preble was held in such high esteem that President Jefferson offered him the position of Secretary of the Navy in 1805.

firmness with Tripoli and downright thankful for his destruction of *Philadelphia*. He received a congressional gold medal. Indeed, Preble was held in such high esteem that in 1805 President Jefferson offered him the position of secretary of the navy. He had to decline; his health was worsening. He died the following year of tuberculosis.

He was buried in his hometown, Portland, Maine. The local paper gave this description of the ceremony:

> [He was interred amid] military honors and the ceremonies of religion and masonry. The bells were tolled from 8 to 9 O'clock in the morning; the colors were displayed at half mast from the shipping in the harbor, from the Observatory and other public places. At 1 O'clock the stores and offices were shut, followed by a total suspension of business and labor for the remainder of the day.

While the Frigate *Essex* had many years left, her first captain was dead.

As for William Bainbridge, he again landed on his feet. He was not censured for the loss of the *Philadelphia*, even though her capture had drastically altered the course of the war. As Preble had written, "Were it not for that loss, I have no doubt that we would have had peace with Tripoli in the Spring [of 1804]." Preble had decided that Bainbridge was not at fault—that he had shown initiative in chasing the Tripolitan ships and had run aground on an uncharted reef. The war's eventual outcome—the surrender of Tripoli— also might have worked in Bainbridge's favor.

Bainbridge's embarrassment, along with the fact that he had a family to support, led him to take a naval furlough and to enter the merchant service. He steered clear of naval life, except to make a trip to Washington, D.C., in 1805, with Samuel Barron and Preble, to lobby the government in favor of a stronger navy. Their efforts had little effect.

Bainbridge was in St. Petersburg, Russia, in 1811, when he received news of impending war with England. Upon returning to the United States, he was given command of *Constitution*, which had just returned from her stunning victory over HMS *Guerriere* (thirty-eight guns) on 19 August 1812. It was a major blow to Britain's notion of total naval superiority; Joshua Humphreys's fortified frigate had done its job. *Constitution*'s captain, Isaac Hull, had declined another tour, due to poor health, and Bainbridge took command, joining a squadron that included *Essex*, now under command of Captain David Porter, in October 1812. Sailing alone thirty miles off the coast of Brazil, *Constitution* encountered the thirty-eight-gun British frigate *Java*, Captain Henry Lambert, with four hundred men, on 29 December 1812. The firing began. Bainbridge was wounded early in the fierce battle, and his ship's steering wheel was destroyed. However, he refused to give up, steering the ship by shouting orders from the quarterdeck to the deck below, where his crew had rigged emergency steering cables. The battle raged on for two hours.

When the smoke cleared, *Java* had struck her flag. Lambert and sixty-four of his crew were wounded; sixty more were dead. *Java* was beyond salvage, and after British survivors were taken aboard *Constitution*, she was burned. The Americans had nine dead and twenty-five wounded. It was another extraordinary triumph for the United States.

Bainbridge's victory was celebrated with a parade and naval ball. With *Java* destroyed, there was no vessel to bring into prize court. Nevertheless, Congress awarded the crew $100,000 for the victory, which put $7,500 in Bainbridge's pocket. After reveling in his honors, Bainbridge was ordered to the Charleston Navy Yard, where he oversaw the building of *Independence*, the nation's first ship of the line. However, the War of 1812 ended before the ship could put to sea. He stayed in the navy, helping to establish the first school for officers, lobbying regularly against naval downsizing, and overseeing various shipyards and naval stations. Upon his death, in 1833, Bainbridge would go down in the nation's annals as the victor over *Java* and, in a smaller way, as another of the men who had captained *Essex*.

CHAPTER FIVE

America Defeats the Bashaw

The poor Bashaw must shortly be disturbed,
By an unwelcome visit from his enemy;
The grand mustaches, soon must quiver on his lip,
And make him seem not quite so fair as Paris:
Into his bomb-proof room he speedily will scud,
And like a champion, wonderously brave,
Sit there, and wish for morning;
Within a hundred fathoms of his castle they approach;
And in the nautick way most handsomely salute it;
Powder and ball, without reluctance is bestow'd,
For they well know the great Bashaw deserves it.

— JOSEPH HANSON, "THE MUSSELMEN HUMBLED" (A
POEM IN CELEBRATION OF THE BRAVERY DISPLAYED BY
AMERICAN SAILORS IN THE WAR WITH TRIPOLI)

*T*he ketch *Intrepid*, used by Stephen Decatur to destroy the captured *Philadelphia*, again would make history in the Barbary war. Edward Preble, with his bombardments having seemingly little effect on the bashaw's resolve, loaded the tiny vessel with explosives and dispatched it with thirteen volunteers, under cover of night, deep into Tripoli's harbor. The crew had plans to light a long fuse, escape in small boats, and hope that the ketch, holding five tons of gunpowder, would decimate the bashaw's fleet of naval and merchant vessels.

In charge of the mission was Lieutenant Richard Somers, who departed with his men at 8:00 P.M. on 3 September 1804. Preble and the fleet anxiously awaited the outcome. The night was black, and the vessel was soon lost in a rising mist. Two hours later, there was a burst of gunfire and then a flash of light. Shore batteries opened fire. There was a monstrous explosion, and the ketch blew up, well short of the target area. The sky lit up for miles, as planks and shells flew into the night. All thirteen Americans perished. The following day, the bashaw had Captain Bainbridge removed from prison and taken to the harbor to view the bodies that had washed up on the beach. They were too horribly burned and disfigured to make any identifications.

There were any number of reasons for the premature explosion. One of the most popular is that Somers and his men, having been detected by the enemy, chose to blow themselves up rather than surrender their supply of precious gunpowder. Preble said that Lieutenant Somers

> *put a match to the train leading directly to the magazine, which at once blew the whole into the air, and terminated their existence. My conjectures respecting this affair are founded on a resolution which Captain Somers and*

*[his men] . . . had formed, neither to be taken by the enemy
nor suffer him to get possession of the powder on board the*
Intrepid.

(In contrast to this purported heroism, William
Bainbridge had been criticized for not blowing up the
grounded *Philadelphia* before she was captured. He replied,
"I never presumed to think I had the liberty of putting to
death 306 souls because they were placed under my command.") It also seems plausible that the ketch, having been
spotted by Tripolitan gunboats, was blown up by the shore
batteries.

Whatever the reason, the failed mission was Preble's
last attempt to wrest a surrender from Tripoli; six days later,
Samuel Barron arrived, flying his commodore's pennant.
Preble's tour was over.

The United States was very serious about putting an
end to the Mediterranean standoff. Commodore Barron
had come with the lion's share of the American navy:
President (forty-four guns), *Constitution* (forty-four guns),
Congress (thirty-six guns), *Constellation* (thirty-six guns),
Siren (sixteen guns), *Argus* (sixteen guns), *Vixen* (twelve
guns), *Nautilus* (twelve guns), *Enterprise* (twelve guns),
Hornet (ten guns), and *John Adams* (which was used as a support vessel). *Essex*, which had been in ordinary between July
1802 and December 1803, was also part of the squadron,
having arrived in mid-August. At the helm was Captain
James Barron, brother of the commodore. Captain Barron
and his crew were ordered to watch the Strait of Gibraltar
and the coast of Morocco, where the emperor was again

making threats, despite Preble's earlier warning that America would negotiate through the mouths of her cannons. The U.S. Consul at Tangiers, James Simpson, had discovered that the emperor had amassed $145,000 with the intent of "increasing his marine" (i.e., buying warships) at Lisbon. Barron took *Essex* on a reconnaissance mission to Lisbon, where he spotted two Moroccan ships being painted and provisioned.

In November 1804, *Essex* sailed east to join the rest of the American squadron in Malta. It was now too late in the season to take action against Tripoli, though plans for the bashaw's defeat were in the works.

Far in the east, at Alexandria, Egypt, the United States was mounting an invasion force headed by William Eaton, the former American consul at Tunis. Eaton had been named "Navy Agent to the Barbary States" and given a ragged army of four hundred Arabs and Greek Christians and ten U.S. Marines. Also accompanying Eaton was Ahmad, Bashaw Yusuf Qaramanli's surviving brother (the oldest brother, Hassan, had been murdered by Yusuf in 1790 in a power struggle). Ahmad had served as bashaw for a brief time in 1795, before Yusuf overthrew him in a bloodless coup. The American plan, which had been kicking around for years, was to capture the Tripolitan port of Derne, six hundred miles east of Tripoli—where Ahmad supposedly had a loyal following—and then march on to Tripoli. Ahmad's arrival, it was thought, would trigger an uprising by people who believed Yusuf had usurped his brother's power. Commodore Barron's American squadron would support Eaton's land force by applying pressure from the harbor.

(COURTESY OF U.S. NAVY)

AHMAD QARAMANLI AND WILLIAM EATON ON HORSEBACK, WITH THEIR
RAG-TAG ARMY. THEIR PLAN WAS TO MARCH TO TRIPOLI AND SEIZE POWER
FROM AHMAD'S BROTHER, YUSUF, WHILE THE AMERICAN NAVAL SQUADRON
APPLIED PRESSURE FROM THE SEA.

Eaton and his troops marched from Alexandria and,
with firepower from the sixteen-gun *Argus*, under Isaac
Hull, as well as the twelve-gun *Nautilus* and ten-gun *Hornet*,
captured Derne on 27 April 1805. Meanwhile, Commodore
Barron was trying, unsuccessfully, to make preparations for
his assault on Tripoli. Gunboats were vital in any attack on
the city's shallow and treacherous harbor, but unfortunately, the ones Preble had obtained for his earlier bombardment were now wanted back by the king of Sicily, who
needed them because of a threat of war with France.

Commodore Barron, therefore, dispatched his brother aboard *Essex* in search of gunboats in March 1805. Captain Barron spent several weeks looking for boats in a few cities but returned to Tripoli empty-handed.

There were other problems facing the American squadron. The health of Commodore Barron, who suffered from a liver disease, was failing rapidly. He required hospitalization and, by 22 May, was forced to hand over com-

(COURTESY OF U.S. NAVY)

THE AMERICAN FLEET FIRES ON TRIPOLI IN AN ATTEMPT TO
"WE . . . MUST ENDEAVOR TO BEAT AND DISTRESS HIS SAVAGE HIGHNESS INTO A

mand to Captain John Rodgers, who was next in seniority. Commodore Barron, hoping to keep his brother and *Essex* center stage in any negotiations with the bashaw, wrote to James:

> *You are directed to proceed off the Harbor of Tripoli, and on falling in with the* Constitution, *deliver to Captain John Rodgers the accompanying Letters with the*

GET THE BASHAW TO SURRENDER. SAID COMMODORE PREBLE:
DISPOSITION MORE FAVORABLE TO OUR VIEWS THAN WHAT AT PRESENT HE POSSESSES."

Contents of which you have been made acquainted. In consequence of my Resignation of the Command of the Squadron to that Officer, communicated to him in said Letter, you will place yourself in all respects under his Orders, and receive his Instructions.—You will take on board your Ship the Consul General, Col. Tobias Lear [U.S. consul general at Algiers and chief negotiator], with whose intentions in going to Tripoli you are also acquainted. . . . I have expressed my wishes with regard to the Essex, in a private letter to Captain Rodgers & have no doubt he will acquiesce in them.

Despite the setback of losing Commodore Barron, the bashaw's defeat now seemed very plausible. When he looked beyond the entrance to his harbor, he could see the American squadron poised for battle. His brother's army was approaching from the east. The bashaw also received word that some of his own troops were deserting. It was under these conditions that he began to consider a peace treaty not entirely on his own terms, though he still had to find a way to save face. As William Eaton put it: "Though the Bashaw is heartily sick of the war, he swears he will not give up the prisoners without ransom: His *Honor* forbids it! And that in a dernier [last] extremity he will retreat with them to the mountains."

On the other side, the Americans were also ready to negotiate, anxious to secure the freedom of Captain Bainbridge and his crew, as well end this conflict, which had been dragging on for four years.

On Monday, 27 May, a flag of truce was hoisted and two guns fired aboard *Essex*. They were answered by guns from the bashaw's castle. A representative of Tripoli came aboard, and with Tobias Lear, John Rodgers, and James Barron, negotiations commenced. The parley took a week, with the bashaw vacillating on America's terms: There would be no ransom for the crew of *Philadelphia* and no more tribute money. John Rodgers—cut from the same mold as Preble—was in no mood for compromise and kept his forces poised for battle. Even during the negotiations, *Essex* gave chase to a ship thought to be attempting to break the blockade, though the vessel turned out to be USS *Nautilus*.

On 4 June 1805, the two sides finally agreed to the following:

1. the United States and the bashaw agreed to a one-on-one prisoner exchange, with America also paying $60,000, because Tripoli had more prisoners. (The ransom figure was drastically less than the $1 million the bashaw had demanded upon capturing *Philadelphia* and considerably less than the $200,000 Preble had thumbed his nose at during his bombardment of Tripoli. In a sense, the $60,000 allowed the bashaw to save face with his people).

2. America would pay no more tribute money.

3. U.S. forces would abandon Derne and agree to stop fomenting plots to put Ahmad on the Tripolitan throne.

Carpenters aboard *Constitution* fashioned a spar into a flagpole to replace the one chopped down by the bashaw years earlier. Stationed in the harbor for a twenty-one-gun salute for the bashaw were *Constitution*, *Constellation*, *Vixen*, and *Essex*. The Americans could see the burned remains of *Philadelphia* on a nearby shore. The crew was released a day later. Of the 306 aboard, 6 had died during the nineteenth-month captivity.

There was much to do during the postwar days. Commodore John Rodgers oversaw the prisoner exchange. He also kept an eye on Tunis, where the bey was threatening to seize American shipping in a dispute over the seizure of two of his vessels, which had attempted to break the Tripoli blockade. Captain James Barron had left *Essex* for *President* to accompany his brother to Syracuse, a port on the east coast of Sicily, where it was believed a change in climate might improve Samuel's condition. The Salem frigate's new commander was George Cox, who was faced with the problem of a sick crew. It is quite possible that many were suffering from yellow fever, which was ravaging Gibraltar that year. The ship was ordered to Syracuse for the purpose of placing her sick in a hospital and from there sailed to Malta to pick up Tripolitan prisoners, who were shuttled back to Tripoli.

Conditions aboard a nineteenth-century frigate, especially for seamen, were hardly conducive to good health. The captain had commodious accommodations in which to sleep, work, and entertain guests. Warrant officers such as the gunner and sailmaker at least had tiny cabins. Midshipmen shared a large room. Sailors, on the other hand, were packed tightly into the lower decks of the ship, where air quality was poor and the atmosphere was dank. Suffice it to say that these conditions often gave the surgeon plenty to do in terms of taking care of colds and other mild illnesses and that he "earned his wages," which were among the highest on the ship's crew. The medical man wore a distinctive uniform, a dark green coat with black velvet lapels and a standing collar. Underneath was a red vest and green trousers.

The sick bay was located two decks below in the bow of the ship—a place, ironically, that lacked fresh air but, like the magazine, was well protected during battle. Each morning, men who felt sick reported their symptoms. There was an incentive against feigning illness: Those who stayed in sick bay missed their daily ration of grog. On larger ships, the surgeon had an assistant who helped dispense medicine and care for the patients.

One of the worst problems aboard the ships of that era was scurvy, which was caused by a steady diet of salt beef and other foods that lacked vitamin C. Fresh fruits and vegetables ran out soon after a ship left port, and on long cruises, scurvy was a constant concern. Its symptoms were weakness, swelling of the joints, sore gums, and the opening of healed wounds. Untreated, it ended in death. So severely did it hit some ships that their crews were rendered helpless, unable to go aloft to handle the sails.

A remedy had been discovered in 1747 aboard HMS *Salisbury*, by its surgeon, James Lind, who put a number of scurvy victims on different treatments. While all men ate the regular diet, some were given vinegar, others cider, and some lemon juice. Those who had the last course were soon well. However, the Royal Navy did not adopt the cure, which also included lime juice, until over fifty years later. As an incentive, on some vessels, sailors received their grog only after taking the much detested juice. (Unfortunately, lime juice's antiscorbutic powers were not universally accepted. In 1911, scurvy appeared on the South Pole expedition of Robert Scott, who believed the disease was caused by bad meat.)

In addition to scurvy, another constant worry for captains and their surgeons was yellow fever, a virus borne by mosquitoes. It caused high fever, vomiting, and jaundice, and it was often fatal.

The other enemy at sea was the dampness below decks, particularly during cold weather. Combined with the ship's watch schedule, it was easy to understand why so many men succumbed to colds, pneumonia, and other pulmonary problems. Watches were divided into four-hour shifts, which meant that a sailor rarely slept more than four hours in his hammock without being awakened for duty. After a sailor finished his watch at midnight, for example, he went below to sleep. Too bad if his clothes were wet; there was no place to hang them. Had he been able to find a place to hang his clothes, they probably would not have dried, anyway. The stoves had been banked for the night, and the air below was especially cold and damp. The sailor slept until four A.M., when he was roused from slumber to slap on his wet clothes and go topside for another shift on watch. It was enough to trigger the grippe in the hardiest soul.

During the day, some commanders tried to alleviate the clamminess by burning fires in stoves below decks and scrubbing the insides of the ship with vinegar to purify the air, but this did little to improve conditions. Perpetually hanging in the air was the odor of decaying stores, bilge water, and unwashed bodies.

After delivering prisoners to Tripoli, *Essex* was dispatched to the Tunisian coast to return sailors of Tunisian vessels captured by the U.S. Navy. Commodore Rodgers agreed to repatriate the men, who had been caught trying to run the blockade of Tripoli, but he would not return the ships without consulting his superiors back in Washington. Rodgers wrote to Cox that the

> *mission to Tunis is merely to deliver up these People [prisoners] and to make me acquainted through Mr. Davis [George Davis, U.S. chargé d'affaires in Tunis], with the state of our affairs with that Regency. You will be pleased to return to this port [Syracuse], so soon as you have completed the object of your mission and await my further orders.*

Essex, its crew still plagued by illness, returned to Rodgers with nine more men "unfit for duty." A letter from the surgeon's mate, John Butler, to a friend in Massachusetts gives an idea of how bad things were aboard the ship:

> *And now, Sir, altho' I have written over so many pages I scarcely know what they contain; for since I have*

been writing, I have been continually perplexed with the damned Infernal Sailors, some sick, some lame, and some lazy—Calling upon me for help—Sickness has been so prevalent on board the Essex, for six weeks past, that we have had from fifty to seventy on our Day List of Sick— principally with fevers.

On the bright side, Butler did note at the end of his letter that "the sickness, however, is now abating."

In July, *Essex*, with a new commander, Captain Charles Stewart, was ordered, with *Congress, Constellation, Constitution, Syren, Vixen, Nautilus, Enterprise,* and *Hornet,* off the coast of Tunis. Rodgers felt it was now time to show the bey the firepower that had forced the bashaw to the peace table. America wanted to close the Barbary chapter in its history books; she wanted a guarantee from the bey that he would not interfere with U.S. commerce. Negotiations under the experienced Tobias Lear commenced, and by August, a peaceful settlement was reached, with the bey agreeing to send an ambassador to Washington as his guarantee.

Rodgers then sent a number of ships home, including *President*, on which James Barron conveyed his ill brother. *Essex* was dispatched to Gibraltar with *Vixen* to watch the western Mediterranean. The goal for the winter of 1805 was to protect American shipping and to pay occasional visits to Barbary ports to make sure the peace was holding. The bashaw was more than behaving himself. When an American sailor deserted while on a port call at Tripoli, he was returned to his ship, even though he claimed he had wanted to convert to Islam. The bashaw informed the

Americans that he would have done this for no other "Christian nation."

During the winter tour at Gibraltar, *Essex* received yet another commander, Captain Hugh Campbell (Charles Stewart returned to the United States aboard *Constellation*). Though the American navy was reducing its force in the Mediterranean, the picture was anything but rosy. Captain Campbell certainly had his hands full. In addition to convoying American ships through the Strait, he also had to keep an eye on Morocco, which continued to arm itself. As if there were not enough problems, Algiers—where the dey had been murdered in a recent coup—had to be monitored to ensure that the dey's successor would honor American treaties.

While stationed at Gibraltar, Hugh Campbell became aware of another problem, perhaps more serious than those involving the Barbary States. As he put it in a letter dated 30 September to Secretary of the Navy Robert Smith:

> *My situation here is both tantalizing and provoking, the British on one side of the Bay, distress our Commerce partly by Necessity, while the Spaniards on the other are daily practicing it in a most Wilfull manner. . . . I find it impossible to look with common patience on the daily depredations committed about this place.*

Campbell was trying hard to keep clear of European entanglement. In fact, staying neutral had been the major theme of America's foreign policy since the nation had won its independence twenty years earlier. The American people wanted nothing more than to go about their business in their promised land. By 1805, however, isolationism was increasingly less of an option for the young nation, partly because the political situation in Europe was as unstable as ever. France, under Napoleon, had smashed the Russian and Austrian armies at Austerlitz, giving the French superiority on land. That same year, the Royal Navy had routed the Spanish and French navies at Trafalgar, making the British masters of the sea. Neither of these nations wanted the United States to trade with its enemies, a fact Americans could comprehend, having just repatriated Tunisian prisoners for running a U.S. blockade. The European powers were becoming aggressive in their demands. A recent order from the British government, for example, demanded that "all American Vessels having on board the produce of French or Spanish Colonies" be adjudicated—that is, brought into port and examined. Campbell was distressed at the manner in which American vessels had "been acted upon in the most prompt and energetic manner, much to the prejudice of our trade."

However, Campbell could be of no service to his country with a leaking ship—and *Essex* was leaking—so he sailed her into Malaga for repairs, leaving *Vixen* to watch the Strait. These repairs must have needed immediate and extensive attention, as the ship anchored there from early October through December before sailing to Cadiz for a new anchor cable.

Still, the repairs were of a temporary nature. It was nearing the time to bring *Essex* home. By the end of the year, Rodgers had informed Secretary Smith that "Essex . . . will require to be reliev'd—The Essex will require from representations made of her to me a thorough repair." Rodgers also was ready to return to the United States, and

in May 1806, he transferred his pennant to the Salem frigate
and sailed home. He placed Captain Campbell in command
of the reduced Mediterranean fleet, which included only
Constitution, *Enterprise*, and *Hornet*. Rodgers was not opti-
mistic about the small squadron's effectiveness in discour-
aging Barbary mischief. He wrote: "No doubt the gunboats
will be sent directly back to the Mediterranean after their
arrival in America. This is singular work. God bless our
country!" (His words were prophetic. A few months after
the United States signed the Treaty of Ghent, on Christmas
Eve 1814, with Britain, ending the War of 1812, the dey of
Algiers would expel the U.S. consul and attack American
shipping.) For a while, however, there was some degree of
peace and prosperity in the trading lanes of the
Mediterranean. In the years after the Barbary war, American
trade with the Italian states, for example, tripled. In addition, insurance rates for shippers dropped, a sure sign that
insurers were confident that the American navy had quiet-
ed the bey, dey, and bashaw.

When *Essex* arrived in America on 27 July 1806, she was
put in ordinary. Naval Constructor Josiah Fox reported
from the Washington Navy Yard at the end of 1807 that
Essex was now "undergoing a thorough repair; such parts as
lie under the surface of the Water have been nearly completed and Coppered, therefore great progress may be made
also on this ship in a Short time, provided the Winter is
favorable." He had good things to say about the construction of Salem's frigate: "The White Oak Timber and Plank
with which this Ship was built is Superior in quality to any
White Oak I have seen made use of in the Navy—It appears
to have been cut from trees, young and Thriving."

It was good that her timbers were solid. America would need them soon enough, in a conflict involving a familiar but formidable power: the Royal Navy.

Like a serpent with innumerable tentacles, the British fleet sailed the seas without rival. Often enough, one of her tentacles reached out, plucked crewmen off an American merchant vessel, and made them Royal Navy sailors, whether they liked it or not (most often, they did not). The practice was called impressment, and it had been going on for centuries. Its latest manifestation had occurred just eight days after America made peace with Tripoli, when members of the British Mediterranean squadron impressed three sailors from a U.S. merchant vessel off Cadiz, Spain.

There was a rational—though not forgivable—reason behind English impressment, which had caused tension between England and her former colonies since the end of the Revolutionary War. A British captain was responsible for recruitment and maintenance of his crew. If he arrived at a British port short of men, he sent press gangs ashore to round up sailors, or he removed them from incoming merchant vessels. Great Britain's constant wars and huge navy created a never-ending need for men. High desertion rates—caused by the harsh conditions aboard Royal Navy men-of-war—further aggravated the shortage. Despite harsh penalties for desertion, nearly twenty-five hundred British sailors per year jumped ship. American merchant ships were attractive sanctuaries because of better conditions, higher pay, and a common language.

From time to time, the United States and Britain discussed ways to curtail impressment. However, the practice never ceased, because the two nations held radically different ideas on naturalization and citizenship. England rested on the concept of "indelible allegiance," which meant that citizenship granted to a native-born Englishman superseded any citizenship acquired later in life, especially in time of war, when the king needed to man his ships.

The United States, meanwhile, took a liberal view, requiring only two years of residence before granting citizenship. This short period was of help to American navy captains, who were not allowed to impress anyone for service aboard their vessels or sign on known deserters. American captains also operated under an additional recruiting burden. They were competing for men against the merchant marine, which, generally speaking, paid better than the navy and offered work that was far less dangerous.

To understand the impressment issue, it is necessary to give a picture of the climate in which early nineteenth-century naval recruiting was done. First, it was an era when there was little difference between the accent of an Englishman and that of an American. Second, it also was a time when the average man on the street did not carry a wallet full of papers identifying his status and personal history (chances are he was illiterate). There were no social security cards, drivers licenses, passports, and the like. Consequently, when a man was signed onto an American warship, he was asked his nationality (which he could fake) and to demonstrate his skill at knotting and splicing (which he could not fake); then he was turned away or signed on as a landsman, ordinary seaman, or able seaman. Case closed. In the end, it was a bigger headache for an American navy captain to sail without a full crew than to later discover that he had on board a deserter or two from the Royal Navy.

Given these conditions, it is not hard to understand why, in 1808, over half of the 419-man crew of the *Constitution* were aliens (though not all British). Over half of the four thousand sailors added annually to American merchant marine, in fact, were of British origin (though not all deserters). During the era, seamen were like coins, passing from one vessel to another, their origin impossible to keep track of. It was not the responsibility of Americans to return British deserters. Nevertheless, the indifferent attitude of Americans toward the issue vexed the British and led to worsened relations between Washington and London.

With the competition for sailors so keen, the two nations were bound to clash. When the captain of a British man-of-war sent his lieutenant to search an American merchantman, seamen had to produce proof not that they *were* naturalized Americans but that they *had never* been British subjects. The number of sailors impressed between 1803 and 1806 numbered about twenty-three hundred—and that was solely the *recorded* number. Not all seamen were fortunate enough to have family with money to trace their whereabouts. A popular line from a song of the Royal Navy went like this: "Not a sail but by permission spreads." The message was clear. Britain ruled the seas and did what she pleased.

Impressment was not the only issue heightening tensions between the Crown and her former colonies. The British were blockading American ports in an attempt to seize American ships trading with France, with whom the British king was at war. Basil Hall, a English midshipman aboard HMS *Leander*, off Sandy Hook, New Jersey, wrote in his journal: "Every morning at daybreak we set about arresting the progress of all the vessels we saw, firing off guns to the right and left to make every ship heave to." The detour was more than a minor inconvenience to captains. Many American ships, Hall added, lost "their fair wind, their tide, and worse than all, their market for many hours, sometimes a whole day, before our search was completed." Even a tincture of evidence that the cargo was bound for France or a French colony triggered seizure of the ship, which was then dispatched to a British Admiralty Court in Halifax for adjudication.

In April 1806, to protest this harassment, the U.S. Congress passed the Non-Importation Act, which placed a ban on the import of British beer, playing cards, clothing, and other goods. At the time, England enjoyed a trade surplus with the United States, and Congress hoped that British manufacturers would pressure their government to end its policies of impressment and aggressive searches and seizures. President Jefferson called the plan a form of "peaceable coercion." However, it had little effect on English behavior.

The impressment issue came to a full boil on 22 June 1807, with the *Chesapeake-Leopard* affair. The USS *Chesapeake*, with a crew of 375, had been ordered to sail to the Mediterranean to replace *Constitution*, which was watching over American interests in the area. *Chesapeake* would sail under the command of Commodore James Barron (who had captained *Essex* during the war with Tripoli) and, under him, Captain Charles Gordon. Before the thirty-six-gun *Chesapeake* departed, the British Minister in Washington, D.C., informed the State Department that there were four English deserters among the ship's crew, and the British wanted them returned. Captain Gordon interviewed the men. While he was reasonably convinced that three were not English, the fourth man's credentials were less believable. Gordon decided to sail anyway. After all, determining the citizenship of sailors in that era was not an easy task.

Chesapeake was no sooner out of Chesapeake Bay than she was hailed by the fifty-six-gun *Leopard*, under Captain S. P. Humphreys. A Royal Navy lieutenant came aboard, presumably to deliver dispatches to *Chesapeake*. Instead, there was a note from Humphreys with orders from Admiral George C. Berkeley in Halifax to search the ship for several deserters. If such men were found and not handed over to *Leopard*, the British would take them by force. Barron informed the lieutenant that he had enlisted no deserters and that it would be illegal for him to give up any of his men. Barron may have believed that the threat of force was a bluff because no American warship had ever been searched by the Royal Navy for deserters. (Only merchant vessels had suffered this affront.) Nevertheless, he was cautious enough to call Captain Gordon into his cabin and ask him whether any of the men on the lieutenant's list were aboard *Chesapeake*. Gordon replied that he was not sure but that he had given recruiters an order not to enlist British deserters.

Barron began preparing his reply to Captain Humphreys, who was getting impatient, probably figuring that the crew of *Chesapeake* were preparing their guns for action, as he had done on his own vessel. He signaled for the lieutenant's return.

The tension mounted. After the lieutenant had departed, Commodore Barron went on deck and observed that the guns of *Leopard* were run out and aimed at his ship. Barron had his captain quietly clear the decks for action—without the drums that normally sent the men to quarters.

Disaster loomed for the crew of the thirty-six-gun *Chesapeake*. Not only was she outgunned, but her commodore and captain had made a fatal mistake: Against naval regulations, they had sailed in a state of unpreparedness. Most of the guns had yet to be mounted, and the decks still were littered with equipment and cargo brought aboard at the last minute. Few of the guns had their flintlock firing mechanisms installed. Nor were the slow matches and linstocks, a pole to which the match was attached, readily available. To make matters worse, most of the crew was green—untrained for battle. In defense of Commodore Barron and Captain Gordon, it must be remembered that the United States was not at war with Great Britain or any other nation at that time. Yet, their lack of preparedness had dire and humiliating consequences.

Leopard and her crew, on the other hand, were in top fighting form. Soon after the lieutenant returned, Humphreys gave the order to open fire. Smoke burst forth from *Leopard's* cannons. Balls screamed toward *Chesapeake*, shattering her walls into splinters. Above, rigging and sails took a beating. The English fired three broadsides at a distance of sixty yards. The Americans could do little but duck for cover. The battle, if it could be called that, lasted only fifteen minutes. The *Chesapeake* crew, to salvage Yankee honor, managed to fire off one shot using a glowing coal carried from the galley stove. With a slaughter in the making, Barron then ordered the flag struck.

Several British officers came aboard, mustered the crew, and took off the men they claimed were deserters. The American officers offered their swords in surrender. They were refused—a further insult. *Chesapeake*, its hold filled with water, limped back to port with three dead and twenty wounded, including Barron. The four sailors removed from the American frigate were taken to Halifax, where one was hanged and the other three punished. After four years of negotiations, two would be repatriated while the third would die in prison. The British government disavowed the orders of Admiral Berkeley (they were delivered by his own initiative), and he was recalled. But the damage had been done.

The American public exploded with outrage. There was talk of war on every street corner. An editor at the *Washington Federalist* wrote: "We have never, on any occasion, witnessed the spirit of the people excited to so great a degree of indignation, or such a thirst for revenge." Poet William Ray captured the anger and fighting spirit of Americans in "War, Or a Prospect of It," published a month after the *Chesapeake* affair:

> *Vot'ries of Freedom arm!*
> *The British Lion roars!*
> *Legions of valor, take the'alarm—*
> *Rush, rush to guard our shore!*
> *Behold the horrid deed!*

Your brothers gasping lie!
Beneath a tyrants hand they bleed—
They groan—they faint—they die.
Vet'rans of Seventy-six,
Awake the slumbering sword!
Hearts of your murd'rous foes transfix—
'Tis vengeance gives the word.
Remember Lexington
And Bunker's tragic hill;
The same who spilt your blood thereon,
Your blood again would spill.

The government, however, was forced to move with more caution than advocated by poets and pundits. There was no declaration of war, though President Jefferson ordered all British ships out of American waters. The Mediterranean squadron was called home. American longshoremen refused to service British vessels in port. Envoys were dispatched to London for negotiations, but they could not resolve the same old issues that were rapidly souring relations.

Short of actually declaring war, the United States could do little to deflect British intimidation. The voice of Treasury Secretary Albert Gallatin, not Navy Secretary Robert Smith, prevailed with President Jefferson. Gallatin was intent on paying off the national debt, and he did this partly by preventing any expansion of the navy. Smith's plans to build bigger and better vessels fell on deaf ears.

Jefferson was convinced that America could exist without a large, established sea force. He favored a plan for creation of a naval militia comprised of a fleet of gunboats.

Under his strategy, sailors would be called into service to man the gunboats when trouble struck. Typically, these vessels were seventy-four feet long, with a beam of eighteen feet and a draught of five feet, and wielded a single twenty-four-pound cannon (which had to be stowed in the hold during storms lest it capsize the light vessel.) Congress had authorized the construction of 15 gunboats in 1803, 25 in 1804, 50 in 1805, and 182 the following year, at a cost of $9,000 each. (The $2.5 million total could have built many fine frigates.) The gunboats only created the semblance of a navy. They were useless against Barbary depredations across

(COURTESY OF U.S. NAVY)

CONVINCED THAT AMERICA COULD EXIST WITHOUT A LARGE ESTABLISHED NAVY, THOMAS JEFFERSON BEGAN BUILDING A NAVAL MILITIA COMPRISED OF GUNBOATS. MEASURING ABOUT 74 FEET IN LENGTH, THEY WERE USELESS IN FIGHTING BARBARY DEPREDATIONS ACROSS THE OCEAN, LET ALONE THOSE OF BRITISH WARSHIPS WITHIN SIGHT OF THE U.S. COAST. STILL JEFFERSON CONTINUED TO BUILD THE GUNBOATS— 182 IN 1806 ALONE. "GUNBOATS ARE THE ONLY WATER DEFENSE WHICH CAN BE USEFUL TO US, AND PROTECT US FROM THE RUINOUS FOLLY OF A NAVY," HE SAID.

the ocean, let alone those of a fifty-gun warship like *Leopard*, within sight of the U.S. coast.

Nevertheless, Gallatin mostly had his way with President Jefferson and was successful in reducing the nation's debt, between 1801 and 1812, from $83 million to $45 million. There was, however, a price to be paid. Without a respectable navy, America was forced to fight her battles with economic warfare, and the Congress, at President Jefferson's request, passed a series of acts that had an adverse effect on commerce. The Non-Importation Act already has been mentioned. Its successor was the disastrous 1807 Embargo Act, which went into effect on the heels of the *Chesapeake* affair. It prohibited American ships from trading with *any* foreign nation. Of course, it was despised by shippers, merchants, manufacturers, and farmers—in short, by anyone who had a hand in the export and import of goods. As one businessman put it: "The embargo is like cutting one's throat to cure a nosebleed." It did little to affect the actions of the warring European powers but did much to cripple the American economy, particularly with towns like Salem, Massachusetts. During the term of the Embargo Act, only 25 of the town's 185 vessels remained active in trade, nearly all of it domestic. Unemployed fisherman, shipbuilders, and sailmakers flocked to soup kitchens. In 1808, only 3 ships—with special permits— cleared Salem for European ports. Salemites bitterly complained that the Democrat Jefferson had taken this radical measure to punish New England, where Federalists, who were notoriously pro-English, abounded. The irony was that Jefferson's gunboats now found a useful purpose: They were ideal for detecting and halting American merchant-men trying to break the embargo.

On the first anniversary of the act, in December 1808, Salem's seamen paraded through the streets with a large model of a ship, its flag at half-mast. Guns were fired at North Bridge "in memory of commerce, now dead." Talk of secession was commonplace and easy to comprehend: New England lost $8 million in trade during the fifteen months the Embargo Act was in effect.

The act finally was repealed in March 1809, a few days before Jefferson left office. Within sixty days, about one hundred Salem vessels sailed with one thousand re-employed seamen. While sailors were no doubt glad to be back to work, they were still no safer from impressment than before, and their vessels were just as susceptible to being searched and seized.

In 1809 the U.S. government replaced the Embargo Act with the Non-Intercourse Act; it prohibited Americans from trading with France and England only. Abuses on the high seas continued, however, and the American government soon faced up to the possibility of war. In 1809, the nation enlisted three thousand sailors and readied eleven warships. *Essex*, now ten years old, was among them, going to sea in September, under Captain John Smith. There was no specific mission except to watch over American interests and flex naval muscle.

Day by day, relations worsened. Tension was further heightened by American accusations that the British were inciting Indian attacks in the West. In Congress, Kentucky Senator Henry Clay and his "Hawks" were calling for war to resurrect America's national honor, and they were gaining public support. (The Hawks also believed that Canada, a British colony, could be conquered.) The U.S. government called up an army of twenty-five thousand men, armed merchant ships, and began fitting out more men-of-war.

On 16 May 1811, American cannons finally responded to years of degrading searches. On a dark night, off Cape Henry, Virginia, the forty-four-gun *President*, under Commodore John Rodgers, came upon HMS *Little Belt*, twenty guns, under Captain Arthur Bingham. Each ship hailed the other, but neither would identify itself. Suddenly, shots were fired. The sloop was no match for *President*'s forty-four guns and soon thirteen lay dead and twenty wounded on her decks. When morning light broke, Commodore Rodgers sent a boat over, though Bingham angrily refused all aid. Inquiries followed; both sides claimed the other had fired first. For Rodgers, there was no glory reaped in attacking a smaller vessel; for Bingham, there were questions about why he had antagonized a ship far larger than his own. For American and Great Britain, it was one step closer to war.

Essex had her own tense moments while visiting an English port to deliver state papers early in 1811. This tale, mentioned in a few sources but hard to confirm in British records, involves a sailor from *Essex* who was recognized by an Englishman as a British deserter. The English demanded that the man be removed. Captain Smith interviewed the sailor, who said that he had served in the Royal Navy only because he had once been impressed. He was, he claimed, an American.

Smith informed the sailor that because *Essex* was in English waters, she could not put up much of a fight. Sadly, he would have to turn him over, but he promised to gain his release. The sailor, so distraught, chopped off his hand with an axe and presented it, along with himself, to the British officer who was to take him away. The officer was so repulsed that he left the ship without the presumed deserter. Was the sailor lying or had he decided that his story, however true, would not be believed? In any case, he undoubtedly figured it was better to lose a hand than his life (deserters were sometimes hanged). Whatever the validity of this tale, shortly thereafter, in February 1811, relations with the British were finally severed and *Essex* brought U.S. Ambassador William Pinkney back to the United States.

By 1 June 1812, with American patience exhausted, President James Madison asked the Congress to declare war on Great Britain A few days earlier, Britain had offered an olive branch by repealing its Orders in Council, an act which forbade Americans to trade with France. However, no cable existed to beam the news to Washington, D.C. The war was on.

At the time, *Essex*, with a defective foremast and rotting hull, was at the Brooklyn Navy Yard. She was awaiting not only repairs but a new captain, David Porter, who would lead the vessel through the best and worst times of her life. One dramatic change had made her a completely different ship from the one built at Winter Island in 1799. The navy had replaced many of the ship's twelve-pounder cannons with thirty-two-pound carronades, which delivered a heavier shot but at shorter range. It was a change in armament that did not please Captain Porter.

CHAPTER SIX

Porter Takes Command

Captain Sir James Yeo . . . would be glad to have a tête à tête anywhere between the Capes of Delaware and Havana, where he would have the pleasure to break his own sword over his [Captain David Porter's] damned head, and put him down forward in irons.

—CAPTAIN JAMES YEO OF HMS *SOUTHHAMPTON*,
MESSAGE TO CAPTAIN DAVID PORTER (PHILADELPHIA
NEWSPAPER, 1812)

Capt. Porter . . . accepts with pleasure his [Yeo's] polite invitation. If agreeable to Sir James, Captain Porter would prefer meeting near the Delaware, where Captain P. pledges his honor to Sir James that no other American vessel shall interrupt their tête à tête. The *Essex* may be known by a flag bearing the motto "Free Trade and Sailors' Rights;" and when it is struck to the *Southampton* Capt. P. will deserve the treatment promised by Sir James.

—CAPTAIN DAVID PORTER, REPLY TO CAPTAIN YEO

*I*t is one of those quirks of history that David Porter's first great act of naval heroism—the first of many—involved a set of circumstances strikingly similar to those surrounding the Battle of Valparaiso, the most significant action of his career. In 1799, Porter was a midshipman of the foretop aboard *Constellation* when that vessel defeated the French frigate *Insurgente*. As was noted earlier, Porter saved the foretopmast from falling by lowering a portion that had been damaged during the fierce fighting. Left hanging, the section would have pulled down the entire mast. This action was critical: with her mast gone, *Constellation* would have been nearly impossible to maneuver and a veritable sitting duck for the blazing cannons of the enemy. *Insurgente* had been armed with carronades—short, squat cannons capable of delivering a heavy shot, but only at a short distance. The range of carronades was far less than that of long guns, which comprised the lion's share of cannons aboard most large men-of-war. Porter's action allowed *Constellation* to move out of range of *Insurgente*'s carronades, while the Americans pounded their enemy with long guns from a distance. In 75 minutes, the French frigate was a mass of splinters and hanging sails.

David Porter, therefore, was well acquainted with the shortcomings of carronades. One can imagine his chagrin and disgust when, in 1811, he found himself in command of *Essex*, whose long guns had been exchanged almost entirely for carronades. Porter complained often about the carronades to Navy Secretary Paul Hamilton and even once went as far as to inform the secretary that he did not want command of *Essex* until her armament was modified. The secretary agreed to his demands, but the gun changes were never made.

Porter sailed with *Essex*, anyway. He was a gutsy sailor loathe to turn away from any challenge. He took his vessel boldly onto the seas, even offering to fight one-on-one battles with British frigates whose long guns, under the right set of circumstances, could have cut *Essex* to pieces.

David Porter was a complex man. His courageous spirit at times bordered on recklessness and even crossed the line of insubordination.

(COURTESY OF U.S. NAVY)

DAVID PORTER, CAPTAIN OF *ESSEX* DURING HER MOST FAMOUS CRUISE, MADE A SURPRISE ATTACK ON ENGLAND'S PACIFIC WHALING FLEET IN 1813, BUT THAT WASN'T ENOUGH TO SATISFY HIM. AS HE WROTE, HE HOPED "TO SIGNALIZE MY CRUISE BY SOMETHING MORE SPLENDID BEFORE LEAVING THAT SEA."

This chapter's opening quotes are evidence of his carelessness. The invitation from Captain James Yeo had been triggered by an incident aboard *Essex*, in June 1812, in which a sailor named John Irving (also spelled Erving) refused to take the oath of allegiance to the United States. Irving, who had been living in the United States since 1800 and been a member of the *Essex* crew for eight months, was a British subject who had bought a protection for four shillings.

A protection was a document from a local judge or government official testifying to the fact that the holder was a native-born American and, therefore, immune to impressment in the Royal Navy. Some of these documents were real, others were forged, and a fair number were "lost" by the bearer, who really sold it and obtained another. Irving had probably bought his. The buyer and seller had to look somewhat alike because the protections contained a brief physical description. Given the possibility of fraud, some Royal Navy officers paid no attention to these documents when they were presented.

Irving told Captain Porter that he couldn't fight against his countrymen because, if captured and recognized, he would be hanged. Apparently, Irving must have had little faith in his protection. Porter agreed to a discharge, but as the *Essex* crew was rowing Irving to shore, he was tarred and feathered. It is not clear whether Porter gave permission for this outrageous act, but he did little to stop it. When Secretary Hamilton learned of the incident, he was livid, writing to Porter: "I do exceedingly regret that an officer of your high rank and intelligence should have permitted the proceeding in question." An editorial in the 27 June 1812 edition of the *New York Post* put it very simply:

> *The story shall be closed by asking the reader a simple question; suppose the captain of an English frigate should suffer his men to tar and feather an American sailor in the port of London, because he would not join in a cruise to fight against his own country; what would you think of such an action?*

No Englishman seemed angrier than Captain Yeo, though the rendezvous with Porter would never take place.

David Porter's vigor and his love for sea life was handed down from his father, also named David, who commanded several ships in the American War of Independence. Born in Boston on 1 February 1780, young David listened to sea tales on his father's knee. By the age of sixteen, he had accompanied his father to the West Indies aboard the merchant vessel *Eliza* and had had his first scrape with the British. After landing in Haiti, the Porters met up with John Reynolds, captain of the English privateer *Harriet*, who was illegally impressing sailors from many ships at the port. When Reynolds came to *Eliza* to round up a few recruits, the American crewmen—with no arms or cannons—beat him back with wood, stones, and tools. Reynolds returned with a group of men bearing firearms and swords but again was driven back. In this second engagement, men from both sides were wounded. When Reynolds returned a third time, however, *Eliza*'s crew had fled, and the British proceeded to cut up the sails and cables and trash the ship. The harrowing experience stayed with the impressionable young Porter and no doubt fueled his fury against England years later.

After his tour aboard *Constellation*, Porter was promoted in October 1799 to second lieutenant aboard the aptly named *Experiment*, a shallow-draft schooner with twenty guns, designed for shoreline action in the West Indies. It was on this tour that Porter first exhibited the stubborn independence he would be known for in the navy. In this case, his actions could be called mutinous.

The Caribbean basin was a hotbed of combat during the 1790s, as the French, Spanish, and British fought over its many islands—rich in sugar, livestock, mahogany, and many other commodities. Each of these nations was quick to stop and search vessels of neutrals to make sure they were not carrying cargo for an enemy. The Caribbean, replete with tempting prizes, also was a popular cruising ground for pirates. Given this atmosphere, as well as the commencement of the Quasi-War with France, American merchantmen needed protection, and *Experiment* was assigned to escort vessels along the coast of Haiti.

One day, her convoy was set upon by ten pirate vessels. Lieutenant William Maley, commander of the schooner and unpopular among his men, lost the last tincture of their respect when he decided to surrender without a fight. For Porter, striking the flag without firing a shot was not an option. There was only one thing to do. He took command of the ship, rallied the men, and beat back the pirates by sinking three of their vessels. The pirates soon marshaled their forces, returned to cut out two vessels from *Experiment*'s convoy, and fled.

While the incident was not a total victory, Porter and his men at least had saved several U.S. merchantmen from capture, as well as the honor of the American navy from disgrace. Lieutenant Maley chose not to report the incident. But his reputation for abrasiveness, drunkenness, and cowardice caught up with him, and he was eventually dismissed from the service.

Porter had another cruise aboard *Experiment*, this time under the command of a more competent leader, Master Commandant Charles Stewart. During the mission, Porter had further opportunity to develop his coolness under pressure, after *Experiment* defeated *Deux Amis*, an eight-gun French privateer on 1 September 1800. After Porter and a few men were sent aboard to take possession of the prize, the enemy vessel became separated from *Experiment*. The situation aboard the prize vessel suddenly grew precarious, for Porter and his men were now outnumbered 40 to 5. The young lieutenant loaded one of the vessel's guns with canister and drew a line on the deck. He then informed his captives that the first man who crossed the line would cause an American sailor to put a match to the cannon. Four intense days ensued before Porter sailed the prize safely into harbor at the island of St. Kitts.

After peace with France in the Quasi-War and the navy's downsizing, Porter—given his solid reputation—was chosen to remain in the navy as one of thirty-six lieutenants. He was sent aboard the schooner *Enterprise*, under Lieutenant Andrew Sterrett. The ship was dispatched to the Mediterranean under Commodore Dale and, on 1 August 1801, defeated the fourteen-gun *Tripoli*, as mentioned previously. After this tour of duty, Porter returned to the United States. He found his way back to the Mediterranean in April 1802 as a first lieutenant aboard *Chesapeake*. Little of importance happened to Porter under Commodore Morris's sluggish tour of command, except that he was allowed to make an assault on grain vessels along the Tripolitan shore. Unfortunately, the enemy put up a strong fight, and

Porter—shot once in each thigh—and his crew pulled away without having accomplished their mission.

Porter was then moved to the ill-fated *Philadelphia*, which under Captain William Bainbridge, ran aground in Tripoli's harbor. Porter made the best of his nineteenth-month stay in a Tripolitan prison, leading classes of officers in tactical warfare training and brushing up on his scant education with books provided by the Danish consul. He also took up drawing and taught himself French. After being released in June, 1805, he was given command of *Enterprise* and assigned to the bland but important task of convoying merchant ships and delivering mail. The tour, however, wasn't entirely without excitement.

During the summer of 1806, at the island of Malta, a drunken sailor from the Royal Navy insulted several American officers. When the sailor refused to apologize, Porter had the man brought aboard his ship and whipped. When the British commander at Malta heard of the incident, he refused to allow *Enterprise* passage out of the port until the matter was resolved.

A tense war of words ensued. Porter would not back down. He demanded to know whether the United States and Great Britain were at war. The British said no. Then, replied Porter, *Enterprise* would sail as scheduled. The British responded that they had orders to shoot should *Enterprise* try to depart. Porter said he would sail anyway, fight until he was defeated, then surrender as if he were at war. That evening, *Enterprise* weighed anchor and sailed, its guns poised for battle. No shots were fired, and the episode eventually fizzled away.

Was Porter courageous or reckless? In naval matters, the line between the two is often murky. Certainly, he could have shown wiser discretion by appealing for redress to the captain of the drunken sailor, as Captain Bainbridge had done when his crew was insulted by the Spanish officers of *San Sebastian*. On the other hand, America was the new kid on the block and could not be seen running to higher authorities whenever she had a problem. She had to handle problems herself; she was too small to be always on the defensive. Undoubtedly, the boldness of Porter and other American officers was the reason behind the survival of the young American navy. It could win only by acting with a spirit of confidence, courage, and, on occasion, audacity. During the War of 1812, in fact, those qualities took Porter to the Pacific, where no American warship had ever sailed, to prey on Britain's whaling fleet.

Porter returned to America in October 1807 and spent some time in New York, where he joined up with a group of *bon vivant* bachelors led by the young Washington Irving, the country's newest literary sensation. The group, having dubbed themselves the "Lads of Kilkenny," met at Dyde's Tavern for cavorting and drinking. They were known throughout the burgeoning metropolis at various restaurants and balls. Porter's very apt nickname was Sinbad.

In early 1808, Porter found himself faced with more heady business: He was sitting on a court of inquiry judging the actions of Commodore James Barron in the *Chesapeake* affair. Among others on the board were former *Essex* captains William Bainbridge and Hugh Campbell.

John Rodgers and Stephen Decatur also sat on the court, which was convened on board *Chesapeake* herself.

The board's task was not a pleasant one. They had to pass sentence on a brother officer who had been glaringly negligent in his duty. Bainbridge, whose actions as captain of the grounded *Philadelphia* once had been the subject of such inquiry, must have been keenly sensitive to Barron's plight. Barron, in fact, had served as president of Bainbridge's proceedings, during which he was exonerated. *Chesapeake*'s commodore, unfortunately, did not fare as well. While he was acquitted of charges of cowardice and unnecessary surrender of his ship, James Barron was found guilty of neglecting to have his vessel ready for battle and was suspended from the navy for five years.

The trial would have repercussions thirteen years later, when Barron killed Stephen Decatur in a duel at eight paces. During his banishment, Barron found employment in the merchant marine. In 1819, he petitioned the navy for reinstatement of his commission. Barron wrongly believed that Decatur had spoken out against his return to the navy; such an action would have been a grave insult. Barron also held a grudge because Decatur had been a member of the court martial board that had suspended him. After an exchange of letters, which could save the honor of neither man, the two met at a dueling field called the Valley of Chance, near Bladensburg, Maryland, just north of Washington, D.C., on 22 March 1820; William Bainbridge acted as umpire. Both men were wounded, Decatur mortally. Congress refused to adjourn to pay Decatur homage—despite that he was (and remains) one of the nation's greatest naval figures—because the government forbade dueling. It was bitterly ironic that Decatur had made his officers sign pledges that they would not engage in duels to settle their scores. Despite the reprobation of Congress, Decatur remained a revered figure among officers and sailors of the U.S. Navy, while Barron was shunned.

David Porter's life changed dramatically soon after the *Chesapeake* proceedings, though the circumstances had nothing to do with the navy. He proposed marriage to Evalina Anderson, the daughter of a future congressman from Chester, Pennsylvania. The family objected to the match; at fifteen, she was too young, they said. Moreover, they argued, Porter, like all naval men, would be frequently absent and too often broke. The story goes that Porter was confronted by Evalina's brother, who ordered him out of the house. In characteristic fashion, Porter countered by informing his future brother-in-law that he would throw him out the window. Porter prevailed, as he often did, and the couple was married, after a brief courtship, on 10 March 1808. They were soon off to New Orleans, where Porter had been ordered to take command of the city's naval station.

The assignment was anything but a honeymoon. New Orleans was hot, humid, and a haven for pirates. Porter had his hands full. He arrived to find rotting gunboats, low morale, yellow fever, a high desertion rate, and, perhaps worst of all, a letter from the secretary of the navy refusing his request for an increase in pay. Treasury Secretary Gallatin was chipping away at the federal debt by mothballing ships and holding the line on salaries.

Another piece of bad news awaited Porter in New Orleans. His father, who had been stationed as a sailing master in the city a few month's before his son's arrival, was gravely ill, the victim of heatstroke. He was under the care of Elizabeth Farragut, the wife of George Farragut, an old crony and fellow veteran of the Revolutionary War. Porter's father soon died, and his death was followed hours later by that of his caregiver, who succumbed to yellow fever. The young David Porter, wanting to show his gratitude to George, as well as give the widower a helping hand, adopted one of Farragut's five children (though not legally), a nine-year-old boy named David Glasgow. The boy would one day serve aboard *Essex* and, climbing through the ranks in a stellar naval career, would be the first U.S. naval officer promoted to rear admiral, in 1862, when that rank was created by Congress.

After the funerals, Porter got down to business. The navy had charged him with the task of capturing French and Spanish privateers. They had been preying on American shipping entering and leaving the port of New Orleans, which had been acquired from a cash-starved Napoleon Bonaparte in 1803 in the Louisiana Purchase. Porter also was ordered to enforce the despised Embargo Act, not an easy task in the long, swampy shoreline of Louisiana. For this job, however, Jefferson's gunboats served a useful purpose.

Porter's two-year tour at New Orleans ended in June 1810. He had had mixed success in hampering smuggling and fending off pirates, and he sailed back to the East Coast on the eleven-gun brig *Vesuvius* with thirty men. Though he was anxious to leave behind dilapidated gunboats and torpid summers, he couldn't resist detouring by way of Cuba to inquire about reward money due him for the capture of a French privateer. Clearly, Porter was in need of money and wanted his due. He was becoming saddled with familial responsibilities—a wife, pregnant with their second child (eventually, they would have ten), as well as the adopted Farragut. Upon arriving back in Chester, Pennsylvania, in August, Porter must have been grateful to return to a mansion, given to him and Evalina as a wedding present by her father.

After a brief respite, Porter was off to Washington, D.C., where he introduced Farragut to Navy Secretary Paul Hamilton, who promised to make the boy a midshipman. The rest of the meeting had mixed results. Hamilton granted Porter leave to return to Cuba to pursue his prize money but turned down his request for promotion to the rank of captain. However, Porter did leave with another prize. He was given command of the frigate *Essex*, with the lower rank of master commandant, and took charge of the vessel in the summer of 1811.

Essex had undergone a major overhaul in the Washington Navy Yard between 1806 and 1809. In addition to work on her frames and topsides, her gunports were modified to accommodate a revised main armament—thirty-two-pound carronades.

At the beginning of the nineteenth century, the carronade was a relatively new weapon, though hardly "experimental," as Porter was wont to claim. The first one had been built in 1776 by the Carron Works (hence the name "carronade") of Falkirk, Scotland, which produced everything from pots and pans to ploughs and spades. Carronades began appearing on British men-of-war in 1779. The gun's appeal was that it threw a heavy ball, which did a tremendous amount of damage at short range, and that it could be fired with a smaller gun crew and more rapidly than a long gun. Herman Melville, who had served for eighteen months aboard the USS *United States*, called the carronades "Iron Attilas." Royal Navy sailors dubbed them "smashers," for the way they downed masts, created irregular-shaped holes that were hard to repair, and sent splinters flying. It should be pointed out that flying splinters, not cannonballs, were the chief hazard for sailors during battle.

The most famous carronades in naval history were two sixty-eight-pounders on Horatio Nelson's *Victory* that blasted away at the Battle of Trafalgar in 1805. Because the carronades weighed less than long guns—a thirty-two-pounder tipped the scales at twenty-two hundred pounds, versus thirty-two hundred for the twelve-pound long guns, such as those removed from *Essex*—they were frequently placed on quarterdecks and forecastles, areas of the ship that could not carry heavier guns. That is where they were placed on HMS *Victory* and on American frigates *Constitution* and *United States*. Carronades were also well suited to smaller warships, like sloops and brigs, both because of their lighter weight and because these smaller vessels could close quickly on an enemy, to the point where the smashers could wreak their havoc. That was probably the Navy's thinking when it replaced most of Essex's long guns with carronades.

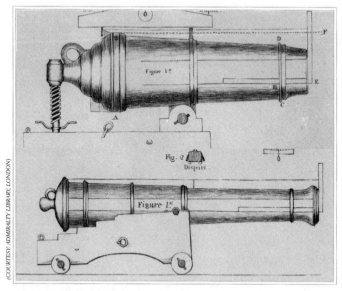

CARRONADES (TOP), DEVELOPED IN SCOTLAND IN 1776, THREW A HEAVY BALL AT SHORT RANGE. BRITISH SAILORS DUBBED THEM "SMASHERS," WHILE HERMAN MELVILLE, WHO SERVED ABOARD A U.S. MAN-OF-WAR, CALLED THEM "IRON ATTILAS." LONG GUNS (BELOW) THREW A SMALLER SHOT A LONGER DISTANCE.

She was a small frigate and, after ten years, still considered a fast sailer who could close quickly on an enemy.

Despite their advantages, carronades remained controversial. The shortness of the gun, for example, allowed the powder charge to burn the ship's side and rigging (a thirty-two-pounder carronade was four feet in length, a twelve-pounder long gun nine and a half feet). The biggest problem, however, was their range. The stubby gun could not shoot nearly as far as a long gun, making it imperative to fight at close quarters. This presented no problem for a frigate like *United States*, which wielded an ample number of twenty-four-pound long guns in addition to her carronades, and, therefore, could do battle at long or short range. However, the captain of a frigate whose armament was comprised mostly of carronades had only one plan of battle: to fight at close quarters. If the wind or other circumstances did not cooperate, the captain and his crew would have to flee or be sitting ducks. Such was the case of the rearmed *Essex*. Porter complained bitterly about his carronades—particularly that they hindered the sailing of *Essex*, though the gun weight that *Essex* carried when she was initially equipped (26 twelve- and 10 six-pound long guns) was approximately the same as that of the new arrangement of weaponry (40 thirty-two-pound carronades and 6 eighteen-pound long guns).

Porter's objection was not strong enough for him to refuse to take command of *Essex*. War with Britain was looming, and the U.S. Navy found itself facing desperate odds. Her tiny fleet amounted to less than twenty vessels compared to more than one thousand for the titanic Royal Navy. A comparison of firepower paints a more striking picture: 27,800 cannons versus 450. Britain certainly could not devote her entire fleet to the war with America; her warships had to protect her interests throughout the world and keep up a wearying blockade against her arch rival, France. Nevertheless, the king had ships to spare, and as the War of 1812 dragged on, more and more vessels were dispatched across the Atlantic to make life miserable for the Americans, particularly after the surrender of France and Napoleon in the spring of 1814.

Given the insurmountable disadvantage, Secretary Hamilton and senior captains worked out a naval strategy that maximized the strength of America's navy, embodied in her superior frigates. Fearing that one major battle could trigger the loss of most of the navy, Hamilton decided to send out the frigates singly, to seek one-on-one combat and destroy as many enemy vessels as possible before England formed the inevitable blockade. In response to this idea, President James Madison said, "It is victories we want; if you give us them and lose your ships afterwards, they can be replaced by others." This was exactly the course the naval war would take, except the blockade and invading British troops would make it almost impossible to get new vessels out of port. During the attack on Washington, D.C., in August 1814, for example, Americans burned the frigates *Boston*, *New York*, *General Green*, and *Columbia* to keep them from falling into British hands.

Desperate odds were not all that faced Secretary Hamilton, who found the office and its functions nearly as primitive as those in Benjamin Stoddert's day, over a decade earlier. An undersized staff forced Hamilton, who had been appointed in 1809, to be involved in minutiae that were the territory of clerks. Still, he could boast of a number of accomplishments during his three-and-a-half-year tenure, including mounting a fight against the slave trade, establishing naval hospitals, and tightening up wasteful requisitioning policies. His only fault, according to his critics, was a drinking problem that often made him unable to return to his office in the afternoons.

While Secretary Hamilton worried about how to conduct war against the Royal Navy, Porter continued to stew over his carronades. (Even Porter's nemesis, James Yeo, would experience the frustrations of carronade warfare. In an indecisive engagement on Lake Ontario in September 1813, Yeo reported: "We remained in this mortifying situation for five hours with only six guns in the fleet that would reach the enemy. Not a carronade was fired.") Porter wrote to Secretary Hamilton:

> *Considering as I do that Carronades are merely an experiment in modern warfare and that their character is by no means established I do not conceive it proper to entrust the honor of the flag entirely to them. Was this ship to be disabled in her rigging in an early part of an engagement, a ship much inferior to her in sailing and in force, armed with long guns, could take a position beyond reach of our carronades, and cut us to pieces without our being able to do her any injury. Long guns are well known to be effective and management of them familiar to seamen. I have therefore required . . . four long eighteen pounders to mount on gundeck and shall on receipt of them send on shore some defective Carronades. I hope, Sir, reasons I have given will in your opinion justify change.*

One can imagine Porter's disappointment with the Secretary's response: "It is not adjudged advisable to change armament of *Essex*. If any carronades are defective, they are to be replaced by good ones, and not to be changed by long guns." Never one to shrink from expressing his opinion, be it via long gun or letter, Porter wrote again to Hamilton, saying he had discussed the carronade issue with his officers and they, too, thought it best that some be exchanged for long guns. Furthermore, he felt so strongly about the issue that he asked reassignment to a smaller vessel if his request should be denied. This was a bold move for Porter, who had still not made the rank of captain. Having witnessed the failure of carronades aboard the frigate *Insurgente*, however, he obviously felt strongly about their limitations.

The crux of the carronade matter was one of perception. There is no question that for a frigate, *Essex* carried too many carronades. The forty-four-gun *President*, which in truth wielded fifty guns (it was customary for U.S. ships to carry more guns than their official ranking stated), had twenty carronades. *Constellation* rated thirty-eight guns but carried forty-six, of which eighteen were carronades. These vessels also had a solid broadside's worth of long guns: thirty on *President* and twenty-four on *Constellation*. To Porter, the guns on *Essex* seemed like an experiment in carronade warfare, using him and his men as guinea pigs. The thirty-two-gun frigate really mounted forty-six guns, forty of them carronades. That amounted to a large percentage of carronades, 85 percent, compared with 40 percent on the other ships. There is no way Porter could have been expected to go up against even a small Royal Navy frigate of thirty-eight guns unless he had a tremendous advantage.

This is where the perception comes in. Hamilton probably saw *Essex* not so much as a small frigate as a large sloop-of-war, fit to seize merchantmen and privateers. American sloops, such as *Wasp* and *Hornet*, also carried large percentages of carronades. Both vessels mounted 16 carronades and two twelve-pound long guns (or 88 percent carronades). Because *Essex* was larger (850 tons versus 450 tons for an average sloop) and wielded more guns, she could also easily do battle with the Royal Navy's sloops and brigs. Furthermore, as a fast sailer, she had the potential to catch these smaller vessels. For Secretary Hamilton, *Essex* probably fit into a very good niche.

Porter, however, would have been loathe to view *Essex* as a large sloop. He wanted the prestige of commanding a frigate because that was the quickest way to make captain and thus ease his financial burdens. The fact that he was not already a captain infuriated him. He once complained that the navy

> in money matters treated me in the most shameful and illiberal manner. As respects honor I have no cause to complain. They have given me more of that than I wanted, and so long as I am fool enough to do captain's duty for the pay of master commandant, so long will they do me the honor to order me to do it.

It would also be safe to assume that Porter, like many of the daring officers of the young American navy, wanted his share of glory and immortality. A captain was more apt to get his name into the history books by sending a British frigate, rather than an eighteen-gun sloop, to the bottom of the sea. All this led Porter, after a highly successful raiding cruise off the Galapagos Islands, to return to Valparaiso to seek one-on-one combat with the frigate HMS *Phoebe*.

Porter's persistence with Hamilton on the carronade issue paid off in word, though not in deed. The secretary agreed to exchange four carronades and two twelve-pounders for eighteen-pounders. However, this modification was never carried out, and Porter stayed with *Essex*.

The first cruise of *Essex* began on 3 July 1812. Though she had been assigned to sail with a squadron that included *President*, *United States*, *Congress*, *Hornet* (eighteen guns), and *Argus* (sixteen guns), repairs to her masts and hull, being done in the Brooklyn Navy Yard, took longer than expected, and she sailed alone. (It should be pointed out that the squadron was led by Commodore John Rodgers, who disagreed with the naval strategy of one-on-one combat. However, his disappointing results on this mission would convince the navy of the superiority of single-ship cruises in the future.)

Porter and his crew took their thirteen-year-old vessel to sea. Eight days into the cruise, while off the coast of Bermuda, *Essex* came across a British convoy under the protection of the thirty-six-gun frigate *Minerva*. Under the cover of night, *Essex* captured the last ship of the convoy, *Samuel and Sarah*, without the knowledge of the other vessels. The ship proved to be quite a plum—a transport ship with about two hundred soldiers bound for Quebec. This was not enough for Porter. The following day, he challenged the *Minerva* captain to a one-on-one battle but was turned down. In lieu of taking prisoners, Porter took

$14,000 from *Samuel and Sarah*'s safe and let the vessel go free. Ransoming a vessel was highly unorthodox and possibly illegal. It is not clear why Porter did this or what money, if any, he and his men earned from the capture. It is quite possible that he had to give the money back. However, the capture was successful in the sense that Porter's English prisoners, dispatched to Halifax, were eventually exchanged for American prisoners of war.

In the coming days, *Essex* sailed northward and captured the rum brig *Lamprey* and then *Leander*, which was carrying a cargo of coal and salt. Both vessels were sent to Baltimore as prizes. Five more merchant vessels were captured during the first half of August. Two were dispatched as prizes (although one of those was recaptured), two were burned, and one was sent to St. John's as a cartel ship. The *Essex* crew also recaptured a number of American merchantmen taken by a British privateer. While Porter had not struck it rich, his captures would eventually put about $927 in his pocket.

On 13 August, however, Porter and his crew earned a prize of infinite value, a place in the history books, with the first American capture of a British warship in the War of 1812. Off the coast of Newfoundland, Porter lured HMS *Alert* into his clutches by making *Essex* look like a merchantman. The gunports were shut, and the sails were set in a sloppy manner, hardly the picture of a crack U.S. man-of-war. *Alert* was a converted collier armed with sixteen eighteen-pound carronades. Under the command of Captain

Thomas Laugharne, she had aboard 98 men who were hungry for an easy victory. The British vessel closed rapidly.

When Captain Laugharne got within two miles of *Essex*, he decided that the strange vessel was a warship, but it was too late to try to flee. *Alert* continued to close; the crew gave three cheers and fired. The broadside did little damage to *Essex*. Her gunports burst open and out came a broadside that shook *Alert* down to her keel. Many of the crew ran below for cover, deserting their guns in the face of a thirty-two-gun frigate. The battle ended in less than ten minutes.

When Porter boarded his prize, he discovered one reason for the rapid surrender: *Alert*'s hold was filled with seven feet of water. Porter acted quickly to save the ship and transferred the enemy sailors to *Essex*.

Four days later, on 17 August, he wrote to the secretary of the navy:

> *I have the honor to inform you that on the 13th his Britannic Majesty's Sloop of War* Alert, *Captain T. L. P. Laugharne, ran down on our weather quarter, gave three cheers and commenced an action (if so trifling a skirmish deserves a name) and after 8 minutes firing struck her colors. . . . I need not inform you that officers and crew of* Essex *behaved as I trust all Americans will in such cases, and it is only regretted that so much zeal and activity could not have been displayed on an occasion that would have done them more honor. The* Essex *has not received the slightest injury.*

The danger with *Alert* was not quite over for Porter. A few days after her sailors were transferred aboard *Essex*, David Farragut, eleven years old at the time, discovered a plot among the prisoners to take over *Essex* in the middle of the night. He ran to tell his captain, who jumped out of bed yelling "Fire! Fire!" The American sailors rushed to their stations, and in the confusion, the mutineers saw their plan fizzle away.

Captain Laugharne and his officers had to face more than the disgrace of defeat. Every navy commanding officer who lost his ship for whatever reason had to face a trial by court-martial to establish the facts and, if warranted, mete out punishment. The court that tried Captain Laugharne wanted to find out why *Alert* had struck her flag with such alacrity. Questions arose about the conduct of First Lieutenant Andrew Duncan, whom Laugharne found "neglectful." The captain told the court:

> *On going round to see everything clear I found many things deficient at the guns and from the commencement of the action till we struck I hardly knew where he was. In giving my orders once or twice he certainly was not to be found on the quarterdeck. He did not appear to know what he was about. I think arising from incapacity.*

In his defense, Lieutenant Duncan called a fellow lieutenant, the purser, the carpenter, and others to testify that he had been on the quarterdeck during the battle, that he had shown no signs of cowardice, and that he was extremely deaf. Two gun captains testified that the guns were in a state of readiness—the first lieutenant's responsibility—before the battle began.

Other officers besides Duncan also were on the hot seat. The court was considering the accusation that some had gone to the captain during the battle to ask him to strike the flag.

The court exonerated Captain Laugharne, finding

> *that he did not strike the colors of* Alert *until it became utterly impossible to continue the action against so superior a force with any prospect of success.*

Secondly, it found the conduct of Lieutenant Duncan

> *reprehensible, and though the court acquits him of cowardice, still it appears that he failed to give that assistance to his captain and encouragement to the ship's company which ought in a more peculiar manner to have been expected from his situation.*

He was dismissed from the service. On the issue of striking the flag, the court was

> *of the opinion that the remaining officers and the ship's company behaved with gallantry during the action, but it cannot pass over the circumstance of them having gone aft to advise their Captain to strike, without expressing the strongest disapprobation: nor would such a proceeding under any circumstances be justified.*

Alert would be condemned and sold in New York for $13,416. Commodore Rodgers received his percentage of the money (commodores got prize money from all captures made by their squadron, even if their ship was not involved in the actual fighting). The *Essex* crew received theirs. Porter was left with $643, for a cruise total of $1,570—hardly a killing, but nevertheless about a year's pay for two months' work. Moreover, Porter had lost only one man and captured over four hundred prisoners. Never one to shy away from trumpeting his own exploits, the *Essex* captain estimated that he had done $300,000 worth of damage to the British Empire, showing his penchant for exaggeration. It had been an easy cruise, with only one close call. On 5 September, he tried to come to the rescue of an American merchantman, only to find himself suddenly being chased by a pack of British frigates. He eventually eluded them and arrived in the United States two days later.

Though relieved to have prize money and be home with his family, Porter still was uncomfortable with his carronades. He wrote again to Secretary Hamilton, this time requesting command of the twenty-eight-gun ship *Adams*. Porter said that his "insuperable dislike to carronades and the bad sailing of the *Essex* render her in my opinion the worst frigate in the service." *Adams* was not available, and Porter was ordered to remain with the Salem frigate.

She departed for her second cruise at the end of October. Porter and his 319 men had orders to make a rendezvous in the South Atlantic with eighteen-gun sloop *Hornet*, under Captain James Lawrence, and *Constitution*, now under the command of William Bainbridge. The latter vessel had recently returned from Isaac Hull's stunning victory over the thirty-eight-gun HMS *Guerriere* on 19 August 1812. The battle, which had taken place seven hundred miles east of Boston, had filled the American public with joy. The British frigate had been so badly damaged that she had to be scuttled, and American casualties were light compared to those of the enemy. When the *London Times* took note of Hull's victory, as well as Stephen Decatur's trouncing of *Macedonian* by *United States* on 25 October, its editors cried, "A national disgrace!" Clearly, Secretary Hamilton's plan of one-on-one engagements was working.

A rendezvous among warships during that era, even in waters as expansive as the South Atlantic, was not as difficult as one might believe. Before the invention of the wireless, captains had primitive but surprisingly successful methods of communication. For example, sailors often looked for floating waste, such as bottles, cask heads, and orange skin peelings, that signaled the proximity of a ship. Captains also agreed on prearranged meeting places. Many ports had "post offices," boxes crudely nailed to trees, where visiting captains dropped messages they hoped would be received by appropriate parties.

Porter did not find Bainbridge at the first rendezvous point, Porto Praya, in the Cape Verde Islands, three hundred miles off the coast of Africa. The island was ruled by a local governor who commanded a ragtag army of four hundred soldiers with broken swords and hardly a working musket. However, the stopover was not a total loss. After dining with the governor, Porter took aboard badly needed fresh fruit, including oranges, coconuts, limes, and lemons.

He reported that "many of the seamen bought monkeys and young goats as pets and when we sailed thence the ship bore no slight resemblance as respected the different animals on board to Noah's Ark."

The ever-alert Porter, wanting no one to know his ship's movements, noted in his journal that

> *on leaving the port we shaped our course to the S.E., with a view of deceiving the people of Praya, and impressing a belief that we were bound to the coast of Africa. When, however, we were at such a distance that the ship could no longer be seen from the town, I stood S.S.W. by compass with a view of falling in with the Island of St. Pedro de Ponedro.*

As *Essex* crossed the equator, her crew held the traditional "crossing the line" ceremony, in which Neptune and his cohorts introduced the uninitiated crew members into the "mysteries" of the South Sea. The colorful ceremony, which ended in a good drunk for many, is captured in the journal of Midshipman William W. Feltus:

> *[Neptune and his entourage rode in a] carriage drawn four men, some with their shirts off and their bodies painted and others with their trousers cut off above the knees and their legs painted and their faces painted in this manner, accompanied by his [Neptune's] barbers with their razors [and with a] band of music they marched on where he dismounted with his wife and spoke to the captain for permission to shave [the heads] of such as had not crossed the*

line before officers excepted, provided that they would pay some rum, this was granted.

On 12 December, Porter lured another ship into his clutches by running up British colors and recognition signals he had learned during his battle with *Alert*. Captains of captured vessels were supposed to drop their records of secret signals overboard in a weighted bag *before* the enemy took possession. Nevertheless, captains sometimes memorized signals displayed by enemy vessels and later used them to their advantage, as Porter did here. The prize turned out to be the British packet *Nocton*, carrying ten guns and, more importantly, $55,000 in specie (coin). Porter dispatched *Nocton* with a prize crew to the United States, but first he moved the money aboard *Essex*. The money would come in useful when Porter rounded the Horn into the Pacific to buy supplies and to pay his crew. *Nocton* sailed toward the American coast but, unfortunately for Porter, was recaptured three weeks later by HMS *Belvidera*.

On 14 December, *Essex* dropped anchor at Fernando de Noronha, a Portuguese penal island four degrees south of the equator. Because Portugal was allied with Great Britain, Porter was careful not to reveal his true identity. He posed as captain of the British merchantman *Fanny* and sent ashore several of his men, who reported that the mailbox there contained a letter for Sir James Yeo, captain of the thirty-two-gun *Southampton*; Yeo, it is recalled, had once challenged Porter to a "tete a tete." Porter also learned that the HMS *Acasta* and *Morgiana*, with forty-four and twenty guns, respectively, had visited the port and set sail for Rio de Janeiro.

Porter informed the locals that he would be happy to transport the letter to his countryman Yeo (and sent over some cheese and porter [a light stout] as an incentive). He was given possession of the letter, which read:

> *My dear Mediterranean Friend: Probably you may stop here. . . . I learnt before I left England, that you were bound for the Brazil coast; if so, perhaps we may meet at St. Salvadore or Rio de Janeiro; I should be happy to meet and converse on our old affairs of captivity; recollect our secret in those times.*

The letter had a special ring for Porter. The "captivity" was a reference to imprisonment in the Tripoli; the "secret" was the use of lemon juice to write hidden words. This epistle, whose handwriting Porter recognized, was from William Bainbridge, Porter's commanding officer when the two were imprisoned in Tripoli after the grounding of *Philadelphia*. The letter was clearly intended for Porter. Addressing it to Yeo had been a ruse. The invisible handwriting revealed the following: "I am bound off St. Salvadore, thence off Cape Frio, where I intend to cruise until the 1st of January. Go off Cape Frio, to the northward of Rio de Janeiro, and keep a look out for me. Your friend."

Porter proceeded to Cape Frio, but not finding Bainbridge, he sailed on to the isle of St. Catherine, the final meeting spot, five hundred miles south of Rio. He arrived on 19 January 1813. Neither *Constitution* nor *Hornet* was anywhere to be found and, finding St. Catherine to be as backward at Porto Praya, Porter sailed on. A week later, he met up with a Portuguese ship, whose crew informed him about a great sea battle in which an American ship had sunk a powerful British frigate. This, Porter would discover later, was *Constitution*'s defeat of HMS *Java* on 29 December, another stunning victory for the U.S. Navy.

Now Porter had to think like a nineteenth-century captain—in short, on his feet. There were many options to consider. He could continue to look for Bainbridge, though it seemed possible that *Constitution*, having met such a formidable opponent, might be heading back to the United States for repairs. Porter also had to entertain the possibility that the South Atlantic would soon be filled with Royal Navy ships; having gotten word of *Java*'s defeat, they would crisscross the area in search of *Constitution*. Thus, it seemed wise to move on. But where could Porter take *Essex?* He could always return to the United States for further orders, but it hardly seemed worth the risk of encountering a tightening British blockade.

The pieces of the puzzle probably fell together for David Porter at this moment. He had been toying with plans to round the Horn into the Pacific. In fact, months earlier, he had floated the idea with Captains Rodgers and Bainbridge, and they had approved of it. Now a foray into the Pacific seemed to be his only option. The strength of *Essex*, after all, lay more in the capture of merchant vessels rather than of British frigates. The English regarded the Pacific Ocean as their domain, though with the Royal Navy always stretched to the limits, they rarely patrolled the immense body of water. There would be few, if any, Royal Navy frigates around, but plenty of merchantmen to take as easy prizes. Porter and his crew could intensify the economic discomfort of the enemy.

Inasmuch as sea captains of the era were required to follow orders, the lack of modern communication gave them a trump card. They could follow their own designs and hunches. Now Porter would follow his into the Pacific, where *Essex* would wreak havoc on the whaling fleet of the world's most powerful nation.

CHAPTER SEVEN

The Glorious Pacific Cruise

A single frigate lording over the Pacific in saucy defiance of
their thousand ships, reveling in the spoils of boundless
wealth, and almost banishing the British flag from these
regions where it had so long waved proudly Predominant.

—WASHINGTON IRVING, ON THE *ESSEX*

A few months before *Essex* rounded the Horn into the
Pacific, David Porter offered each crewman a clean
slate. As he later wrote, "I now gave a general pardon for all
offenses committed on board; recommended the strictest
attention to the discipline of the ship; held out prospects of
reward to those who should be vigilant to the performance
of their duty." Porter, however, was hardly a lax captain and
was quick to make known the consequences that would
befall those who did not tow the line. It was Porter, in fact,
who once said that "a man-of-war is a petty kingdom, and is

169

governed by a petty despot. . . . The little Tyrant, who struts his few fathoms of scoured plank, dare not unbend, lest he should lose that appearance of respect from his inferiors which their fears inspire."

To that end, he told his crew that "the first man I was under the necessity of punishing should receive three dozen lashes; expressing a hope, however, that punishment during the cruise would be altogether unnecessary." Porter's amnesty was more than a symbolic gesture. The crew of *Essex* was about to embark on a cruise whose challenges, deprivations, temptations, and, especially, final battle, would demand the deep loyalty of her men.

The first test was upon them soon enough. By the end of January 1813, *Essex* slammed into the roiling seas around Cape Horn. Porter readied the ship for stormy waters by lessening the weight aloft and moving weight toward the ship's center:

> *I had taken measures to prepare the ship for the worst, by sending down our royal masts and rigging, unreaving all our running rigging not absolutely necessary, sending every heavy article out of the tops, as well as all the light sails, such as royals, stay-sails, topgallant-studding-sails, &c. . . . I also caused all the shot to be put below except six to each gun, on the gun-deck; removed the guns from the extremities to midships; set up the main rigging; and bent the storm-stay-sails.*

The crew of *Essex* faced other dangers. Porter was in possession of an imperfect ocean chart; the ship was in dire need of cordage; and provisions were low, despite that the crew had been on half rations (with the exception of rum) since leaving the United States in October 1812. The men were getting tired, cold, and weak. They were heading into the Pacific Ocean, and friendly ports, where rest and comfort could be obtained, were few and far between. An eclipse on 1 February 1813 could not have failed to further unsettle the sailors, traditionally prone to superstition. The celestial event, Porter wrote, gave him "reason to expect unsettled weather."

On 18 February, Porter and his crew were blasted by a three-day storm that tossed *Essex* about like a cork and forced her to run with the wind. After she had rounded the Horn and was edging her way into the Pacific, she was hit by another gale that, according to Porter's journal entry, "blew with a fury even exceeding any thing we had yet experienced, bringing with it such a tremendous sea, as to threaten us every moment with destruction." *Essex* held up well under the storms, though the same could not be said for the men. In addition to being absolutely exhausted, they were slammed against bulwarks and thrown down hatchways by the violent rolls of the ship. If that wasn't enough, 3 March saw the arrival of a third blow, this one wielding a wall of water that swept over the ship and poured down the hatchways, igniting panic even among experienced crew members. David Farragut would recall that sailors fell on their knees in prayer and had all but given up, when Boatswain's Mate William Kingsbury bucked up the crew with these words: "Damn your eyes, put your best foot forward, there is one side left of her yet!"

The weather wasn't Porter's only worry. He also was concerned about what he called "that dreadful scourge, the scurvy." He wrote that he

> *therefore gave the strictest orders to the cook, not to permit any person to use slush from the cask, for the purpose of frying their bread &c., as this practice is very common among seamen; and on board of many ships, but particularly Captain Vancouver's [George Vancouver (1757–98) was an English explorer], the disease has been traced to this cause.*

Porter was wrong to believe slush—nothing more than grease and fat from cooking—was the cause of scurvy. However, he must be given more credit than many captains of his day (and even one hundred years later) because he had some inkling about the remedy for scurvy—limes and lemons. He states: "Yet we have not had the slightest symptom of scurvy on board. To be sure, the fruit they [his men] brought with them from Praya, and the onions from St. Catharines, were powerful anti-scorbutics." Overall, Porter's crew was very healthy.

Porter's insistence on cleanliness of his ship and men—and his strict enforcement of it among *all* on board—could not but have raised morale. Put succinctly, Porter ran a tight ship. *Essex* was cleaned twice daily. Every deck was fumigated by pouring vinegar on red-hot shot. Lime was provided for whitewashing and sand for dry scrubbing. While these methods truly did little to purge the vessel of filth and foul odors, they were the best the navy had to offer, and they certainly imbued the crew with a spirit of cleanliness. Porter gave orders that no wet clothes or provisions be permitted on the berth deck. The crew was not allowed to eat anywhere but on the gun deck, except in bad weather.

Among the men themselves, Porter, following the example of other captains like James Cook, required

> the utmost cleanliness from every person on board, and directions were given for mustering the crew every morning at their quarters, where they were strictly examined by their officers. It was recommended to them to bathe at least once a day, and the officers were requested to show them the example.

In warm weather, Porter allowed the crew to sleep in hammocks on the gun deck—instead of in the cramped, airless berth deck below—because it was cooler. This meant that more time was needed to stow the hammocks at the approach of danger, but it showed that Porter had great confidence in the ability of his crew to clear the decks for action swiftly.

Porter's regimen was absolutely necessary. *Essex* was entering an area of the world where there were few, if any, friendly ports in which to safely anchor in the event disease was rampant on his ship. His insistence on scrubbing, scraping, and bathing paid off. *Essex* had a remarkably illness-free cruise in the Pacific. Porter did not neglect the mental health of his men, either. He exhorted the officers to keep the crew occupied with tasks during working hours and to be "particularly careful not to harass them by disturbing them unnecessarily during their watch below."

Supplies continued to dwindle and were further reduced by spoilage. It is not hard to reckon why a sailor's pet monkey disappeared. On the bright side, there was enough fresh water to make hot tea, which the crew sorely needed as they set and took in sail to keep the Salem frigate afloat. More than a few were suffering from frostbite due to sodden clothing and a lack of decent footwear. Porter rather glumly stated in his journal that "we have now been three months from the United States; in the course of which time, we have been but seven days in port." But, the men remained in what Porter called "extraordinary spirits." They "continued their usual diversions during the gales, labored with cheerfulness when labor was requisite, and all seemed determined to share with their officers every fatigue and to exert themselves to the utmost to conquer every difficulty." *Essex* herself wore well, despite her age. Porter reported: "In the heaviest blows and worst sea we have yet had, I find the ship to be remarkably easy and comfortable."

By March, *Essex* had rounded Cape Horn, thus becoming the first American warship to fill her sails in the Pacific (she had attained the honor of being first to round the Cape of Good Hope under Captain Preble in 1800). A few days later, on 6 March, the ship landed at the island of Mocha, off the Chilean coast, six hundred miles south of Valparaiso. There the crew obtained fresh meat by shooting wild hogs. Porter kept a very low profile during his first few weeks because he wanted to make a few surprise captures before word got out that an American frigate was cruising the coast of South America. Unfortunately, *Essex* was plagued by fog, and by the middle of March, when she arrived at Valparaiso, she had found no enemy vessels.

Porter sailed into the Chilean port flying English colors, because Chile was a Spanish colony, and Spain at that time was aligned with Great Britain. After dropping anchor, however, he received the shocking news that the Chileans, inspired by the American and French revolutions, had declared their own independence after Napoleon removed Spanish Monarch Ferdinand VII from his throne. Though Chile would not gain her full and lasting independence until 1817, Porter could only have been elated at the news. While the nation could not be counted as an ally, Chile—for the time being, at least—was not allied with the British. The Chileans were elated over the arrival of the Americans, believing it was a sign that the United States planned to aid their struggle for independence. Cannon salutes were exchanged, and *Essex* became the first warship to honor the Chilean flag in this manner.

There was more exciting news for the crew of *Essex*. Peru, which had remained loyal to Spain, had sent out cruisers against vessels trading with the rebellious Chileans—most notably, American whalers in the Pacific. It was clear that *Essex* had arrived at an opportune time. The cruisers were no match for the Salem frigate, and the neutrality of Chile was one less thing Porter had to worry about as he and his men sought after lucrative prizes.

The local governor feted Porter and his officers at a Chilean ball. While grateful for the hospitality, the

American captain found many of the provincial customs bizarre and startling. A local dance, Porter relates,

> consisted of the most graceless and at the same time fatiguing movements of the body and limbs, accompanied by the most indelicate and lascivious motions, gradually increasing in energy and violence until the fair one, apparently overcome with passion and exhausted with fatigue, was compelled to retire to her seat. . . . They [the women] disfigure themselves most lavishly with paint, but their features are agreeable, and their large dark eyes are remarkably brilliant and expressive. Were it not for their bad teeth, occasioned by the too liberal use of matti [an herb sweetened with sugar and sucked through a straw] they would be thought handsome.

Business was mixed with pleasure during these affairs, and in time, Porter learned about the extent of British whaling. The news was good. The king's whalers were plentiful in the Pacific. Many cruised the seas around the Galapagos Islands, twenty-three hundred miles northwest of Valparaiso. The vessels were armed, though none with more than twenty guns, and they certainly were not manned by as large or as well-trained a crew as that of *Essex*. These whalers were powerful enough, however, to take by surprise and capture American merchant vessels whose crews had been out at sea for years and had not heard about the fighting between the two countries. Moreover, two Spanish ships recently had left Valparaiso for Lima, where they were sure to spread the warning to their allies, the

English, that a thirty-two-gun U.S. frigate had sailed into the Pacific. Porter stated wryly: "It seemed beyond a doubt that they would conjecture my designs were not confined to doubling Cape Horn merely for the pleasure of visiting Valparaiso." To be productive, Porter and his men had to move fast.

On 23 March 1813, *Essex* sailed for the Galapagos Islands. Two days out, she met up with a Nantucket whaler, *Charles*, whose captain informed him that his ship, along with two other American whalers, *Walker* and *Barclay*, had been attacked by a Peruvian vessel. The crew of *Charles*, Porter was told, had been released only after paying ransom.

The following day, Porter met up with the suspected perpetrator of the depredations, a fifteen-gun Peruvian cruiser by the name of *Nereyda*. In actuality, she was a sloop disguised as a whaler. Porter had prepared his own disguise. *Essex* was flying British colors. When a lieutenant from the *Nereyda* came aboard *Essex*, he informed Porter that he was searching for American vessels and that he was the one who had earlier captured *Barclay* and *Walker*. The American crews were imprisoned aboard his ship. The seizures had provided a rich haul because the American whalers were just about to sail for home laden with whale oil and spermaceti. The crewmen had also been robbed of their personal possessions, Porter learned.

Porter asked *Nereyda*'s lieutenant to bring over the captain of *Walker* and one of the crew of *Barclay*. When these two men came aboard, Porter took them aside and revealed his American identity, no doubt to their elation. Porter's journal takes it from here: "The *Nereyda* was now under the muzzle of our guns, and I directed the American flag to be hoisted, and fired two shot over her, when she struck her colors." In one swift move, Porter had liberated two crews and captured a hostile ship bent on making life miserable for American merchantmen. In disposing of *Nereyda*, however, Porter had to exercise caution. Relations between Spain and the United States at that time were very strained, and America did not need a war breaking out with Spain when she had all she could handle with England. In lieu of claiming the Peruvian cruiser as a prize, Porter ordered her armaments thrown into the sea and sent the ship to Callao with a letter to the viceroy calling the ship's attack on American whaling "piratical."

Porter now turned to the American whalers. How many British whaleships were in the area, he asked them. They estimated eighty. One can only imagine Porter's glee at the response. After all, it now seemed certain that his risk in taking *Essex* around the Horn, without sufficient provisions and without *official* naval orders, was about to pay off. Porter wrote:

> *Their cargoes [the whalers] in England would be worth two hundred thousand dollars each, which, agreeable to this estimate, would be upwards of four millions of British property now exposed to us. . . . Beside the capture and destruction of those vessels, I had another object in view . . . the protection of the American whaleships; and if I should only succeed in driving the British from the ocean, I conceive [it] be considered a justification for departing from the letter of my instructions.*

(The accuracy of Porter's computations will be discussed in Chapter 8.)

A good amount of British cargo was now potentially exposed to the muzzles of *Essex*. A valuable commodity, whale oil had many uses in the early nineteenth century, such as in lighting street lamps and lighthouses. Because of its ability to withstand heat and cold, it served as a good lubricant for the machinery of the Industrial Revolution. Spermaceti, a waxy substance taken from the head of a sperm whale, was used to make fine ointments and candles. Whalebone, another product of the hunt, brought in cash as well. Harvested from the mouth of the right whale, the bone was made into horsewhips, brushes, corsets, and ribs for parasols.

Porter's ruse of flying English colors had worked well against *Nereyda*; he decided to try a similar tactic with other vessels. He had his crew paint the ship to look like a Spanish merchant vessel.

On 29 March, *Essex* recaptured the American whaleship *Barclay*, whose captain elected to stay with the Salem frigate so as not to risk capture again. Porter cruised the waters around the Galapagos, obtaining information on British whalers from letters left in a "mailbox" known as "Hathaway's Post Office," on one of the islands. With their stunted trees and rocky fissures, the Galapagos Islands were a strange, uninhabitable place, which Porter described as having "the most dreary, desolate, and inhospitable appearance imaginable."

A month-long search paid off on 29 April 1813, when *Essex* captured the whaler *Montezuma* (270 tons, two guns, twenty-one men) with fourteen hundred barrels of whale oil. Using a false identity, Porter invited the ship's captain to come aboard and give him information about other British whaling ships in the area, before informing him that his ship had been captured by an American frigate.

A short while later, *Essex* captured two other whalers: *Georgiana* and *Policy*. The former was a good-size vessel with twenty-five men, six guns, and a good supply of spermaceti. She was pressed into the service of the U.S. Navy by adding ten guns from *Policy*. Both whaling vessels had surrendered handily, not surprising given that many of the sailors aboard the British whalers were Americans. Many men were willing to enlist, and in this way, Porter manned his prizes without heavily depleting his own crew.

Georgiana's sailing was improved by taking down the boilers used for rendering whale oil from the blubber. These massive boilers, made of brick and mortar, with huge kettles, weighed down the ship and made for sluggish sailing. Command of the vessel was given to the first lieutenant of *Essex*, John Downes. He was ordered to sail eastward in pursuit of more British whalers.

These captures buoyed Porter and his men not only in the name of victory but also, more practically, because whalers carried provisions for a three-year cruise, and these stores were sorely needed by the crew of *Essex*. "From them [the captured vessels] we obtained an abundant supply of cordage, canvas, paints, tar, and every other article necessary for the ship, all of which she stood in great need, as our slender stock brought from America had now become worn out and useless," Porter wrote. His men, however, were

(COURTESY OF U.S. NAVY)

ESSEX AND HER FLEET OF PRIZES OFF PERU. PORTER WAS SO SHORT OF NAVAL
OFFICERS TO COMMAND THE VESSELS THAT HE PUT HIS MARINE LIEUTENANT IN
CHARGE OF ONE AND HIS CHAPLAIN IN COMMAND OF ANOTHER.

probably most excited about the haul of tortoises captured
from the whaling crews, who had obtained them from the
Galapagos Islands, where they thrived in abundance. Porter
wrote: "Hideous and disgusting as is their appearance, no
animal can possibly afford a more wholesome, luscious, and
delicate food than they do. The finest green turtle is no
more to be compared to them in point of excellence than
the coarsest beef is to the finest veal." Tortoises were an
ideal source of protein aboard sailing vessels because the
animals could live for long periods without food or water
and could be stored readily in the vessel's hold. In short, 29
April was a memorable day for the crewmen of the Salem

frigate. As Porter wrote: "The satisfaction which the possession of these valuable vessels gave us made us forget for a
moment the hardships of Cape Horn."

Porter continued to cruise around the Galapagos, at one
time anchoring to paint his prize vessels so that they might
bring a higher price when he had opportunity to put them
up for sale on the South American coast. While at sea, his
crew searched the waters for "the garbage of whales floating
on the surface," a sure sign that a vessel was in the vicinity.
He used the *Georgiana*, *Barclay*, and *Policy* to cut as wide a
swath through the sea as possible. Each ship stayed within
signaling distance, ready to alert Porter and his *Essex* crew
should any strange vessel appear.

On 27 May, the sails of the British whaler *Atlantic* hove
into view. She was a vessel of 355 tons, with a crew of twenty-
four and six guns. After a chase that lasted a night and a day,
Essex pulled alongside the vessel and hoisted British colors.
As *Atlantic*'s captain came on board, another sail was sighted. He was ushered below. Porter sent Lieutenant Stephen
McKnight and some crewmen aboard to secure the prize,
then ordered his crew to set off in pursuit of the distant sail.

Porter then went below to play host to his guest. He
offered him a glass of wine and soon learned more about his
identity. The captain was Obadiah Weir, an American from
Nantucket, and he gladly passed on information to a man he
thought was the captain of a Royal Navy man-of-war. When
Porter asked him how he reconciled himself to sailing
against his own nation, he replied that "though he was born
in America, he was an Englishman at heart." It must have

given Porter great pleasure to introduce Weir to the imprisoned captains of *Montezuma* and *Georgiana*, "who soon undeceived him with respect to our being an English frigate."

Later that evening, *Essex* caught up with and captured the ship she had been chasing, but not before firing a menacing shot between the stranger's masts. She was *Greenwich* (388 tons, ten guns, and twenty-six men). Her captain was John Shuttleworth, who was intoxicated and none too happy to be taken aboard an American frigate. Porter wrote that after Shuttleworth and Weir were shown to their quarters,

> *they gave full vent to their anger . . . and lavished on me, in particular, the most scurrilous epithets, giving me appellations that would have suited a buccaneer. . . . I determined next day to make them sensible of the impropriety of their conduct and did so without violating the principles of humanity or the rules of war. I let them feel that they were dependent entirely on my generosity [and they] were now so humbled by a sense of their own conduct that they would have licked the dust from my feet had it been required of them to do so.*

Porter was now in command of a small fleet, which included *Atlantic*, *Greenwich*, *Montezuma*, *Policy,* and *Georgiana*, a total of thirty-four extra guns to add to forty-six on *Essex*. In addition, some of the prisoners agreed to serve in the American navy and received their full allowance of provisions. In his own eyes, at least, Porter had become something of a commodore.

However, all was not bliss for the *Essex* captain, who had a very unusual problem. He did not have enough lieutenants to man his prizes, a situation aggravated by the drinking problem of Lieutenant James Wilson, whom Porter had put under arrest. Porter was forced to recall Lieutenant McKnight from *Atlantic* and replace him with Chaplain David Adams. In addition, Porter had no choice but to give command of *Greenwich* to Marine Lieutenant John Gamble, who was accompanied by two of the best seamen from *Essex* to make up for his lack of ship handling experience. At any rate, it was another first for *Essex*: the first U.S. Marine ever to be given command of a "navy" vessel. *Greenwich* was used as a store ship for the wealth of supplies Porter had captured.

The shortage of experienced officers to man the whalers should have sent a signal to David Porter. He was spreading his resources too thin and would have been better off burning the ships. True, he and his crew would have forfeited the opportunity for prize money. On the other hand, what was the possibility of getting the prizes to a port with a legitimate prize court? Certainly there was none in Chile, which was in a state of civil war. To get to a U.S. court, the whalers—notoriously slow sailers—would have had to squeeze through a tight British blockade, because there was little chance a whaler could outrun a man-of-war. It is possible that Porter, during his initial visit to Valparaiso, made arrangements with officials to get his prizes condemned and sold. However, he does not mention it in his book, *Journal of a Cruise*, with good reason—that is, it might very well have been viewed as akin to piracy, since the

Chilean rebels were not an officially recognized government with legitimate courts.

Porter's shortage of officers grew worse on 24 June. He met up with Lieutenant Downes aboard *Georgiana*, which had more captured whalers under her guns. The vessels were *Hector, Rose,* and *Catherine*, each of 270 tons, with about twenty-five men and eight to eleven guns. They had been taken near the Galapagos. Porter began shuffling his men around again. Because *Atlantic* was a superior vessel to *Georgiana*, Porter ordered the former to be mounted with twenty guns and gave her to Lieutenant Downes. She was rechristened USS *Essex Junior*.

John Downes, Porter's first lieutenant and right-hand man, had been handpicked for the cruise. He and Porter went back many years, serving together as midshipmen during the wars against the Barbary States. Downes would go on to his own fame after his *Essex* cruise. As captain of the eighteen-gun brig *Epervier,* he would accompany Commodore Stephen Decatur's squadron of nine vessels to the Mediterranean in 1815 to confront the dey of Algiers.

Downes is best known, however, for a cruise from 1819–21, when he returned to the coast of Chile, this time as captain of frigate *Macedonian*. The navy had dispatched Downes to the area to protect America's merchant interests, which were growing each year, from depredations committed both by Spanish Loyalists and local rebels fighting for independence. While patrolling the seas, Downes carried specie, or "freight," for merchant vessels of all countries, who were susceptible to raiders. As was mentioned, this was against naval regulations because American men-of-war

(COURTESY
U.S. NAVY)

First Lieutenant John Downes, Porter's right-hand man, who made several captures of his own during America's raid on British whalers.

could carry freight only for U.S. citizens. Moreover, Downes charged a fee (a percentage of the freight) higher than allowed by the navy. When his tour ended, it is estimated that he returned home $100,000 richer. In later years, he served as commandant of the Boston Naval Yard and died in Charlestown, Massachusetts, at the age of seventy, in 1854.

Porter and his crews made no more captures during the next three weeks. They simply needed time to consolidate their squadron. Together, they had captured nine whalers, a very successful assault, though Porter's unmolested raiding could not last forever.

Even without telegraphs or telephones, news had a way of traveling amazingly fast during the age of sail. It was as if secrets flew on the winds. Word of Porter's capture of the Peruvian *Nereyda* reached British ears only two months after the event. An intelligence report dated May 1813 stated:

> *The last accounts from Chile mentions that the* Essex *frigate had sailed from Valparaiso to protect the trade of that country against the Lima cruisers some of which the Captain of that vessel had seized and dismantled.*

The author of the report was dead wrong in his predictions on the future course of the American frigate:

> *It is difficult to say which will be the next movement of the Essex. It is said she will remain a short time longer on that [Lima] coast and thence will run across the Pacific to India, where report is given out by the Americans here that she is to join the* Constitution *and the* Hornet, *who were to go thither from the Coast of Brazil. . . . Other reports are that she will come back round Cape Horn and . . . return to America.*

It is quite possible Porter fed his Chilean guests these bogus speculations to hide his true plans. He had, in fact, remained in the Pacific and had much to show for his efforts.

By the end of the summer, a fuller picture of Porter's depredations were known to the British. A letter written by Commodore William Bowles near Buenos Aires to John Wilson Croker, secretary to the Board of Admiralty, stated:

> *I am sorry to inform their Lordships that letters are just received here from Chile giving accounts of the continued success of the American frigate ESSEX on that coast. It appears that on the 11th ultimo the seven English whalers, CATHERINE, HECTOR, POLICY, MONTEZUMA, ATLANTIC, GREENWICH, GEORGE & ANNE had arrived at Valparaiso, and the Americans were fitting out one of them (ATLANTIC) with 20 guns and 90 men to cruise in company with*

ESSEX, which ship was still at sea but expected at Valparaiso in about a month from that date to refit and convoy her prizes to America.

Some of this information was incorrect, but the British had the gist of the story. Porter was raising hell in the Pacific. The Royal Navy could not abide news of *Essex* for long without dispatching men-of-war to capture or sink her. There was, in fact, a British frigate making her way toward the Pacific that summer, though her mission was to aid her countrymen in the battle for the Oregon Territory. She was HMS *Phoebe*, and her captain, James Hillyar, would find news of Porter's raid disturbing enough to make a short but momentous detour to the Bay of Valparaiso.

The War of 1812 had intensified the dispute over control of the Pacific Northwest, prized for its fur trade. There was a lot of money to be made selling the commodity to Asian markets. Claims to the territory known as Columbia were nebulous. Lewis and Clark had been the first to arrive in 1805, but by the War of 1812, English traders had entered the area as well.

By 1811, New York fur entrepreneur John Jacob Astor (1763–1848) was digging in his heels in Columbia. He had dispatched the ship *Tonquin* around Cape Horn to the Pacific coast, where its crew was to build Fort Astoria on the Columbia River. As the war heated up, England decided to foil his plans and to stake a permanent claim in the area. In March 1813, the British sent a fur trading vessel, *Isaac Todd*, twenty guns, and the thirty-six-gun *Phoebe*, under Captain

Hillyar, to the Columbia coast, with secret orders to destroy Fort Astoria and build a new settlement.

The vessels arrived in Rio de Janeiro two months later, just in time to hear news of *Essex* captures. Rear Admiral Sir Manley Dixon of the South American station added two more vessels to the fur mission—the sloops, *Racoon*, twenty-six guns, and *Cherub*, eighteen guns—in the event the tiny squadron should meet up with *Essex*. The mission remained the same: to proceed to the Northwest to "protect and render every assistance in your power to the British traders from Canada, and to destroy, and if possible totally annihilate any settlements which the Americans may have formed either on the Columbia River or on the neighboring Coasts." However, Hillyar was also to keep an eye out for the Salem frigate.

The passage around the Horn was arduous, and *Isaac Todd* became separated and was given up for lost. By the time the ships had sailed north to the equator in early October 1813, Hillyar had heard more about the havoc created by *Essex*, and he decided to cruise the area with *Cherub*, in search of Porter. *Racoon* was dispatched north to complete the mission in Columbia.

The story in the Pacific Northwest, at least in the short term, ended badly for the Americans. Protecting Astoria from the British proved impossible. Astor could get no support from the American navy, which was locked into ports along the eastern seaboard by the British. The Americans at Fort Astoria, after hearing rumors of the impending arrival of an enemy frigate and two sloops, sold their enterprise to the English in October 1813. *Racoon* arrived a month later.

Porter, however, was not finished with the British whaling trade. On 14 July, four days after sending Downes to Valparaiso with orders to sell the prizeships *Hector*, *Catherine*, *Policy*, and *Montezuma*, the Americans seized three more vessels. The first was the 274-ton *Charlton*, with twenty-one men and ten guns. She was "an old vessel and a dull sailer." For a captain short on lieutenants, she was hardly worth keeping. The second whaler was *New Zealander*, with eight guns and twenty-three men.

The crew of the third whaler, the fourteen-gun *Seringapatam*, did not readily submit to capture. Marine Lieutenant Gamble, commanding *Greenwich*, reached *Seringapatam* first, and his crew fired several broadsides, partially disabling the English vessel. The captain hauled down his colors, then attempted to escape. His ruse failed, and the vessel was soon captured. There was a reason why the *Seringapatam*'s crew, unlike the others, had put up a good fight. Previously, the ship had captured an American whaler out of Nantucket. When Porter asked the captain, William Stavers, for his letter of marque (official permission from a government to prey on enemy shipping), he said he had none with him. Technically, that made him a pirate, and Porter put him in irons.

Consolidating his prizes as best he could, Porter moved some of the guns of *Charlton* and *New Zealander* to *Seringapatam*, which now wielded a formidable twenty-two guns, and sent *Charlton* to Rio de Janeiro as a cartel vessel with prisoners.

Ten days later, Porter reconfigured his tiny fleet again. He sent *Georgiana* with $100,000 worth of spermaceti to the

United States, where he believed he could get a better price than along the South American coast. Also aboard the ship were *Essex* crewmen whose terms of duty were set to expire. In command of the vessel was Lieutenant Wilson, whom Porter was glad to be rid of. Though a drunkard, he was popular with the crew, making it difficult for Porter to discipline him. Porter dropped charges against Wilson after his brave conduct during the battle with *Seringapatam*. It seemed an opportune time to bid farewell to the troublesome lieutenant. *Georgiana* got three cheers upon her departure, and Porter wrote, "We had an opportunity, by this vessel, of writing to our friends and enjoyed, in pleasing anticipation, the effect that the news of our great success would produce in the United States."

By the end of July, Porter anchored his small fleet off the Galapagos Islands, where he lost another lieutenant, this time to a duel—"a practice that disgraces human nature." Lieutenant John S. Cowan was buried where he fell. Porter kept the identity of the officer who killed Cowan a secret.

Though saddened by the event, Porter used it to his advantage. By the grave side, he left a bogus note, meant to fool British whalers that happened upon it, that read:

> *The United States frigate* Essex *arrived here on the 21st July, 1813, her crew much afflicted with the scurvy and ship fever, which attacked them suddenly. She lost her first lieutenant, surgeon, sailing master, 2 midshipmen, gunner, carpenter, and 36 seamen. [The* Essex *is in a] leaky state, her foremast rotten in the partners and her mainmast sprung. . . . Should any American vessel, or,*

indeed, a vessel of any nation, put in here and meet with this note, they would be doing an act of great humanity to transmit a copy of it to America in order that our friends may know of our distressed and hopeless situation and be prepared for worse tidings if they should ever again hear from us.

The message, in the eyes of a Royal Navy captain cruising the seas, would make out *Essex* to be an easy prize, and she was hardly that.

The Salem frigate made one last capture. On 15 September, the ship *Sir Andrew Hammond*, with twelve guns and thirty-six men, struck her flag after a short chase. The decks of the vessel were full of blubber that had yet to be rendered into whale oil. Not wanting to pass up any prize money, Porter had his prisoners finish up the messy business, which took three days. Still short of men, Porter placed Chaplain Adams in command of the vessel.

By the end of the month, Porter had a rendezvous with *Essex Junior* and Lieutenant Downes, who brought news that *Phoebe* and *Cherub* were cruising the seas in search of the American frigate. Figuring it was an opportune time to rest his men, reprovision his squadron, prepare *Essex* for battle, and put a lot of distance between himself and the scenes of his depredations, Porter set sail for the Marquesas Islands, twenty-five hundred miles southwest of the Galapagos. The Marquesas, actually a series of ten islands, would provide a remote place where the crew of *Essex* could clean the ship's bottom and repair the copper, overhaul the rigging, and smoke out the rats, which had become a tremendous nuisance, eating through water casks and gnawing on the ship's cartridges. The visit also would give the crew their fill of fresh fruits and vegetables necessary to maintain good health.

As he sailed toward the islands, Porter must have been in buoyant spirits. His gamble in rounding the Horn had paid off handsomely. He had crippled the British whaling fleet in the Pacific by capturing 13 vessels, 105 guns, and countless barrels of valuable whale oil that would not brighten English streets or lubricate machines in her burgeoning factories. Porter also had kept his men supplied with food and grog and his ship furnished with sails and cordage, all taken from captured vessels. The capture of *Nocton* the previous December had helped him meet his payroll expenses. And he had accomplished all this without losing many of his crew to battle or disease. In fact, *Essex* hardly had had to fire her guns (though it is likely that Porter was not happy with that aspect of the cruise).

There was more to raise the spirits of Porter and his men. Lieutenant Downes had brought news of the American navy's early and stunning victories, among them *Constitution* versus *Guerriere*, *United States* versus *Macedonian*, and the *Wasp* versus *Frolic*. It seemed that the American navy, despite its small size, was giving the giant Royal Navy a run for its money.

Essex landed at the Marquesa island of Nukahiva in late October 1813. Porter's contact with the islanders was facilitated by an Englishman named Wilson, who had lived for years among them, spoke their language, and, in Porter's words, was an "inoffensive, honest, good-hearted fellow, well disposed to render every service in his power." His only failing, according to Porter, "was a strong attachment to rum." Porter claimed the archipelago as a U.S. possession and renamed it Madison's Islands, in honor of the newly re-elected president. Porter later would be criticized for his claim, as well as for his actions in the Marquesas. The *Salem Gazette* would condemn him for attempting to conquer "these simple and unoffending children of nature." One of Porter's motives was to establish a base in the Pacific where U.S. men-of-war and merchant ships could land at a friend-ly port, instead of living by their wits, as he had done. The United States could not rely on Chile, whose independence rested on shaky foundations. In the end, however, Porter's claim amounted to nothing. The U.S. government would be too slow in confirming Porter's claim on the islands, and they later fell into the hands of the French.

At the very least, however, Porter gave the islands the semblance of an American port for a few months at the end of 1813. He had his men build huts, a bakery, a sail loft, a sick house, and a cooper's shop. For protection against the British, as well as the local inhabitants, he erected a primi-tive fort with six guns. Work on *Essex*, meanwhile, pro-gressed steadily. During hours of leisure, Porter exchanged gifts with the high chief while the *Essex* crew exchanged intimacies with the local women.

Unfortunately, but hardly unexpectedly, the Americans got mixed up in the politics of the island tribes. Porter's aim during his stay was to protect his men and ship by keeping peace among the islanders. Neutrality, however, eluded him. The Tayees, whom Porter had befriended, were at war

ESSEX AND HER WHALING PRIZES AT NUKAHIVA, MARQUESAS ISLANDS, IN THE FALL OF 1813. IT WAS HERE THAT PORTER REPAIRED HIS SHIP AND REFRESHED HIS CREW FOR BATTLE WITH THE ROYAL NAVY HE WAS DETERMINED TO SEEK OUT.

with an inland tribe called the Happahs, who seemed intent on attacking. Porter had a six-pound cannon dragged ashore and fired it off a few times to frighten the Happahs. The Tayees were certainly impressed by the gun's performance. Porter noted, "They hugged and kissed the gun, lay down beside it, fondled it with utmost delight."

The Happahs, however, took more persuading. Porter was forced to send Lieutenant Downes and forty men to drive them back into the mountains. The Americans had an inauspicious start. Downes was floored by a stone that struck him in the belly; another American received a spear through his neck. The Happahs, who Porter numbered at three thousand, then "scoffed at our men, and exposed their posteriors to them, and treated them with the utmost contempt and derision." Downes was able to recover and led his men "through a shower of spears and stones." The islanders were routed, and five were killed. A peace was brokered between the tribes, and for a while, Porter had calm.

Work continued on *Essex*. Leaky seams and the copper bottom were repaired. Barnacles were scraped off the bottom. The main mast was rebuilt. Rats were smoked out. The ship was painted.

Before long, however, work was interrupted by another hostile tribe, the Typees. (The Typees were made famous by Herman Melville's book of the same name, published thirty-three years later. Melville and a companion, Toby Greene, fed up with the despotic captain of the whaler *Acushnet,* jumped ship. Their adventures were a source for Melville's very successful first novel.) Again, the Americans found themselves dragged into a local conflict. On this occasion, Porter led the troops, which numbered thirty-five Americans and five thousand Tayees and Happahs, to a valley up the coast of the island. His initial assault ended in near disaster when he was ambushed and his island allies fled. Lieutenant Downes once again fell victim to a flying stone, this time breaking his leg. Porter retreated back to his base, gathered up two hundred of his best men, and made a second assault by an inland route. His strategy worked. He pushed the Typees back, though not before burning their village. The tribe sued for peace, though Porter's problems were far from over.

He now faced a captain's worst nightmare: mutiny. The cause of the impending uprising was quite simple. As the ship's repairs were nearing completion and a sailing date was set, a good many men were thinking about refusing to leave their new utopian home, brimming with rich fruits and willing women. By mid-December, with most of the repair work completed and the ship reprovisioned, Porter thought it prudent to confine his men to the ship. Along the beach, the island women lined up and expressed their grief at the loss of male companionship "by dipping their fingers into the sea and touching their eyes so as to let the salt water trickle down their cheeks." Three men were caught sneaking back to shore and were put in irons.

Morale sank lower. There were rumors that the crew was going to seize the ship. Porter apprehended the man he thought responsible for fomenting trouble—Robert White, who had enlisted aboard *Essex* from an English whaler. Porter confronted him with witnesses and then chased him from the ship. While White went over the gangway, Porter ordered his crew to man the capstan and had a fiddler play "The Girl I Left Behind Me."

Rumblings of mutiny behind him, Porter ordered *Essex* and *Essex Junior* to set sail for Valparaiso. Lieutenant Gamble and Midshipman Feltus, along with twenty-two volunteers and six prisoners, were left behind with *New Zealander*, *Seringapatam*, *Greenwich*, and *Sir Andrew Hammond*. Porter wanted to retain a presence on the island in case he needed to return for repairs and provisions after his anticipated showdown with the Royal Navy. Gamble was instructed to stay on good terms with the islanders and to leave the island if Porter had not returned within five and a half months.

As Porter sailed toward Valparaiso, he was filled with hope of meeting up with a British frigate and sending her to the bottom of the ocean. The same confident spirit, however, no longer infused the rest of the tiny American navy. After a handful of stunning victories, the tide had turned against the United States. The reversal was inevitable. As was mentioned, the Royal Navy outnumbered the American navy by 1050 to 20 vessels. Though the American sailor, generally speaking, was better trained and more highly motivated than his English counterpart, the numerical odds were insurmountable. By early 1813, the British had begun to establish a blockade of the American coast. Chesapeake Bay was bottled up by the seventy-four-gun *Marlborough*, under Admiral Sir George Cockburn, who was sending expeditions up navigable rivers to wreck ships and shore facilities. At New London, Connecticut, Sir Thomas Hardy kept shipping—including *United States* and the former HMS, now USS, *Macedonian*—holed up with his seventy-four-gun *Ramilies*.

On 1 June, the *Shannon* laid waste to the American frigate *Chesapeake*, whose captain, James Lawrence, dying in the battle, would shout, "Don't give up the ship!" (Commodore Oliver Hazard Perry would fly the famous words on his battle flag during his notable victory at the Battle of Lake Erie two months later.) The crew of *Shannon* was said to be the best trained in the Royal Navy, while *Chesapeake* seamen were green and untried in battle. In the brief but savage fifteen-minute encounter, over two hundred men were killed or wounded, most on the American vessel. As *Chesapeake* drifted helplessly, the British boarded and a fierce hand-to-hand combat ensued. The contest was witnessed by hundreds of Salem residents who climbed Legge's Hill. They turned away with heavy hearts as the outcome of the struggle became obvious.

There were further U.S. losses at sea. Two months later, the sixteen-gun *Argus*, which had seized twenty British vessels in a daring raid around Ireland and in the English Channel, was captured by the brig *Pelican*, eighteen guns, after a fierce fifty-minute battle. As the war progressed, the blockade grew tighter, and American morale, especially in the New England states, plummeted.

America again was relying on her privateers to take up the slack of her tiny navy. During the first seven months of the war, U.S. privateers, numbering two hundred, took over five hundred British merchantmen. By the close of the war, the figure would quadruple to two thousand captures.

Salem was particularly active in providing privateers for the war effort. A total of forty-one were fitted out, a number surpassed only by the larger cities of New York and Baltimore. One of the fastest and most successful privateers was Salem's *America*, a 350-ton ship, with eighteen long nine-pounders, two eighteen-pound carronades, and a crew of 168, many of them seamen from Salem's first families. The large number of men was needed not only to handle the enormous spread of sails but also to man captured vessels as prize crews. During her cruises, which began in the summer of 1812, *America* took twenty-six prizes worth over

$1 million. Her crew appeared in Salem's harbor with an endless assortment of cargoes taken from English merchantmen. The prize *Thistle*, for example, carried linens, women's shoes, teas, pickles, chintzes, wines, prunes, and gunpowder, all auctioned off. Another haul from *Falcon* included Bibles that were to be distributed at the Cape of Good Hope by the British and the Foreign Bible Society. The Crowninshields sold the Bibles to the Massachusetts Bible Society at a rock-bottom price. The War of 1812 even saw a privateer christened *David Porter*. The two hundred-ton vessel, armed with one eighteen-pound long gun and four six-pounders, made a number of captures under her captain, George Coggeshall.

David Porter could have well used American seamen who were enlisting aboard privateers. His seizure of so many whalers had left him drastically short of men aboard *Essex*, down to 255 from 319. This was a significant percentage for any warship that needed a full crew to fire the cannons, make sail, and board the enemy. Porter's reduced complement of sailors meant that he could not afford to lose many in battle without compromising the fighting abilities of his vessel. *Essex Junior* was not much of a fighting machine, having only ten eighteen-pound carronades, ten six-pounders, and a small crew of sixty.

The manpower shortage makes Porter's decision to confront the British all that more puzzling. The Royal Navy had no idea where *Essex* was exactly. Had Porter run west into the Pacific and the Indian Ocean, the element of surprise might have enabled him to capture more British merchant vessels. His return to Valparaiso was a surprising move for a captain who had little confidence in his ship's cannons, though not all that surprising considering the prize money that would go to Porter should he capture an enemy frigate larger than his own.

And there was something else: "I had done all the injury that could be done to the British commerce in the Pacific," Porter wrote. His two-and-a-half-year tour with *Essex,* in fact, had seen the capture of over twenty vessels. But not a single one gave the captain and crew a real taste of glory. *Essex*'s one-sided victory over the twenty-gun sloop *Alert* had lasted a measly eight minutes. Porter was hoping "to signalize my cruise by something more splendid before leaving that sea."

What is the final assessment of Porter's Pacific cruise? It was a great strategic success, and had he not tried to make it fantastic, it would have been better.

Porter had had the opportunity to put twelve whalers out of commission forever by burning them. Instead, hoping to line his pockets and those of his crew, he gave high priority to selling the vessels and their cargoes. Here, he failed miserably. Except for *Essex Junior* (formerly the *Atlantic*), not a single vessel was sold, with the possible exception of *Montezuma* (records are not clear). It is clear that Lieutenant Downes had no success finding buyers for *Hector*, *Catherine*, and *Policy* when he brought them to Valparaiso in July 1813. It is possible that cash locally was in short supply; it also seems plausible that neither the Rebels nor Loyalists wanted to buy captured vessels belonging to a nation whose warships were rumored to be sailing toward Valparaiso at that moment.

In the end, Porter burned only three of the whalers—and two of those at the last moment, when he was trying to goad *Phoebe* Captain James Hillyar into a one-on-one battle. Two prizes were put to good use by being turned into cartel vessels. However, five of the vessels and much of the total cargo were eventually recaptured by the British (for the fate of each vessel, see the listing at the end of this chapter). Porter would have done more damage to the British Empire and etched his name a little deeper into the history books had he put a match to each of his prizes—and had he not returned to Valparaiso.

But, back he went, arriving on 3 February 1814. *Essex Junior* was directed to cruise off the port to keep an eye out for enemy vessels while Porter spent time entertaining the locals. The festivities did not last long. On 7 February, Lieutenant Downes aboard *Essex Junior* signaled the approach of two unknown ships. Porter recalled his sailors from shore. He had the decks of *Essex* prepared for action while he went out in *Essex Junior* for a closer look. When he returned, *Essex* was battle-ready. A short time later, HMS *Phoebe*, accompanied by sloop-of-war *Cherub*, appeared in the harbor. They, too, had cleared their decks for action.

Captain Hillyar, who had been searching for the Salem frigate for months, had sailed into Valparaiso as a last resort before giving up the chase and rounding the Horn back into the Atlantic. Letters reveal that Hillyar had regretted passing up action in the Oregon Territory to hunt for an elusive frigate, but as he cruised into Valparaiso, he realized that the real action along the Pacific coast awaited him here.

As *Phoebe* ranged up alongside *Essex*, Captain Hillyar, an old friend of Porter's from their days in the Mediterranean, inquired after Porter's health. The two had known each other well. Porter, in fact, had spent many hours with Hillyar and his family. Porter reciprocated, asking after the well-being of Hillyar. Any further sense of camaraderie, however, quickly vanished in the thick atmosphere of brinkmanship. Tension built as *Phoebe* crept closer. An exchange of cannon fire from this range would have created a bloodbath.

Suddenly, awkwardness filled the air. It became obvious that Hillyar's crew had lost control of their ship, which was on a collision course with *Essex*. To Porter, the mishandling could have been a ruse. He was not prepared to take any chances in the Chilean harbor, whose neutrality was open to question. Porter reminded Hillyar that *Essex* was armed to the teeth and his men were ready to board but that he would fire only if the ships touched. Hillyar, whose vessel was in a very vulnerable position, replied, "O, Sir, I have no intention of getting on board you."

Porter's journal picks up the narrative from here:

> *I told him again, if he did fall on board of me, there would be much bloodshed. He repeated his assurances, with the same* nonchalance, *that such was not his intention. Finding, however, that he luffed up so as to cause his ship to take aback, whereby her jib-boom came across my forecastle, I immediately called all hands to board the enemy, directing them, if the hulls touched, to spring upon the deck of the* Phoebe.

For Porter and *Essex*, it was a pivotal moment. *Phoebe* (in Porter's opinion) was in a helpless position. Porter continued:

> *At this moment, not a gun from the* Phoebe *could be brought to bear on either the* Essex *or the* Essex Junior, *while her bow was exposed to the raking fire of the one, and her stern to that of the other.*

Her consort, which proved to be the *Cherub*, of eighteen guns, was too far off leeward to afford any assistance.

> *It is quite impossible for me to describe the consternation aboard the* Phoebe, *when they saw every officer and man of the* Essex *armed with a cutlass and a brace of pistols, ready to jump on board. . . . The* Phoebe *was at this moment completely at my mercy. I could've destroyed her in fifteen minutes. The temptation was great; and the unequivocal appearance of this near approach of the enemy might have justified my attacking him on the plea of self-defence.*

Porter's despised carronades were perfect at this short range. Why did he not give the order to fire? A sense of fair play? Probably not, since Porter was a pragmatist from head to toe. His friendship with Hillyar? This is possible, but certainly it could not have been the overriding reason for any self-respecting navy captain. The desire to have a one-on-one battle off the coast with *Phoebe*? That is certainly possible—after all, David Porter came looking for his pursuers.

Another possibility, one that must not be discounted, is that Porter's advantage in the situation was not as great as he made it out to be. *Phoebe* was a powerful ship wielding thirty eighteen-pounder long guns and sixteen thirty-two-pounder carronades of her own. Her decks were cleared for action. She would not have been destroyed by one broadside from *Essex*. Her crew would have rallied and given *Essex* the fight of her life. *Cherub*, too, might have maneuvered herself into position for the battle. Though he does not say it, the odds were not as great as Porter made them out to be. Hillyar makes no mention of the incident in his early correspondence from Valparaiso, either because he did not consider the moment as significant as Porter or perhaps because he was embarrassed by his mishandling of *Phoebe*.

The description of Hillyar's arrival in Valparaiso—indeed, of Porter's entire cruise with *Essex*—was recorded in Porter's *Journal of a Cruise*, published a few years after the end of the War of 1812. While the book is a fascinating and generally truthful account of the cruise of *Essex*, it was also Porter's apologia for the loss of his ship, which he believed had been attacked in neutral waters. It is, therefore, quite possible that Porter dressed up this incident to his advantage to make Captain Hillyar look all the worse for his attack when Porter would later describe it.

Whatever the reason, Porter did not give the order to unleash a broadside. *Phoebe* drifted past and, in words that rang with prophecy, "anchored on the Eastern side of the harbor, within reach of her long eighteen pounders, but beyond the reach of my carronades."

The day after Hillyar's arrival, the British captain, along with Captain Thomas Tucker from *Cherub*, met Porter at the home of a resident Chilean and, to many locals, acted as if there were no war on. They socialized and discussed Hillyar's hunt for Porter. Porter even released some prisoners in exchange for an agreement from Hillyar that his government would do the same. Most importantly, the two captains agreed to honor the neutrality of Valparaiso. According to Porter, Hillyar said, "You have paid so much respect to the neutrality of the port that I feel myself bound in honor to respect it." Porter replied that the "assurance was sufficient and that it would place me more at ease, since I should now no longer feel it necessary to be always prepared for action." Nevertheless, despite the veneer of cordiality and cooperation, neither man let down his guard. As Hillyar wrote to his superiors three weeks after his arrival, "I expect an awful combat if the two ships meet."

Porter was certainly not content to sit out the duration of the war in a neutral port. He was intent on getting Hillyar to send *Cherub* away so that *Essex* and *Phoebe* could fight one-on-one. Porter wrote, "I secretly resolved to take every means of provoking him to a contest with his single ship." Porter must have retained much confidence in his crew, which was not only diminished in size but also had to go up against *Phoebe*'s long eighteen-pounders with *Essex*'s short range carronades.

To his credit, Hillyar refused the challenge. He had not been ordered to fight for glory and his own reputation but to destroy or capture (or, at the very least, bottle up) an enemy frigate that had inflicted heavy damage on the nation's whaling trade and caused much consternation among the nation's citizens, who had read of her attacks. It was enough for now to keep *Essex* trapped in the harbor, where she could commit no more depredations and where Porter's impatience might cause him to make a foolish move.

Porter continued to goad Hillyar. During one conversation, when Hillyar asked Porter what he intended to do with his prizes, Porter replied that he "would take them to sea and destroy them at the first opportunity. He [Hillyar] told me I dared not do it while he was in sight. I replied, 'We shall see.'"

During the next few days, the crews of both ships struck up songs intended to insult the enemy. The American flag flew with the motto, "Free trade and sailors' rights" while the English flag waved, "God and country; British sailors' best rights; traitors offend both."

On 25 February, while *Phoebe* and *Cherub* were patrolling outside the harbor, Porter made good on his promise to Hillyar. He towed *Hector* and *Catherine* to sea, burned them in sight of the British warships, and returned to the harbor before they could cut him off. "Notwithstanding my own impatience to depart, I determined to keep it under control while I endeavored to provoke my adversary to combat," he wrote.

A day later, Hillyar appeared to have accepted Porter's one-on-one challenge. Outside the harbor, *Phoebe* fired a gun and hoisted a banner as a signal to challenge *Essex*.

Porter grabbed the bait. *Essex* set sail and was closing in on *Phoebe* when the latter signaled for *Cherub*, which lay a few miles away. Porter brought *Essex* to and returned to port. He was indignant at what he believed was Hillyar's ploy to lure him into a one-on-one duel and then disgracefully call for aid, a strange reaction from a captain who lured countless whalers into his clutches with ruses of all kinds.

Porter claimed the behavior cowardly, and Hillyar, getting wind of the comment, sent a lieutenant aboard *Essex* to ascertain whether the American captain really had made the statement. Captain Hillyar, the lieutenant explained, had initially fired his gun and hoisted his flag as a signal to *Cherub*, not to the *Essex*. Porter scoffed at the notion. "There was not a man, woman, or child in Valparaiso that did not think it a challenge," he replied. Tensions remained high.

Nasty letters were dispatched to *Essex*. They insulted American character and encouraged American seamen to desert. Porter wrote of his indignation to Hillyar, who denied he was responsible for such epistles. Porter had his doubts. He wrote: "The crews of the hostile ships continued to carry on the war, in poetry and prose: and some of the poetical effusions of our opponents were so highly meritorious, as to cause a suspicion of their being the production of Captain Hillyar himself." The bantering and ridicule continued for another month. The veteran Royal Navy captain bided his time, waiting for his brash American friend to make his move.

Meanwhile, news of Porter's exploits was trickling back to the United States. In a story that would appear in the

Weekly Niles Register, a crew of a Spanish brig that had made contact with *Essex* reported that she

> had made twenty-two prizes in all; that Captain Porter had taken possession of and fortified three small islands, where he had deposited his prizes; that his fleet … was well manned with hardy and happy crews; that they had everything in abundance and were in good health.… This is the latest news from the Admiral of the Great South Sea.

Porter would have loved the hyperbole.

Fate of Prizes Taken by *Essex* in the Pacific

Date	Vessel/Men/Tonnage (Guns)	Country

25 March 1813 *Nereyda (15)* Peru
FATE: This vessel had harassed at least three U.S. whalers by the time Porter captured her. Because he did not want to provoke the Peruvian viceroy and Spanish government, he did not destroy or take the vessel. Instead, he disarmed her by throwing her guns into the sea and sent her to Callao, Peru.

20 March 1813 *Barclay* U.S.
FATE: This American whaler was captured by *Nereyda* and recaptured by *Essex*.

29 April 1813 *Montezuma*/21/270/(2) U.K.
FATE: *Montezuma* was sent to Valparaiso, where her cargo, fourteen hundred barrels of whale oil, was to be sold, though there is no evidence that Porter did make a sale.

29 April 1813 *Georgiana*/25/280/(6) U.K.
FATE: Her cargo of whale oil was sold. Ten guns from *Policy* were moved on board, along with sixteen more men, giving the vessel sixteen guns and forty-one men. It was pressed into service under Lieutenant Downes and sailed off. On 28 May, the crew captured three whalers (see below). On 25 July 1813, Porter sent the vessel to America with $100,000 worth of whale oil, along with American sailors whose terms would be soon expiring. It was under the command

DATE	VESSEL/MEN/TONNAGE (GUNS)	COUNTRY

of Lieutenant Wilson, whose drunkenness gave Porter much trouble. Porter and his crew did not profit from this move, as the vessel was captured off the U.S. coast by HMS *Barossa*, a thirty-six-gun frigate.

29 April 1813	*Policy*/26/275/(10)	U.K.

FATE: After this prize was captured, the guns were moved to *Georgiana*. Eventually, she sailed to Valparaiso with *Essex Junior.* When Lieutenant Downes could not sell the vessel or cargo, he ordered her to America, where she was taken by the privateer *Loire*.

28 May 1813	*Atlantic*/24/355/(6)	U.K.
	renamed *Essex Junior*	

FATE: Fourteen guns and thirty-six men were added to this vessel, giving it twenty guns and sixty men. It was commanded by Chaplain Adams and then by Lieutenant Downes, when she was renamed *Essex Junior*. On 9 July 1813, Porter ordered Downes to escort the *Hector*, *Catherine*, *Policy,* and *Montezuma* to Valparaiso to sell the ships. *Barclay* also sailed in this convoy, with Midshipman Farragut in charge. When Downes arrived in the Chilean port, he discovered that war had been declared between Chile and Peru and was unable to sell his prizes. *Essex Junior* later accompanied *Essex* to the Marquesas, then back to Valparaiso for the final battle, though the ship did not participate. After the defeat, she was converted into a prisoner cartel and sailed, under Porter's command, for America. The vessel was

DATE	VESSEL/MEN/TONNAGE (GUNS)	COUNTRY

condemned in a prize court at New York, with the U.S. government buying her for $25,000, the only prize money Porter and his crew made on the second cruise.

28 May 1813   *Greenwich*/26/338/(10)   U.K.
FATE: *Greenwich* was converted into a store ship and commanded by Marine Lieutenant Gamble, who would later burn the ship at the Marquesas Islands because it was judged unseaworthy.

13 July 1813   *Seringapatam*/31/357/(14)   U.K.
FATE: The ship fought, escaped, and was recaptured. Porter had carpenters and gunners fortify the fast sailing vessel. She accompanied *Essex* to the Marquesas. As she shoved off, with Lieutenant Gamble in command, the ship's crew—many of them whalers from English vessels—rose up and took command; Gamble and two other Americans were set adrift in a small boat. Thus, *Seringapatam* fell back into the hands of English whalers. They sailed her to Australia; the vessel eventually was returned to her owners. Gamble and his compatriots rowed back to the Marquesas.

13 July 1813   *Charlton*/21/274/(10)   U.K.
FATE: Her guns were moved to *Seringapatam*. The vessel, which Porter considered "a dull sailer," was ordered to Rio de Janeiro, with whale oil and the prisoners of *Charlton* and *Seringapatam*.

DATE	VESSEL/MEN/TONNAGE (GUNS)	COUNTRY

13 July 1813   *New Zealander*/23/259/(8)   U.K.
FATE: She accompanied *Essex* to the Marquesas. She was eventually loaded with whale oil and ordered to sail to America, where she was captured by *Belvidera*, thirty-six guns, off the coast.

15 Sept 1813   *Sir Andrew Hammond*/36/301/(12)   U.K.
FATE: The vessel, carrying sperm oil, was captured by *Essex* because, in the words of Porter, "the captain assured me that our ship had been so strangely altered that he supposed her to be a whaleship." She accompanied *Essex* to the Marquesas Islands. Lieutenant Gamble, who was left behind at the Marquesas, made his escape in this vessel as the islanders were trying to capture him. He sailed the vessel to the Sandwich Islands (Hawaii), where it was soon recaptured by *Cherub*, in the summer of 1814.

Fate of Prizes Taken by *Georgiana* in the Pacific

DATE	VESSEL/MEN/TONNAGE (GUNS)	COUNTRY

28 May 1813   *Catherine*/29/270/(8)   U.K.
FATE: Stripped of equipment, she was a sluggish sailer. She was burned at sea with *Hector* (see below) to bait Hillyar into a one-on-one combat.

28 May 1813   *Rose*/21/270/(8)   U.K.
FATE: Her sperm oil cargo was thrown overboard. The vessel was stripped of guns, made into a prisoner cartel, and dispatched to St. Helena.

28 May 1813   *Hector*/25/270/(11)   U.K.
FATE: The crew of this vessel put up a fight, but after five men fell dead, the captain surrendered. Porter later burned her at sea, within sight of Hillyar, as a provocation for one-on-one combat.

CHAPTER EIGHT

Valparaiso:
The Final Battle

Heave the topmast from the board,
And our ship for action clear,
By the cannon and the sword,
We will die or conquer here.
The foe, of twice our force, nears us fast:
To Your Posts, my faithful tars!
Mind Your rigging, guns, and spars,
And defend Your stripes and stars
To the last.

—"THE BATTLE OF VALPARAISO"

*T*he Battle of Valparaiso, among the fiercest of the war, did not commence on a dramatic note. There was no thrilling chase or shot across the bow. Rather, a heavy southern wind parted *Essex*'s port cable, which held one of two anchors, and began pushing *Essex* out of Valparaiso's bowl-shaped harbor, which faces north. As the ship began dragging her anchor, there was no alternative but for *Essex* to make a dash for open seas, past *Phoebe* and *Cherub*, which were patrolling outside the harbor.

Porter's move was more than serendipitous. A day earlier, on 27 March 1814, he had learned that three additional British men-of-war were on their way to destroy *Essex*—or at the very least, to bottle her up at Valparaiso. Porter's continuous challenges and taunts to the English, offering "to put an end to all this nonsense of singing, sporting, hunting and writing which we know less about than use of our guns" and to meet in one-on-one combat, were resisted by Hillyar. Porter had waited too long to make his escape. But the weather finally forced his hand, and *Essex* raced for the mouth of the bay. The attempt to escape had a good chance of success because *Essex* was the fastest sailer of the three vessels.

Essex was up against a frigate that, though not the Royal Navy's finest, was every bit a match for the Salem frigate. *Phoebe*'s keel was the same length as that of *Essex*—118 feet. Her breadth and depth of hold were only slightly larger. One report on her stated that

> she rides very badly at anchor, in a heavy sea and under sail is very crank [a description of a vessel that heels too easily in a wind]. She does not carry her lee ports well, but roles carry in the trough. She pitches very heavy when pressed with sail. Generally, a very easy ship if not pressed with sail. . . . She wears well and stays well. She behaves well lying to.

Despite any deficiencies, the well-armed *Phoebe* had seen her share of action. She had been built in the Royal Dockyard at Deptford on the Thames River in 1795. After several years of service in the English Channel, the frigate, under the command of Robert Barlow, captured the thirty-eight-gun French *Africaine* on 19 February 1801, off Ceuta (opposite Gibraltar). The French ship, which was transporting troops, put up a fierce fight, but after a two-hour action, she was forced to surrender, with five feet of water in her hold and

(COURTESY: NATIONAL MARITIME MUSEUM, LONDON)

HMS *Phoebe* Captain James Hillyar, whose heroic exploits had once earned him an audience with Horatio Nelson. As battle with *Essex* loomed, Hillyar wrote to his superiors: "I expect an awful combat if the two ships meet."

heavy casualties among her crew of 315. Aboard *Phoebe*, by contrast, casualties were minor, with only 1 killed and ten wounded out of a crew of 239. *Africaine* was taken into the Royal Navy, and Barlow was knighted.

Phoebe would reap other glories. She would be present at the Battle of Trafalgar in October 1805. In 1811, she captured the French vessel *Renommee* and was awarded a battle honor from the British government. Several days later, her crew received another battle honor for assisting in the capture of two more enemy ships.

As for *Cherub*, a report on the 422-ton vessel hardly cast her as the jewel of the British Navy:

> *All ships of war and good sailing merchant ships beat her constantly and she is leewardly. Tolerable in light winds, goes 5 knots only on a bowline. Very slow. The most she will run before the wind is 10-1/2 knots. She rolls very deep. The only thing she does well is lying to. Pitches much very deep.*

Launched at Dover at the end of 1806, *Cherub* had no significant captures to her credit but had been part of large squadrons that had taken the French islands of Martinique and Guadeloupe. Her presence during the standoff at Valparaiso cannot be underestimated. Because Porter refused to fight *Phoebe* until *Cherub* withdrew, the presence of the sloop allowed Hillyar to bide his time and wait for circumstances to fall his way.

The wind off Valparaiso was blowing hard when the crews of the British men-of-war spotted *Essex* trying to make her escape. *Cherub*'s Captain Tucker stated in his log: "At 3 observed the Essex coming out of the bay. Made sail and cleared for action." As the British ships set off in pursuit, their crewmen observed what was the start of trouble for the Salem frigate. Tucker wrote, "At 3:10 observed her main topmast go over the side." As *Essex* rounded the point of the harbor—called, ironically, Angels' Point—a heavy squall struck the ship and carried away her main topmast—the result of carrying a very heavy press of sail so as to beat her enemies to sea. The men who were aloft fell into the sea and were drowned, but that was the least of the crew's problems. The loss of sail made it impossible to outrun her pursuers.

Porter's only option was to get back to Valparaiso, presumably a neutral port. Because the winds made it impossible to return to the harbor, he ran *Essex* into a neighboring bay called Viña del Mar, where he thought he could repair the mast. The bay was three miles north of Valparaiso, and in Porter's words, *Essex* came to anchor "within pistol shot [a few hundred yards] of the shore."

Meanwhile, *Phoebe* and *Cherub* were closing in with banners hoisted: "God and Country. British sailors best Rights. Traitors offend both." Porter's plan to repair *Essex* in neutral waters was jettisoned when he saw the enemy bearing down in a belligerent manner. He cleared the decks for action and attempted to get springs on his cable, which would allow him to turn his ship while at anchor and thus prevent the British ships from attacking his lightly defended bow and stern.

Was *Essex* close enough to shore to be considered in Chile's neutral waters? The question must have arisen in the minds of all three captains. From Porter's perspective, *Essex* should have been safe. After all, he and Hillyar had made the agreement to honor Chilean neutrality six weeks earlier—when *Phoebe* and *Cherub* had first arrived at Valparaiso.

For Hillyar, however, the issue was not so cut and dry. First, there was the issue of Chile's right to independence. The nation was in the midst of a civil war and was not recognized as an independent state—certainly not by Spain, Britain's ally. It was questionable whether Chile could claim neutrality. Another factor that put Chile's neutrality in jeopardy was an unofficial but nevertheless real alliance between the United States and the Chilean rebels, orchestrated by U.S. Consul Joel R. Poinsett.

Poinsett had been dispatched to South America to expand U.S. influence in the southern hemisphere. His mission was to improve ties with established countries, as well as those nations being born of democratic revolutions. In the latter case, the United States sensed a real opportunity to gain a foothold in the region, as America served as the example for many revolutionaries.

There is no question that David Porter had the expansion of American influence in mind when he declared the

WHEN *ESSEX* SAILED AROUND THE HORN IN THE WINTER OF 1813, IT WAS MORE THAN A HISTORIC FIRST FOR A U.S. MAN-OF-WAR; IT WAS THE COMMENCEMENT OF A BOLD SURPRISE ATTACK ON ENGLAND'S PACIFIC WHALING FLEET.

Marquesas Islands a U.S. possession. With his claim, America now had a base of operations in the area. Porter stated, with the usual hyperbole of a conqueror, that "the natives, to secure to themselves that friendly protection which their defenseless situation so much required, have requested to be admitted into the great American family." Porter even assumed that the island's inhabitants, by virtue of this agreement, were *ipso facto* at war with Great Britain and should "prevent the subjects of Great Britain (knowing them to be such) from coming among them until peace shall take place between the two nations."

Correspondence between British diplomats in 1813 and 1814 reveals that Porter's claim to the Marquesas would be challenged. In the end, as was mentioned, the United States, preoccupied in other areas of the globe, lost control of the islands to the French. It was just as well. Welcoming islanders into the American fold would not have been simple. Porter's actions during his stay had turned many local inhabitants against him. The journal of F. Ross, a crew member of HMS *Targus*, recounts that when his ship appeared at the Marquesas several months after Porter had departed, the inhabitants fled to the mountains, fearing *Essex* had come again. According to Ross, whose account is possibly exaggerated, the locals accused David Porter of taking all their hogs, including those needed for breeding. They "expressed great satisfaction on being informed we were enemies of Captain Porter and had taken him prisoner," Ross wrote. "They very naturally inquired whether we had eaten him, and no doubt longed to have a share themselves."

After lobbying for good relations in Buenos Aires, Consul Poinsett arrived in Chile in December 1811. He was well received by the rebel junta, which was then skirmishing with Peru. The Peruvian viceroy, loyal to the Spanish king, had sent out privateers to seize Chilean ships, as well as those of nations (including America) trading with the junta. The junta requested Poinsett's help in securing arms for their cause, but with the approach of war with England, the United States could spare none. Still Poinsett assisted in other ways. He encouraged the junta in its drive for independence, defused tensions among leaders, and gave advice on constitutional and commercial questions. American influence was strong enough that junta leaders even toyed with the idea of making a declaration of independence on 4 July 1812, but they called off the plan in the name of caution.

When David Porter showed up in his frigate in March 1813, the junta and its followers thought the United States had sent a frigate in support of their cause, a notion the American captain and Poinsett did little to dispel. After Porter went off on his raiding tour, Poinsett got in deeper with the Chilean rebels, actually participating in skirmishes with the Loyalists. Junta leaders referred to him as "el mejor chileno" and they even gave Porter permission to sell his captured whalers and their cargo on Chilean soil.

Great Britain was keeping a close eye on Poinsett. One British naval officer, stationed in Brazil, said Poinsett was "contaminating the whole population on that side of the continent." Hillyar, too, was well aware of America's play for interest in the region. On 24 January 1814, two weeks before arriving in Valparaiso, he wrote to John Croker, secretary to the board of admiralty:

> *The Americans . . . are the only people likely to benefit by the contest in the event of the Revolutionists being successful—they are* making friends, *and while pretending to advocate the cause of liberty and free trade, are successfully striving to irritate the minds of the Natives against the old Spaniards, at the same time espousing ideas that tend to lessen the British in the estimation of both.*

The American assistance to the junta, of course, was not free of charge. In February 1814, when a battle seemed imminent between *Essex* and *Phoebe*, Poinsett exacted a promise from junta officials that they would fire on the Royal Navy vessel with their port batteries if *Essex* was attacked in neutral waters. The Chileans agreed but did not follow through, knowing that as the *Essex* mast went by the wayside, so did the junta's ties to America.

Hillyar, too, was not one to shy away from exerting English influence. He made careful observations of the living conditions in Chile and suggestions about how they could be improved:

> *The wealthy are deprived of property to support the [civil] war, the poor are becoming disconcerted from the total stagnation of commerce and consequent want of employment, and I believe, a very great majority would prefer a return to the old system, bad as it was, to the continuance of the present.*

Hillyar counseled putting in power a government that was not as radical as the rebels but not as oppressive as the previous rulers.

> *Only men of integrity, more intent on public good than personal emolument, more disposed to suppress vice in all classes, than encourage it by bad example, should be sent to preside over these people.*

In fact, Hillyar would himself broker a peace treaty between the rebels and loyalists, though it didn't last long.

Essex's battle against *Phoebe* and *Cherub* was not just an engagement between enemy frigates. It was a fight between the Americans and the British for the upper hand along the South American continent and in the vast Pacific Ocean, both laden with opportunities for trade and unknown treasures.

And the question of neutrality? It is safe to assume that the issue was used by both the Americans and the British to further their own ends.

On 28 March 1814, at 3:54 P.M., the British answered the neutrality question with their long guns.

David Porter must have been cursing his situation. Perhaps echoing in his mind were the words he had once written to Navy Secretary Hamilton: "Was this ship [*Essex*, with her preponderance of carronades] to be disabled in her rigging in an early part of an engagement, a ship much inferior to her . . . armed with long guns, could take a position beyond reach of our carronades, and cut us to pieces without our being able to do her any injury." The prophecy had come true.

For David Porter, however, the battle was not over by any means. The unpredictable winds of Valparaiso Bay had foiled his plans for escape. They could just as easily foil the designs of Captains Hillyar and Tucker—perhaps push them within range where *Essex*'s "smashers" could bring down a mast or two, perhaps even allow the Americans to board for hand-to-hand combat.

Captain Hillyar, as he closed in on his injured prey, must have rejoiced at his good fortune. He had been plain lucky that *Essex* had lost her main topmast. Her speed probably would have enabled her to elude her pursuers and go on to raid more British shipping. But the veteran Hillyar knew that the outcome of the battle was anything but a foregone conclusion. Porter's reputation for boldness and resourcefulness was known among officers of the Royal Navy. He was a seasoned captain capable of turning battle circumstances to his advantage. Should the dismasted *Essex* be able to defeat her enemies, Hillyar—notwithstanding his personal humiliation—would probably have been censured or worse. The Royal Navy captain had to keep his head and, above all, his distance, and allow his long guns to do their bloody work.

Cherub reached *Essex* first, firing off a broadside. Both Royal Navy vessels must have looked particularly ominous as they closed in on the struggling *Essex*.

The *Phoebe* had a 320-man crew and was equipped with fifty-two guns—including sixteen thirty-two-pound carronades, thirty long eighteen-pounders, and six three-pounders in the tops. The *Cherub* had 180 men and was armed with twenty-six guns—including eighteen thirty-two pound carronades, eight twenty-four-pounders, and two nine-pounders on the quarter deck and forecastle.

The combined power of the English vessels (eighty guns and 500 men) greatly exceeded that of the *Essex* and *Essex Junior* (sixty-six guns and 315 men). In addition, Porter and his men were up against a seasoned naval officer.

Born in 1769, James Hillyar, like Porter, came from a naval family. He was the eldest son of a Royal Navy surgeon who was also named James. After his wife died, the surgeon took his son to sea when he was hardly more than an infant. The younger James formally entered the Royal Navy in 1779 on HMS *Chatham* and was present at the capture of the French ship *Magicienne* off Boston in 1781. He earned for himself a solid reputation and, after the war with America, had no trouble procuring a berth on other ships. While serving in the Mediterranean, he made David Porter's acquaintance during the Barbary conflicts.

In 1800, he was given command of *Niger*, a frigate of thirty-two guns. Hillyar saw action in nearly every part of the British empire and performed heroically on a number of occasions, including the daring capture of two Spanish corvettes that same year. His exploits earned him an audience with Lord Nelson in 1803, who asked him to dinner to give the particulars of his attack on the corvettes. "You have not been treated well, but never mind," Nelson told Hillyar, who had been passed over for promotions. The following year, Nelson wrote to the first lord of the admiralty:

"Capt. Hillyar is most truly deserving of all your Lordship can do for him; and in addition to his public merits, he has a claim on us." Nelson asked that *Niger* be refitted with more powerful guns and that Hillyar's rank be raised to captain, a promotion long overdue.

Hillyar was given command of *Phoebe* in July 1809 and was present in May 1811 at the bloody capture of the island of Mauritius, when the Royal Navy took three forty-four-gun French frigates. *Phoebe* returned to England for repairs and, after being variously employed during 1812, was dispatched to the Pacific Northwest to destroy American fur interests. Hillyar would retire as a rear admiral in 1837 and his sons, Henry and Charles, continued the family's naval legacy, both working their way up to the rank of admiral.

Back in the bay of Viña del Mar, *Cherub* took up a position off *Essex*'s starboard bow. *Phoebe* arrived soon after and placed herself under *Essex*'s stern. In the early moments of battle, the fighting was intense. By attaching springs to the ship's anchor cables, Porter attempted to pull *Essex* ship into a position that would enable her men to fire broadsides. However, each time the maneuver was attempted, the lines were shot away. Nevertheless, the accurate shooting of the American gunners eventually forced the British to pull back. Porter records in his journal: "I had got three long 12-pounders out of the stern ports, which were worked with so much bravery and skill that in a half an hour we so disabled both [enemy vessels] as to compel them to haul off to repair damages." *Essex*'s long twelve-pounders had not only damaged the mainsail, jib, and mainstay of *Phoebe* but also severely wounded Captain Tucker of *Cherub,* though

Hillyar would report to the admiralty that his fellow captain remained on deck throughout the action.

An hour after the initial firing, damages to the British ships were repaired, and the fighting resumed in an even more intense manner. Knowing he was up against carronades, Hillyar kept his distance. Porter writes: "[The enemy] now placed himself, with both his ships, on my starboard quarter, out of reach of my carronades, and where my stern [long] guns could not be brought to bear: he there kept up a most galling fire, which it was out of my power to return." Porter's constant complaints about the carronades must have echoed in his ears—even above the crushing din of *Phoebe*'s guns. With *Essex*'s maneuverability hampered by the loss of her main-topmast, she was little more than a hulk for target practice.

The Americans began falling, and the cockpit began to fill with wounded. A battle between frigates was not for the timid. One well-timed broadside was sufficient to litter the gun decks with limbs and spatter the bulkheads with blood. A cannonball could smash the side of a vessel and turn its wooden planking into flying splinters—some as large as four feet—that pierced flesh and arteries. Some sailors were killed instantly after being struck by the balls themselves—mercifully decapitated in some cases. Others were cut to ribbons by langradge or canister. The latter was a cylindrical metal case, like a large tin can, filled with musket balls. When fired across the decks of an enemy vessel, it acted like the blast from a titanic shotgun. Sailors exposed on the upper decks or repairing rigging aloft were often cut down by gunfire from enemy marines. Cannon smoke filled the air and mingled with the scent of blood. The wounded were taken below, where the surgeon and his assistants worked. Amputation was common; the anesthesia was rum.

As the injured poured in, medical facilities on *Essex* quickly became overloaded and chaotic. Above, on the gun decks, the dead were dumped overboard so as not to encumber the gun crews. The fire from *Phoebe* and *Cherub* laid waste to sails and rigging, as the one-sided assault continued.

Now ninety minutes into the battle, Porter "saw no prospect of injuring him [the enemy] without getting under way and becoming the assailant." In other words, Porter would attempt to move *Essex*—despite that her sails and rigging were in shambles—toward *Phoebe*, in the hope that the ships would collide and his men could board for hand-to-hand combat (at which they were said to be among the best on the seas). He managed to cut his cable and to close on *Cherub*, no small feat considering his sails and rigging were heavily damaged. *Essex* got off one broadside that forced both enemy vessels to pull back. *Cherub*, in fact, did something of a retreat at that point, keeping her distance from *Essex* for the remainder of the battle (though her crew would continue good use of her long guns). *Phoebe*, meanwhile, remained within range where she could smash *Essex* with her eighteen-pounders which, Porter recounts, "mowed down my brave companions by the dozen."

The decks of *Essex* were now strewn with dead. Many guns had been destroyed and their crews killed. One cannon, in fact, had been manned by three different five-man crews—all fifteen were killed during the battle. In the chaos, Midshipman Farragut was ordered to hunt down and execute three men, the sentence for those who had deserted their battle posts.

Porter's plan to close and board the enemy had failed, but he had another trick up his sleeve. He decided to move in the opposite direction—that is, to run for shore, where he could scuttle his ship to keep it from falling into enemy hands and where he and his unwounded crew could make their escape. Again, however, the winds whipping off the Chilean coast were against him, and they pushed *Essex*—now hardly more than a hulk—back toward sea for a final raking by *Phoebe*.

Even now, Porter refused to give up. As the drifting *Essex* moved toward *Phoebe*, he fired a broadside that did further damage to enemy sails and cordage. But, it was *Essex*'s last blow.

The ward room now was filled with wounded, though there was no lack of bravery. When Lieutenant Cowell was carried into the cockpit with half his leg shot off, the surgeon turned to assist him before attending to seamen who had been wounded earlier. Cowell said, "No, doctor, none of that; fair play's a jewel. One man's life is as dear as another's." He died before the surgeon could get to him.

Heavy casualties and wrecked cannons were not all Porter had to worry about. Fires were inching their way toward the magazine and threatening the Americans with complete annihilation. Porter gave his men permission to jump ship and swim ashore, a gesture that the English did not look kindly upon. Hillyar later wrote to the admiralty that he was *much hurt on hearing that [the men of the Essex] had been encouraged, when the result of the action was evidently decided, some to take to their boats, and others to swim to shore; many were drowned in the attempt; 16 were saved by the exertions of my people, and others, I believe between 30 and 40, effected their escape. I informed Captain Porter, that I considered the latter, in point of honor, as my prisoners; he said the encouragement was given when the ship was in danger from fire, and I have not pressed the point.*

The British *Times*, however, had stronger words for Porter and his actions:

The conduct of Captain Porter, however, on conniving at the escape of some of his men after surrender, agrees pretty well with the character we have before given of him, and shows that his sentiments of honor are but American.

Porter makes it clear in his diary that the men leaped overboard *before* surrender. The truth may never be known, but it seems likely that no captain would reduce his crew while still fighting.

With his crew depleted, Porter considered the inevitable: surrender. His journal picks up the action:

I now sent for the officers of the divisions to consult them; but what was my surprise to find only Acting Lieutenant Stephen Decatur M'Knight remaining, who confirmed the report respecting the condition of the guns on the gun-deck—those on the spar deck were not in a better state. Lieutenant Wilmer, after fighting most gallantly throughout the action, had been knocked overboard by a

(COURTESY OF U.S. NAVY)

The Battle of Valparaiso, one of the most bloody ever fought by a U.S. (shown in this painting), took a vicious pounding from HMS *Phoebe* Captain David Porter had often complained about, proved useless during

splinter while getting the sheet anchor from the bows, and was drowned. Acting Lieutenant John G. Cowell, had lost a leg; Mr. Edward Barnewall, acting sailing master, had been carried below, after receiving two wounds, one in the

MAN-OF-WAR. *ESSEX* (LEFT) DISABLED BY THE LOSS OF HER MAIN TOPMAST (CENTER) AND THE SLOOP *CHERUB*. *ESSEX*'S 32-POUND CARRONADES, WHICH THE BATTLE. HE WROTE: "THE ENEMY WAS ABLE TO TAKE AIM AT US AS AT A TARGET."

breast and one in the face; and acting Lieutenant William H. Odenheimer, had been knocked overboard from the quarter an instant before, and did not regain the ship until after the surrender. I was informed that the cockpit, the steerage, the ward-room and the berth-deck, could contain no more wounded; that the wounded were killed while the surgeons were dressing them, and that, unless something was speedily done to prevent it, the ship would sink from the number of holes in her bottom. And, on sending for the carpenter, he informed me that all his crew had been killed or wounded, and that he had been once over the side to stop the leaks, when his slings had been shot away, and it was with difficulty he was saved from drowning.

The enemy . . . was now able to take aim at us as at a target; his shot never missed our hull, and our ship was cut up in a manner which was, perhaps, never before witnessed—in fine, I saw no hopes of saving her, and at twenty minutes after six, gave the painful order to strike the colors.

The battle was done after two and a half hours. *Essex*, Salem's fifteen-year contribution to the never-ending American fight for independence, was finished.

And, yet, it was not quite over. In the tumult of battle, Hillyar did not see that *Essex* had struck, and he continued firing. Porter even had his crew shoot a gun in an opposite direction from the enemy, a signal of surrender. But, the firing continued. Americans continued to fall. As Porter wrote: "I now believed that he [the enemy] intended showing us no quarter [mercy shown to an enemy], and that it would be just as well to die with my flag flying as struck, and was on the point of hoisting it, when about ten minutes after hauling the colors down, he ceased firing!"

The scene aboard *Essex* was one of raw carnage. Of the 255-man crew, 58 had been killed, 66 wounded, and 31 missing or drowned. Young David Farragut was found stunned, though otherwise uninjured. The British—with every possible variable in their favor—had very few losses: 4 dead and 7 wounded aboard *Phoebe*, and 1 dead and 3 wounded (including Captain Tucker) on *Cherub*.

There is some difference of opinion on the number killed aboard *Essex*. William James, the British historian, contends that Captain Porter greatly exaggerated the number killed, "to prop up his fame." The discrepancies in the death figures probably arise from the number of men who were listed as missing. James insists that only 69 were killed aboard *Essex*, while Porter gives the final count as 124. Captain Hillyar comes in much closer to Porter at 111. It is unlikely that Porter could have inflated the figure too much, as relatives of the dead sailors would have received pensions. Had Porter exaggerated, many of these pensions would have been revoked and the government would have revised his death toll downward. If, indeed, the highest totals were true, *Essex* would have lost about 50 percent of her crew—an astonishing figure.

Porter's immediate post-battle duty was attending to the wounded. Many were cared for in hospitals and homes by the women of Valparaiso. "I shall never forget their gentle humanity," Porter wrote. Hillyar proved himself as compassionate in peace as he was competent in battle. While

Porter was angry over what he perceived to be Hillyar's attack in neutral waters, he had nothing but praise about his old friend's post-battle assistance. "He has, since our capture, shown the greatest humanity to my wounded . . . and has endeavoured as much as lay in his power, to alleviate the distresses of war, by the most generous and delicate deportment towards myself, my officers, and crew."

The fifty broadsides fired at *Essex* had caused heavy damage. Her hull was so riddled with holes, according to Porter, that the vessel was saved from sinking only by the calmness of the seas. *Phoebe*, too, had not escaped unscathed. Her mainmast and mizzenmasts had been heavily damaged, and the ship had been hulled in several places. And there was the usual damage to canvas and cordage. Porter predicted that *Phoebe* would never make it round the Horn, but his prediction proved wrong: She would escort *Essex* back to England.

Hillyar offered Porter parole, a common arrangement between victors and vanquished in a remote location of the world. Under such an agreement, the losers returned to their country, usually aboard a captured or neutral vessel, and pledged themselves not to fight until they were exchanged for prisoners of the victorious side. This was a good deal for Hillyar, as he would not be burdened with expending men to guard the American prisoners while one of his lieutenants and a prize crew took them around the Horn to a British-held port. (Prisoners occasionally overpowered a prize crew and retook the vessel.) Porter accepted the parole, no doubt anxious to get back to the United States to tell *his* side of the Valparaiso story and to suit up again for battle. (It is important to note that the list of the prisoners released from *Phoebe* to *Essex Junior*, ostensibly the American survivors, support Porter's higher casualty figure.)

Porter and his men made their return aboard *Essex Junior*, which had not fought in the battle and was immediately ready for the trip around the Horn, on 27 April. Hillyar provided Porter with documentation that would allow the ship to sail unmolested to the United States. The exact terms were as follows:

> *1st. Essex, Jr, to be deprived of all her armament and perfectly neutralized to be equipped for voyage solely and wholly at expence of American government and to proceed with a proper officer and crew to any port of U.S. of Am. that you may deem most proper.*
>
> *2nd. Yourself [Porter], officers, petty officers, seamen, marines & composing your crew to be exchanged immediately on their arrival in America for an equal number of British prisoners of equal rank. Yourself and officers to be considered on their parole of honor until your and their exchange shall be affected.*

The two captains, who had known each other for over a decade, had an awkward departure. After thanking Hillyar for his attention toward American wounded, Porter made it clear that he would not hide the fact that *Essex*, he believed, had been attacked in neutral waters. "The tears came into his [Hillyar's] eyes," Porter writes in his journal, "and, grasping my hand, he replied, 'My dear Porter, you know not the responsibility that hung over me, with respect to your ship. Perhaps my life depended on taking her.'" Porter asked for no further explanations and departed without any change of heart. "He [Hillyar] has it in his power, however, to clear up the affair to the world," Porter wrote. It is quite possible that Porter had no right to claim high moral ground. Both Farragut and Hillyar reported (separately) that Porter had tried to make a surprise attack on the *Phoebe* while in Valparaiso harbor, an event the American captain does not mention in his journal.

The rebel junta lost some of its fortitude when *Essex* was defeated. By October 1814, plagued by infighting and losses against Loyalists, junta leaders fled. By that time, Poinsett had had enough of revolutions and was ready to return to the United States. However Hillyar, aware of the American's diplomatic capabilities, refused to let Poinsett, "the arch enemy of England," return to America aboard *Essex Junior.* He was forced to go overland across the continent to the Atlantic coast and did not set foot upon American soil until May 1815.

News of the battle reached England in July 1814. The victory carried special satisfaction for the British, who had little love for David Porter. The *Times*, which dubbed Porter's cruise "a buccaneering expedition," reported:

> *It was yesterday reported with great confidence that the American frigate* Essex, *which has been so long blockaded on the coast of South America, by the* Phoebe, *Captain Hillyar, was captured by the latter in attempting to escape. We have great satisfaction in learning a confirmation of this*

intelligence. Porter was the fellow who in 1805 enticed a man onboard his ship in the harbour of Malta for the purpose of causing him to be flogged; a circumstance which excited much indignation on the part of the British there; that Mr. Porter was obliged to weigh anchor, and make his escape in a few hours to avoid the consequences with which he was threatened.

On 5 July 1814, Porter and his crew came abreast of the British razee *Saturn*, off Sandy Hook, New Jersey (a razee was a two-decked ship of the line with one deck removed, putting her in frigate class). The British captain, James Nash, examined Porter's papers and treated him with civility, providing him with the latest newspapers, as well as some oranges. *Essex Junior* was allowed to sail for New York, though *Saturn* followed her on the same tack.

After two hours, the American ship was hailed again and boarded. The astonished Porter was told that Captain Hillyar had no authority to grant *Essex Junior* safe passage to America. Porter then claimed he was a prisoner and offered Nash his sword, which was refused. The American ship, however, was forced to remain under lee of *Saturn*.

Declaring he had had his fill of arrogant British officers, Porter gave Lieutenant Downes a letter stating that "Captain Porter was now satisfied, that most British officers were not only destitute of honor, but regardless of the honor of each other." He was then lowered into an armed boat with several crew. Porter got off safely, but after a short while, *Saturn* came off in pursuit. Only a sudden fog saved Porter from capture. After sailing and rowing sixty miles, he landed at

Babylon, New York, where he was interrogated because the locals suspected him of being a spy. However, he was able to prove his true identity and was welcomed as a hero.

Porter's escape may have made him less of a hero in the eyes of his crew. One of the oldest laws of the sea—in both naval and merchant service—is that a captain never deserts his crew, no matter what the circumstances. It is quite possible that Porter was afraid that Captain Nash would violate the agreement made with Hillyar and send the Americans to Britain to await the long process of formal prisoner exchange. With Porter gone, his men were "mustered on deck, under the pretence of detecting deserters; her officers insulted, and treated with shameful outrage." The Americans were even "ransacked" for money. *Essex Junior* was eventually allowed to sail to New York, but Porter's actions further illustrate that he was a bold character who could do the rash and dishonorable.

Porter arrived in New York City on 8 July. A Tammany Hall dinner was given in honor of him and his crew. He then proceeded to Washington, D.C., where he was invited to dine with President Madison.

Salem, Massachusetts, had been following news of Porter's cruise, and the *Weekly Register* reported his arrival in Philadelphia, near his hometown of Chester, Pennsylvania, as follows: "Captain Porter of late frigate *Essex* arrived in Philadelphia a few days since. The Hero was met in the suburbs by the populace, who took horses from his carriage and drew it themselves to his lodgings, escorted by military and with repeated cheerings."

Porter then went home to Chester, where, after an absence of one and a half years, he saw his wife and, for the first time, met his son, David Dixon, who himself would make naval history. During the Civil War, David Dixon and his stepbrother David Farragut would score a number of naval victories against the Confederacy. Both would retire as admirals.

Despite the intoxication engendered by parties and dinners, Porter had been defeated at Valparaiso and was anxious to make his case to his superiors. In July 1814, he wrote:

> *We have been unfortunate but not disgraced, defence of* Essex *has not been less honorable to officers and crew than capture of an equal force. I now consider my situation less unpleasant than that of Capt. Hillyar who in violation of every principle of honor and generosity and regardless of rights of nations attacked* Essex *in her crippled state within pistol shot of neutral shore when for six weeks I had daily offered him fair and honorable combat on terms greatly to his advantage. Blood of the slain must be on his head and he has yet to reconcile his conduct to heaven, to his conscience, to the world.*

There is no record in Great Britain's Public Record Office of any protests filed on behalf of the American government against Hillyar for attacking Porter in what he deemed neutral waters, suggesting that Navy Secretary William Jones, who replaced Hamilton in January 1813, didn't consider Porter's cause substantial enough to pursue.

Porter had another point to make with the navy. He added, with an emphasis that would make Jones or any future secretary think twice about questioning him about armament, "I must observe we fought this action with our six twelve pounders, our carronades being almost useless."

Porter continued to salvage his reputation for the history books. He could only have been peeved that Hillyar reported to his superiors that the fight had lasted all of fifty minutes. He parried by describing the condition of the British vessels in terms far worse than Hillyar's: "All Masts and yards of *Phoebe* and *Cherub* are badly crippled, their hulk much cut up, former had 18 twelve pound shot through her below water line some three feet under water. Nothing but smoothness of water saved the *Phoebe* and the *Essex* [from sinking]." Porter also must have taken great pride in informing Secretary Jones that the British had been searching for him as far away as the China Seas and the waters around New Zealand.

The bright news for Porter was that the American government agreed to buy *Essex Junior*, formerly the whaler *Atlantic*, for $25,000, with Porter's share being $1,875. That brought Porter's prize money for both cruises—from July 1812 to July 1814—to just under $3,500.

Roughly speaking, the prize money doubled Porter's salary during this period, a fact that could not have failed to disappoint him when he discovered that more of his prizes, laden with whale oil, did not make it through the British blockade. His fellow captain Stephen Decatur had raked in over $30,000 from his capture of *Macedonian* alone. During the War of 1812, Captain John Rodgers took home nearly

$20,000, and Porter's old friend, William Bainbridge, had walked away $11,276 richer.

While Porter had a right to be disappointed, he made out far better than his crew, who also got a crumb of the prize money pie. Much of Porter's time after the war was used up answering letters from his men (or their surviving family members who received the prize money) inquiring about the amount owed them. Often, letters came in from lawyers because the crew member was illiterate. One particularly telling and touching letter, dated 15 October 1815, came from Marine William M. McDonald, residing in Frederick County, Maryland. It seems that McDonald had already received some prize money but had set his hopes on getting more from a whaler "half full of oil" left at Valparaiso, probably *Montezuma*. He also was hoping to make a few dollars from the cartels filled with captured British whalers that David Porter sent round Cape Horn in exchange for American prisoners of war. Victorious captains sometimes exacted amounts of money from cartel vessels, but it is difficult to say in Porter's case. He makes no mention of it in his journal.

McDonald also mentions "bounty money" and "tickets." The former was money sailors and marines received when enlisting, though some captains did not pay it until the sailor's discharge, fearing he would desert. Tickets, or chits, were given to the sailors in lieu of pay; they were exchanged later for their money. Another form of payment, though not mentioned in the following letter (it is, however, mentioned in others Porter received), was "smart money;" this was extra money given to sailors wounded in battle.

Dear Sir:

I take the liberty at this time to let you know that I am yet alive and living with a farmer near a little town called Woodsberry, how long I don't know. I beg the favor of you to let me know whether I am entitled to any further proportion of prize money, bounty, or head money as Marine Drummer on board the United States Frigate Essex under your command. Between the 11th December 1812 and the 15th Sept. 1813 there was a vessel left at Valparaiso half full of Oil and also the transport let go with prisoners. Be so kind as to let me know whether there is not more than 233 Dollars to my share which is all that I have received of Major Bloom at New York, also what has become of Lieutenant Gamble, whether he has returned to America or not, and where he is—he has got . . . Seven Dollars of mine I let him have for safe keeping. I have Retained my prize Tickets & as I have experienced hitherto the treatment of a father to a son from you I make thus free at this time to solicit your aid in satisfying me on the subject of required if you will condescend to write me. Please direct your letter to the post office at Woodsberry Town to the care of Middleton Smith, the man with whom I at present reside.

I am Sir yours Dutifully,

William M. McDonald

PS I am well & Hearty at this time & hope to hear that Commodore Porter is the same.

Unfortunately for McDonald, $233 was probably all there would be of his prize money. As far as records show, no prize money came from any whalers besides *Essex Junior* (*Atlantic*), and the navy did not give out prize money for cartel vessels. (Whether he ever got his $7 from Lieutenant Gamble will probably never be known!) McDonald, who earned $233, got off better than most of the ship's seamen and marines, who records show came away with around $50 each.

What is the overall assessment of David Porter's Pacific cruise? First, his claim of doing over $5 million worth of damage to Great Britain is drastically overstated. Porter estimated that the value of the twelve prizes he took was half that figure, $2.5 million. That comes to roughly $208,000 per vessel, an absurd figure even when giving Porter the benefit of the doubt in every circumstance.

For example, he states that the whaler *Montezuma* held fourteen hundred barrels of oil, a good-size cargo. In 1813 and 1814, the price of sperm oil was $1.25 per barrel (compared to $.50 per barrel for oil from other whales). Given that a barrel held thirty gallons, this cargo would have been worth $52,500.

Then there was the value of the vessel itself to factor in. *Montezuma* was not among the largest or best whalers, but *Atlantic* was. As just stated, she was sold in New York for $25,000. If every vessel was carrying a cargo the size of *Montezuma* and was as solid a ship as *Atlantic*, each capture would have been worth $77,500, not the $208,000 needed to support Porter's claim.

Porter's estimate is lowered considerably more by a further examination of the facts. It is improbable that all the whalers had fourteen hundred barrels of oil in their holds. And it is certainly true that all the whalers were not worth as much as *Atlantic*. Some of them were hardly seaworthy. Moreover, of the twelve vessels Porter captured, five were retaken by the British, including those—*Georgiana*, *Policy*, and *New Zealander*—he dispatched to America with their holds filled with whale oil. Porter's $2.5 million total plummets under this scrutiny.

The other half of the $5 million is calculated on the assumption that the presence of *Essex* in the Pacific kept American whalers from being captured. This figure is much more difficult to compute and, therefore, dispute. The captains of American whalers in the region told Porter that there were about forty-six U.S. vessels cruising the seas. Many of their crews, away from home for years, may not have known America and Britain were at war and were vulnerable to surprise attack. However, if the total U.S. exposure in the Pacific was really $2.5 million, each of the forty-six vessels and their cargo would have been worth nearly $55,000—very doubtful, indeed.

There is no question that David Porter and his crew did a good deal of damage to Britain's whaling industry. And, as is seen by Porter's disarming the Peruvian cruiser *Nereyda* and recapture of other American whalers, he did protect U.S. interests and perhaps save the whaling families of Nantucket and New Bedford many sleepless nights. Like U.S. captains on other commerce raiding tours, he struck the British where they least expected it and drove fear into the commercial sectors of the economy. Navy Secretary Jones once compiled a list of the captains who had served under him and gave a mark to those who had distinguished themselves with important victories and actions. Porter was among them.

In the end, Porter's $5 million figure is open to dispute. What is not open to challenge is that David Porter could have done more harm to the British had he sent every captured vessel and its cargo up in flames.

By the end of the summer, Porter was anxious to get on with his life. After all, there was a war on. England was using Canada as a base of military operations, and a good deal of the fighting took place along the border and on the Great Lakes. On 10 September 1813, Commodore Oliver Perry, after building a small squadron of ships from nearby forests, went up against the British in the Battle of Lake Erie. The sides were evenly matched, and the fighting was intense. When Perry's vessel *Lawrence* was disabled, he rowed to the *Niagara*, took up the fighting, and eventually captured each enemy vessel. Almost a year later to the day, Commodore Thomas Macdonough, with his squadron of four ships and ten gunboats, defeated a superior British force on Lake Champlain, an action that also precipitated the retreat of eleven thousand British soldiers preparing to advance on the Hudson River Valley.

Despite these victories, America's navy was having mixed success in the war. America's most powerful frigates lay idle, victims of the British blockade. The defeat of Napoleon had allowed Great Britain to dispatch more of her ships to North America, and the balance of power

tipped quickly in favor of the British. The blockade length-
ened and tightened and soon extended up and down the
entire American coast. England's naval tentacles even
reached into Chesapeake Bay, where raiding parties
destroyed vessels and routed troops.

The concentration of American soldiers on the
Canadian border left areas of the eastern seaboard vulnera-
ble to attack. By August 1814, British forces already on U.S.
soil were bolstered by a force of fifty-four hundred troops,
under the command of Vice Admiral Alexander Cochrane.
The English set their sights on Washington, D.C., and routed an American army of sixty-five hundred men at the
Battle of Bladensburg, in Maryland. By 25 August, the
White House and the Capitol were burning. At the Navy
Yard, Americans destroyed the old ships that had sailed with
Essex—*New York, Boston*, and *General Green*—to keep them
from falling into British hands. Also destroyed was the
newly built forty-four-gun *Columbia*, whose command had
been offered to Porter.

Meanwhile, what was happening in the Marquesas?
Porter had left orders with his trusted marine lieutenant,
John Gamble, to remain on the island for five and a half
months and then sail for Valparaiso. If he did not find
Porter, he was to return to the United States after disposing
of the prize ships.

As the months wore on, the islanders were causing
Lieutenant Gamble more and more worry. Restless and
bold now that the impressive *Essex* had sailed off, they were
supplying their American visitors with less fruit and meat.

One day, from his post on *Sir Andrew Hammond*, Gamble watched the natives raid the old fort for iron they could make into weapons. Another factor that worried him was the disappearance of women and children, a sign of impending battle. He suspected that the Englishman, Robert White, whom Porter had turned out of *Essex*, was responsible for stirring up bad feelings.

If that was not enough to keep Gamble awake at night, he also had to consider that most of his men were British whalers who had joined the American navy. He could not count on their loyalty. There were rumors of mutiny, but Gamble could not confine or arrest anyone based solely on his suspicions. On 7 May, however, his worst fears were realized. He and two midshipmen were thrown below decks on *Seringapatam*, and the renegade Robert White, after hoisting British colors, gave the orders to point the vessel toward sea.

A few miles out, Gamble and his men were set adrift in a leaky boat (though not before he was shot in the foot in an unexplained blast of gun fire). The three Americans rowed and bailed back to the Marquesas, where the situation with the islanders had deteriorated even further.

Determining that he had to depart as soon as possible, Gamble ordered sails and other articles moved from *Greenwich* to the *Sir Andrew Hammond*, a more seaworthy vessel. He also dispatched a crew with a raft to gather up the remainder of the American property on shore. That process required several trips, and on the last, his men were attacked. Gamble fired a cannon on two canoes filled with warriors, who were forced to turn back. The sailors who reached *Hammond*, however, brought bad news. Four of their comrades had been killed.

That evening, with angry islanders on shore preparing for another assault, Gamble set fire to *Greenwich*. He then cut the anchor of *Hammond* because there were not enough sailors to man the capstan and put the vessel before the wind with a crew of eight—many ailing from injuries incurred in the earlier skirmishes. Only one man—Seaman Worth—was familiar with the operation of a ship. Miraculously, *Hammond* reached the Hawaiian Islands, two thousand miles away, on 23 May 1814, without even a spyglass to her name.

Gamble hoped to get aid at the islands—a port of call for many American vessels. He and his men were destitute, as Porter's description (received secondhand) illustrates:

> *In coasting along the N.W. side of the Island, several canoes came off in the afternoon, with swine, poultry, fruit and vegetables. . . . They [the natives] left the ship, with the greater part of their swine, &c. not having seen anything on board for which they would willingly exchange them.*

Local Americans helped Gamble pilot his vessel into the harbor and locate much needed provisions. He was entertained and sent gifts of fish by the islanders. He also learned that a week before his arrival, a mysterious ship had been seen standing offshore, seemingly studying vessels moored in the harbor. Gamble suspected it was *Seringapatam*, whose mutinous crew had set him adrift, and he decided to depart as soon as possible.

The Hawaiian Islands were filled with the usual stragglers and wanderers who populate every port; therefore, it was not long before Gamble enjoined nine additional men to sign on. With a crew large enough to sail the ship through inclement weather, the reprovisoned *Hammond* set sail for the United States on 11 June.

Two days out, an unknown sail appeared on the horizon. It was too late to flee. Gamble—thinking it might be *Seringapatam*—ordered his guns cast loose. The distant vessel showed a signal, but Gamble could not make it out because he still had no spyglass! The ship ran up U.S. colors, though this did not instill hope in the *Hammond* crew. Oceans were full of tricksters; they had sailed under one of the best. American hopes were definitely dashed when the ship ran up a British flag; upon closing, it proved to be *Cherub*, which had been ordered to search for *Essex*'s prizes.

Captain Tucker warmly received Gamble and had his surgeon dress the marine's wounded heel. But, as Porter's journal relates,

> *no stroke of adversity came with so much pain to the feelings of Lieutenant Gamble, as the capture of the* Essex, *with which he was now, for the first time, made acquainted. . . . It was some alleviation of his feelings, however, to hear even Captain Tucker confess, that "he never saw a ship make so desperate a resistance; and that 'he expected to see her colors lowered an hour before 'Free Trade and Sailors Rights' came down."*

Although he did not realize it at the time, Gamble's trials were not yet over. Thanks to sluggish vessels, long waits, and naval bureaucracy, it would take him fourteen months to get back to the United States.

Negotiations of a peace treaty between America and Britain had been proceeding in one shape or form since soon after the war had begun. By 1814, talks between the outgunned Americans and inconvenienced British got serious. The British blockade had wreaked havoc on America foreign trade, which had plummeted from $108 million in 1807 to $7 million in 1813. With sea routes blockaded, Americans were forced to ply their trade on rutted, muddy roads that both slowed commerce and made goods more expensive. Food prices skyrocketed, and there were tremendous shortages of sugar and flour. In the New England states, where pro-British sentiment ran high, trade was carried out with the Royal Navy and England's army, which paid good money for hogs, butter, and fruit. The American troops offered only paper money worth sixty cents on the dollar.

In England, the economic picture was certainly not as bad, but vessels like USS *Argus*, as well as privateers, made life uncomfortable for many of the nation's shipowners. Five English merchant ships had been captured at the mouth of the Thames River—such was the courage and audacity of American privateers. English businessmen were putting pressure on their government for a treaty because they wanted to commence trading with the United States, traditionally a strong market for their goods. They also wanted to resume unimpeded trade with Europe, which, with the defeat of Napoleon, was open for the first time in twenty years. In the end, the United States and Great Britain dropped their demands and simply agreed to return all prisoners and restore all previous boundaries—in other words, reestablish the status quo.

The Treaty of Ghent was signed on Christmas Eve 1814 (though news of the peace did not get to New Orleans soon enough to keep Andrew Jackson from routing the invading British army on 8 January 1815). The treaty was ratified by Congress on 17 February, thus officially ending the war.

The U.S. government, however, did not immediately downsize its navy—as it had done after every conflict since the Revolutionary War. The ink on the Treaty of Ghent had hardly dried before warships were sent to the Mediterranean, where the Barbary States had resumed harassment (with British encouragement) of American merchantmen. The War of 1812 had forced America to recall her warships from the region, and the Barbary States took full advantage of the void in U.S. naval presence. The Salem brig, *Edwin*, for example, was seized by the dey of Algiers because he was not happy with tribute being paid to him.

On 2 March 1815, the United States declared war and ordered Commodore Stephen Decatur to the Mediterranean (Porter had wanted to lead the squadron but was passed over). Decatur sailed in mid-May, with *Guerriere* (forty-four guns), *Constellation* (thirty-six guns), and *Macedonian* (thirty-eight guns), as well as some smaller vessels. The dey must have been chagrined to see *Guerriere* and *Macedonian*—which he had known as Royal Navy frigates—now flying the Stars and Stripes.

There was no long standoff this time. Decatur and his crews quickly captured the forty-six-gun Algerian frigate *Mashouda* and disabled the twenty-two-gun *Estedio,* and the dey sued for peace. He, along with other Barbary leaders, not only relinquished all claims on future tribute money and released prisoners without ransom but also paid indemnities for the damage of their recent depredations.

The postwar years saw a number of important developments for the navy, including the cessation of impressment by British men-of-war. Also, in 1816, Congress passed the Gradual Increase Act, which provided for the stockpiling of shipbuilding timber (which took years to season) at naval shipyards. This would allow America to be better prepared for war by having shipbuilding materials ready at hand.

Perhaps the most important change in naval policy was the establishment (ten days *before* the Ghent treaty was ratified) of the Board of Navy Commissioners, a permanent body of three captains to oversee naval construction, equipment, and repairs. The first three commissioners were John Rodgers, Isaac Hull, and David Porter. Their goal was to wrest control of the navy from civilians who, they believed, didn't always act in the best interests of the crews and ships. The three captains set out to professionalize the American navy by creating standard rules of conduct for officers and sailors, instituting a system of ranks and promotions, procuring and stockpiling materiel and supplies, establishing navy yards, and—one can imagine David Porter taking the lead on this—*determining the suitable armament for ships*. While none can say whether *Essex* would have prevailed at the Battle of Valparaiso had she had better guns, few would argue that she could have put up a better fight.

CHAPTER NINE

A Fitting End

For Sale: The Prison Hulk *Essex*, lying at Kingston, Ireland
—22 JUNE 1837

Sold to a Mr. Galsworthy for £2,010
—6 JULY 1837

O n 11 February 1824, *Essex*—now HMS *Essex*—sailed with the cutter *Dwarf* from England to Kingstown, Ireland (now Dun Loaghaire, a port town about ten miles south of Dublin). Plans had been made to convert the Salem frigate into a prison hulk. On this short voyage, she was commanded by Sam William Augustus Raven, first assistant master attendant of the dockyard at Plymouth, where she had been moored for nine years. On board was a small crew of officers, riggers, and a Royal Marine sergeant as a passenger. The ship was unarmed.

During the voyage, a Dutch smuggling ship was sighted, and *Essex* and *Dwarf* gave chase for over sixty miles. True to her history as a swift sailer, *Essex* left the cutter miles astern as she continued in hot pursuit.

Essex, built with the best timber the residents of Salem had to offer, had plenty of life left in her after her defeat at Valparaiso. Captain Hillyar had gotten the battered frigate around Cape Horn and arrived in Rio de Janeiro by late July 1814. Within a few days, carpenters, smiths, and sailmakers, from the British warships *Achilles* and *Indefatigable*, swarmed over *Essex* to assess her condition. She was condemned and purchased by Admiral Manley Dixon, British commander

(COURTESY OF MARINER'S MUSEUM)

THE HULK *JERSEY*, IN NEW YORK HARBOR, DURING THE REVOLUTIONARY WAR. IT SERVED AS A PRISON FOR AMERICAN SEAMEN—AMONG THEM, FUTURE *ESSEX* CAPTAIN EDWARD PREBLE. *ESSEX* SERVED OUT HER LAST DAYS AS A PRISON HULK IN IRELAND.

in chief of the seas around South America, on behalf of his government, at six pounds per ton. Thomas Sumter, the U.S. minister at Rio de Janeiro, objected to the sale and remonstrated the Brazilian government for permitting it in its territory (a ridiculous protest given the fact that Captain Porter had been peddling British whalers and their cargoes up and down the coast of Chile a year earlier). Sumter's objections fell on deaf ears. On 4 August, *Essex* was commissioned officially into the Royal Navy as a thirty-six-gun frigate. She was manned by a crew of officers taken from *Phoebe* and other men-of-war at the port.

A month later, Captain Hillyar received orders to proceed to England with *Phoebe* and *Essex* and report his arrival to the commander in chief at Plymouth Sound. The ships arrived in England on 11 November 1814, with Hillyar cautiously avoiding the usual sea lanes so as to keep his damaged ships away from U.S. men-of-war.

Essex was placed in ordinary. Though her rating was later increased from thirty-six to forty-two guns, she remained unmanned, unrigged, and unarmed. By 15 December, less than two weeks before the signing of the Treaty of Ghent, which would end the war, the Salem frigate was moored next to the hulk *Egyptienne*. A few days later, probably in anticipation of the end of the war with America, the Royal Navy hauled down her pennant. She was out of service.

Essex received little notice (though a brief report in 1817 found "HMS Essex (42) in want of between small and middling repair") until 1824, when the Admiralty saw fit to convert her into a prison ship, dubbing her "the Convict

Hulk *Essex*." Her old nemesis, *Phoebe*, also remained at Plymouth, and no major repairs were made to her. She would be hulked in 1826, eventually becoming a slop (store) ship, and was sold for scrap in 1841.

From 1824 to 1837, *Essex*, built in the cause of freedom, was consigned to holding prisoners in Ireland. She turned up again in the records on 16 March 1837, when the Irish Prison Commission, having no further use for her, put her up for sale. The highest bidder was Peter Jones, a Dublin merchant who offered £1,205. He planned to sail her to Liverpool and break her up for scrap wood. When Jones came for the ship, however, he was informed that the sale had been blocked by the British Admiralty, which claimed that the government of Ireland had no right to sell *Essex*. Records revealed that the ship had been lent, not sold, to the Irish government, which had only paid the costs of converting the vessel to a prison hulk.

A few days later, the Admiralty ordered a survey of the ship. A letter dated 7 April 1837, from foreman Henry Bois at the Northumberland Hotel in Dublin, reported that *Essex* was not in fit enough condition to sail. The letters also stated her value at £2,393. The Irish government was allowed to remove its stores and fittings, and the Admiralty gave the order to sell *Essex*.

She was advertised on 22 June as "the *Essex*, then lying at Kingston" and was sold to a Mr. Galsworthy for a little over £2,000. It can be assumed that the only thing Galsworthy could have done with the thirty-eight-year-old frigate was to break her up for wood. At the time of the sale, 6 July 1837, only sixteen of the ninety-nine *Essex* subscribers were still living.

David Porter was still alive, though he, like *Essex*, had been humbled. The War of 1812, while improving ties with Great Britain, did not end depredations against U.S. merchantmen by vessels from other nations. Americans continued to suffer, especially in areas where Spain's loss of control over her colonies had opened up opportunities for pirates. In 1822, the U.S. government dispatched *Macedonian*, under Captain James Biddle, to protect its interests in the southern hemisphere. The cruise turned into a disaster when a third of Biddle's crew fell victim to yellow fever. Biddle's successor was Porter, who was finishing up eight years as a member of the Board of Navy Commissioners.

Porter had lost none of his spunk in the decade following the defeat of *Essex*. Not long after taking command of *Macedonian*, he ran into trouble when two of his officers, in pursuit of pirates in Puerto Rico, were captured and jailed by local officials. Without permission from Washington, Porter dispatched his marines ashore to get his men back, which they successfully did, and to demand an apology, which he also got. The U.S. government strongly objected to his actions, and he was recalled. Rarely one to hold his tongue with superiors, Porter made matters worse by criticizing U.S. foreign policy in the region. A court of inquiry found him guilty of violating Spanish territory, and he was suspended for six months.

The action triggered Porter's resignation from the U.S. Navy, an institution that had been his life for nearly thirty years. However, he could not leave naval life for long. In 1826, he became commander in chief of the Mexican navy, which had only four vessels of any worth. He had some success in helping the newly independent nation build up a respectable force, but eventually resigned because of political backstabbing and low salary.

Back in the United States, financial woes continued to dog Porter. A large family and lavish spending contributed to his problems. Porter often had to beg and borrow from friends, particularly his former first lieutenant, John Downes. Porter turned to the administration of President Andrew Jackson for help in finding employment. He declined many offers (he considered them below his status) before accepting a post as chargé d'affairs at Constantinople, at a time when America had aspirations of opening up trade with the Ottoman Empire. He held the position from 1831 to 1843, when he died of heart failure, after outliving his faithful *Essex* by six years.

It is unlikely that Porter knew about *Essex*'s last capture—the Dutch smuggler, in 1824. *Essex* finally caught up with her after the long chase and, without cannons, rammed the vessel and carried away her bowsprit. The smuggler broke away, but her captain soon thought better of his actions and struck his flag. *Essex* sent over a boat to take the prize, which was the *Twee Gerusters*, with a crew of thirty-three and 850 bales of tobacco. *Essex* arrived with the smuggler at Kingstown on 18 February. The former Salem frigate, whose captains and crew bravely defended the interests of the young American republic for fifteen years, was down, but not *out*. Before she was to suffer her final ignominy as a prison hulk, she had taken one last prize to add to dozens of others.

Epilogue

"The *Essex*?! Well, for goodness sakes, I've got a print of that hanging in my basement. Come have a look!"

That was frequently the response we got when we told people we were writing this book. We descended into basements, visited grill rooms at men's clubs, and were handed old books with fine engravings. On every single occasion, the *Essex* in question was not our vessel, but a whaleship out of Nantucket that was rammed and sunk by a sperm whale in the Pacific Ocean in 1820. The plight of the vessel was so evocative that Herman Melville used it as the basis for his great opus, *Moby Dick*.

The 238-ton whaler *Essex* went down two thousand miles west of the Galapagos Islands. There was a crew of twenty-one, but only eight survived (by making their way in open boats across the sea toward the South American coast).

The survivors, who had to resort to cannibalism to stay alive, were reunited in Valparaiso, Chile.

There is clearly room on the bookshelves for the two vessels called *Essex,* especially in light of the fact that they have a few things in common. Both tell tales of great adventure in the Pacific. Both have at their core the whaling trade. Owen Chase, author of *Shipwreck of the Whaleship Essex* and a survivor of the disaster, even mentions the importance of Porter's cruise. In Chase's day, as in Porter's, the real danger to whalers was not so much belligerent whales but depredations committed on American merchantmen from rebel forces and pirates spilling off the volatile South American continent. "We require a competent naval force in the Pacific for the protection of this important and lucrative branch of commerce," he wrote. "Captain Porter's skillful, spirited, and patriotic conduct . . . imparted a protection and confidence to our countrymen."

The frigate *Essex*, built exactly 200 years ago, was emblematic of the new American navy, paving the way for the expansion of American commerce in the shipping lanes of the Pacific and beyond. She was the first U.S. man-of-war to round both the Cape of Good Hope and Cape Horn, and she flew her pennant in the Mediterranean. She shepherded convoys. She was part of large U.S. naval squadrons that showed the world that America would not be pushed around. She was a harasser, a thorn in the side to a seemingly omnipotent enemy. And she was a fighter. She was captained by the first fathers of the American navy—Preble, Bainbridge, James Barron, and Porter—and she could boast of a midshipman named David Glasgow Farragut.

The memory of *Essex* and her crewmen lives on. On a grand scale, an entire class of aircraft carriers, vital to victory in World War II, is named after the frigate. The present-day reincarnation of the ship is a forty-thousand-ton amphibious assault carrier christened in 1991. She carries a technological complexity that would have baffled Preble, Bainbridge, and Porter—but only for a moment. The qualities that define success in any naval

DAVID PORTER'S GRAVE IN
WOODLAND CEMETERY IN
PHILADELPHIA.

(JOSEPH MCCLEARY)

battle—courage, leadership, prudence, and fortitude—are timeless.

The memory of the Salem frigate lives on. The National Society of the U.S. Daughters of 1812 erected and continue to maintain a monument in Valparaiso's Protestant Cemetery, dedicated to American crewmen killed in 1814. The city of Valparaiso, Indiana, located in Porter County, is proud to send you a pamphlet describing how the town got its name. During the course of our research, we encountered a woman in search of one of her ancestors, whom she believed to be a doctor aboard *Essex*. And, recently, a retired naval officer, visiting Philadelphia's Woodland Cemetery, came across Porter's grave. After looking over his shoulder to make sure the authorities weren't around, the officer pulled out his flask of fine Scotch whiskey, and took a nip in honor of Captain Porter.

It is hoped that this book will serve to preserve remembrance of all the men who served in the young American navy but especially of those who sailed on *Essex*, the thirty-two-gun Salem frigate.

Bibliography

Allen, Gardner W. *Massachusetts Privateers of the Revolution*. Boston: Massachusetts Historical Society, 1927.

———. *Our Naval War with France*. Boston: Houghton Mifflin, 1909.

Ansted, A. *A Dictionary of Sea Terms*. Glasgow: Brown and Son and Ferguson Ltd., 1933.

Balinky, Alexander. *Albert Gallatin, Fiscal Theories and Polices*. New Brunswick, NJ: Rutgers University Press, 1958.

Bassett, Fletcher. *Legends and Superstitions of the Sea and of Sailors*. Chicago: Belford, Clark and Co., 1885.

Bell, Frederick J. *Room to Swing a Cat, Being Some Tales of the Old Navy*. New York: Longmans, Green and Co., 1938.

Bowen, Frank S. *Men of the Wooden Walls*. London: Staples Press, 1952.

Bradford, James, ed. *Command Under Sail: Makers of American Naval Tradition 1775–1850*. Annapolis: Naval Institute Press, 1985.

Brewington, M. V. *Shipcarvers of North America*. Barre, MA: Barre Publishing Co., 1962.

Brooks, Elbridge S. *The Story of the American Sailor in Active Service on Merchant Vessel and Man-of-War*. Boston: D. Lothrop Company, 1888.

Carr, Albert H. Z. *The Coming of War, An Account of the Remarkable Events Leading to the War of 1812*. Garden City, NY: Doubleday and Co., Inc., 1960.

Chapelle, Howard I. *History of the American Sailing Navy, the Ships, and Their Development*. New York: W.W. Norton and Co., 1949.

Clark, George. *A Short History of the U.S. Navy*. Philadelphia: J. B. Lippincott, 1911.

Clissold, Stephen. *The Barbary Slaves*. New York: Barnes and Noble Books, 1992.

———. *Bernardo O'Higgins and the Independence of Chile*. New York: Frederick A. Prager, 1969.

Coggeshall, George. *History of the American Privateers and Letters of Marque.* New York: published by author, 1856.

Coletta, Paolo E., ed. *American Secretaries of the Navy*. Annapolis: Naval Institute Press, 1980.

Cousins, Frank, and Phil M. Riley. *The Wood-Carver of Salem: Samuel McIntire, His Life and Work*. Boston: Little, Brown and Co., 1916.

Davies, George F. "Robert Smith and the Navy." *Maryland Historical Magazine* 14(4) (December 1919): 305–22.

Donovan, Frank R. *The Tall Frigates*. New York: Dodd, Mead and Company, 1962.

Dudley, William S., ed. *The Naval War of 1812, a Documentary History*. Washington, DC: Naval Historical Center, Department of the Navy, 1985.

Dye, Ira. *The Fatal Cruise of the Argus*. Annapolis: Naval Institute Press, 1994.

Emmons, George F. *The Navy of the United States from the Commencement 1775 to 1853*. Washington, DC: Gideon and Co., 1853.

Folayan, Kola. *Tripoli During the Reigh of Yusuf Pasha Qaramanli*. Ile-Ife, Nigeria: University of Ife Press, 1979.

Forester, C.S. *The Age of Fighting Sail*. Garden City, NY: Doubleday and Co, 1956.

Frere-Cook, Gervis, ed. *Decorative Arts of the Mariner*. London: Cassel and Co., Ltd. 1966.

Guttridge, Leonard F., and Jay D. Smith. *The Commodores*. New York: Harper and Row, 1969.

Horsman, Reginald. *The Causes of the War of 1812*. New York: Octagon Books, 1972.

Hoyt, Edwin P. *America's Wars and Military Excursions*. New York: McGraw-Hill, 1987.

Jackson, Gordon. *The British Whaling Trade*. London: Adam and Charles Black, 1978.

James, William. *Naval Occurrences of the Late War Between Great Britain and the United States of America*. London: T. Egerton Whitehall, 1817.

Kilmarx, Robert A., ed. *America's Maritime Legacy: A History of the U.S. Merchant Marine and Shipbuilding Industry Since Colonial Times*. Boulder, CO: Westview Press, 1979.

Knox, Dudley W., ed. *Naval Documents Related to the Quasi-War Between the United States and France*. Washington, DC: U.S. Government Printing Office, 1935.

———, ed. *Naval Documents Related to the United States Wars with the Barbary Powers*. Washington, DC: U.S. Government Printing Office, 1939.

———. *The Naval Genius of George Washington*. Boston: Riverside Press, 1932.

Laing, Alexander. *American Ships*. New York: American Heritage Press, 1971.

———. *Seafaring America*. New York: American Heritage Publishing, 1974.

Laughton, L. G. Carr. *Old Ship Figureheads and Sterns*. London: Halton and Truscott Smith Ltd., 1925.

Lewis, Charles Lee. *David Glasgow Farragut: Admiral in the Making*. Annapolis: U.S. Naval Institute, 1941.

Long, David F. *Nothing Too Daring, A Biography of Commodore David Porter, 1780–1843*. Annapolis: U.S. Naval Institute, 1970.

Lovette, Lt. Commander Leland P. *Naval Customs, Traditions and Usage*. Annapolis: U.S. Naval Institute, 1939.

Maclay, Edgar Stanton. "Early American Wireless." *American Irish Historical Society Journal*. 8 (1909): 195–202.

Mahon, John K. *The War of 1812*. Gainesville, FL: University of Florida Press, 1972.

Masefield, John. *Sea Life in Nelson's Time*. New York: MacMillan and Co., 1925.

Maxtone-Graham, John. *Safe Return Doubtful: The Heroic Age of Polar Exploration*. New York: Charles Scribner's Sons, 1988.

McKee, Christopher. *A Gentlemanly and Honorable Profession: Creation of the U.S. Naval Officer Corps 1794–1815*. Annapolis: Naval Institute Press, 1991.

———. *Edward Preble, a Naval Biography 1761–1807*. Annapolis: Naval Institute Press, 1972.

Melville, Herman. *White Jacket; or, The World in a Man-of-War*. New York: Harpers, 1850.

Morison, Samuel Eliot. *The Maritime History of Massachusetts 1783–1860*. Boston: Houghton Mifflin, 1941.

Nash, Howard P. *The Forgotten Wars, The Role of the U.S. Navy in the Quasi-War with France and the Barbary Wars 1798–1805*. London: A. S. Barnes and Co., 1968.

Nesser, Robert W. "American Naval Gunnery—Past and Present," *North American Review* 96 (December 1912): 780–91.

———. *Statistical and Chronological History of the United States Navy*. New York: MacMillan, 1909.

Padfield, Peter. *Guns at Sea*. London: Hugh Evelyn, 1973.

Palmer, Michael A. *Stoddert's War: Naval Operations During the Quasi-War with France 1798–1801*. Columbia, SC: University of South Carolina Press, 1987.

Paullin, Charles Oscar. *Commodore John Rodgers*. Annapolis: U.S. Naval Institute, 1909.

Porter, David. *Journal of a Cruise Made to the Pacific by Captain David Porter in the U.S. Frigate Essex in the Years 1812, 1813, and 1814*. New York: Wiley and Halstead, 1822.

Reilly, Robin. *The British at the Gates, the New Orleans Campaign in the War of 1812*. New York: G. P. Putnam's Sons, 1979.

Rippy, J. Fred. *Joel R. Poinsett: Versatile American*. Durham, NC: Duke University Press, 1935.

Robertson-Lorant, Laurie. *Melville: A Biography*. New York: Clarkson Potter, 1996.

Robotti, Frances Diane. *Chronicles of Old Salem, a History in Miniature*. Salem, MA: Newcomb and Gauss Co., 1948.

———. "The U.S. Frigate Essex." *The Nautical Research Journal* (three-part series) 8(6) (November/December 1956): 153–68; 9(1) (January/February 1957): 13–26; 9(2) (March/April 1957): 48–51.

———. *Whaling and Old Salem, A Chronicle of the Sea*. New York: Fountainhead Publishers, 1962.

Roosevelt, Theodore. *The Naval War of 1812*. New York: G. P. Putnam's Sons, 1882.

Shepard, Betty, ed. *Bound for Battle: The Cruise of the United States Frigate Essex in the War of 1812 as Told by Captain David Porter*. New York: Harcourt, Brace and World, 1967.

Sievers, Allen M. *The Mystical World of Indonesia*. Baltimore, Johns Hopkins University Press, 1974.

Spears, John R. *A History of the United States Navy*. New York: Charles Scribner's Sons, 1908.

———. *The Story of the American Merchant Marine*. New York: The MacMillan Co., 1915.

Stackpole, Edouard A. *The Sea Hunters: New England Whalemen During Two Centuries 1635–1835*. New York: Bonanza Books, 1953.

Stevenson, Burton E., ed. *Poems of American History*. Boston: Houghton Mifflin, 1936.

Sweetman, Jack. *American Naval History: An Illustrated Chronology of the U.S. Navy and Marine Corps, 1775–Present*. Annapolis: Naval Institute Press, 1984.

Takakjian, Portia. *Anatomy of a Ship: The 32-gun Frigate Essex 1799*. Cedarburg, WI: Conway Maritime Press, 1990.

Tily, James C., and Thomas Yoseloff. *Uniforms of the U.S. Navy*. New York: A. S. Barnes and Co.,1964.

Tindall, George Brown. *America: A Narrative History*. New York: W. W. Norton and Co., 1984.

Toner, Raymond J. "The Cruise of the Frigate Essex." *American History Illustrated*. 11(9) (January 1977): 4–7, 34–45.

Tucker, Spencer. *Arming the Fleet: U.S. Navy Ordnance in the Muzzle-Loading Era*. Annapolis: Naval Institute Press, 1989.

Turnbull, Archibald D. *Commodore David Porter 1780–1843*. New York: The Century Co., 1929.

Turner, Harriet Stoddert. "Memoirs of Benjamin Stoddert, First Secretary of the Navy." *Columbia Historical Society*, 20 (1917): 141–66.

Valle, James E. *Rocks and Shoals: Order and Discipline in the Old Navy 1800–1861*. Annapolis, Naval Institute Press, 1980.

Van Woerkom, Dorothy O. "Joel R. Poinsett: Patriotic Meddler." *American History Illustrated*, 8(9) (January 1974): 40–46.

Wallace, F.W. *Wooden Ships and Iron Men*. London: White Lion Publishing, 1924.

Whipple, A. B. C. *To the Shores of Tripoli, the Birth of the U.S. Navy and Marines*. New York: William Morrow and Company Inc., 1991.

Wilkinson-Latham, Robert. *British Artillery on Land and Sea 1790–1820*. Newton Abbot: David and Charles, 1973.

Williams, Stanley T. *The Life of Washington Irving*. New York: Oxford University Press, 1935.

Worcester, Donald E. "Sea Power and Chilean Independence." University of Florida Monographs, no. 15 (Summer 1962).

Zimmerman, James F. *Impressment of American Seamen*. Port Washington, NY: Kennikat Press, 1966.

Other sources include the following:

British Library
Historical Society of Pennsylvania
Nantucket Whaling Museum
National Archives, Northeast Regional Branch, New York
New York Public Library—Manuscript and Archives Division
Peabody Essex Museum
Portsmouth Naval Library, Great Britain
Public Record Office, Great Britain
Swem Library, College of William and Mary

Glossary

ABLE SEAMAN. The most senior of the ranks given to seamen in the United States Navy in the nineteenth century. A man with no seafaring experience was rated as a landsman (or boy, if he was under eighteen) on first entering the navy. After learning the basic skills (to hand, reef, and steer), he advanced to ordinary seaman. When he had learned to perform the above skills more proficiently and without supervision, he was promoted to able seaman. The process took about three years. The next step was to become a petty officer.

ARTICLES OF WAR. The basic disciplinary rules that governed the Royal Navy. Every other Sunday at sea, the captain of a Royal Navy ship was required to read aloud the Articles of War to his crew so that no one could claim ignorance through illiteracy. On the other Sundays, a church service was conducted.

BERTH DECK. In a frigate, the deck immediately below the gun deck, so called because this was where most of the crew swung their hammocks at night (i.e., berthed).

BLOCK AND TACKLE Before the middle of the nineteenth century, heavy lifting, pulling, and hauling was done by the brute strength of the crew. In order to assist, ropes were run through combinations of wooden pulleys, called blocks. Such a setup was called a block and tackle.

BRIG. A small vessel with two masts carrying square-rigged sails. A brig was generally larger than a schooner but smaller than a ship.

BROADSIDE. Firing of all the guns on one side of a ship simultaneously for maximum shock effect.

CANISTER. A cylindrical metal container, much like a modern soup can, filled with iron or lead balls. Fired from a cannon, it acted like a huge shotgun.

CARRONADE. A short, light, muzzle-loading gun that fired a heavy round shot at a limited range. Royal Navy sailors nicknamed them "smashers" because of the damage they wreaked.

CARTEL VESSEL. Normally an unarmed merchant ship owned or leased by the government and used to transport exchanged or paroled prisoners of war, under a flag of truce, from their place of confinement to a friendly port.

CLEAR FOR ACTION. A warship preparing for battle took a number of steps to increase fighting efficiency, such as extinguishing all flames and fires, laying out small arms, and spreading sand on the decks to give the gun crews better traction. When these and other steps had been completed, the ship was said to be "cleared for action." A well-trained crew could clear for action in about ten minutes.

COLLIER. A vessel specifically designed and built to carry cargoes of coal. Because coal was such a heavy, dense cargo, colliers were constructed with unusually strong hulls.

COMMODORE. The courtesy title given to a captain commanding a squadron of several ships. In the United States Navy, once a captain had held the title of commodore, he would be addressed as such ever thereafter.

CORDAGE. A naval term that collectively encompassed all the different types of ropes and lines that would be carried in or on a ship.

CORSAIR. A ship fitted out to prey under license on the ships of an enemy, most often applied to vessels belonging to the Barbary States along the North African coast.

FIRMAN. A decree, sanction, or order issued by a Turkish or Oriental ruler or governor.

FIRST LIEUTENANT. A navy officer next in seniority to the captain.

FORECASTLE. The upper deck of a ship forward of the foremast.

FORETOP. A platform located approximately one third of the way up the forward-most mast in a vessel with two or more masts. It was used as a foundation for mounting and spreading rigging and for supporting the other parts of the mast above it. In a three masted ship, the other masts (i.e., the mainmast and mizzenmast) would have similar tops and be named appropriately. In a warship, seamen and marines, armed with muskets, were stationed in the tops to shoot down on the enemy.

FRIGATE. A class of ship employed in almost all navies during the sailing era, a frigate carried three square-rigged masts and was armed with between thirty and forty-nine guns and was known for speed and finesse. Frigates were principally used for scouting, escorting convoys, and commerce raiding and were powerful enough to overwhelm smaller warships.

GROG. An allowance of 90 proof rum, mixed with water, issued daily, on a warship, to all hands eighteen years or older. It was doled out just prior to the noonday meal. Whiskey was sometimes substituted for rum. If he wished, a teetotaler could receive a money allowance instead of grog. The name grog honored the memory of British Admiral Sir Edward Vernon, who was commonly known as "Old Grog," due to the grosgrain cloak he frequently wore.

GUN DECK. In a frigate, the uppermost continuous deck, extending the full length of the ship. It was on this deck that the main battery guns were mounted.

HARDTACK. Also called ship's bread or ship's biscuit, hardtack resembled a large, thick cracker (about four by four inches) and consisted of flour, salt, and yeast mixed with a minimum of water. Long slow baking was used to preserve the biscuit for a long time. By the time it was eaten, a biscuit could be rock hard and infested with weevils. Sailors would frequently rap their biscuits on the table to scare out the beetles.

HULK. An old and otherwise useless ship, usually a former warship, that had been stripped of all masts, rigging, stores, and guns. These vessels, or hulks, were then frequently used as warehouses, barracks, and prisons.

IMPRESS. The term used in Great Britain to describe the lawful process by which British seaman were drafted into the Royal Navy when manpower needs were great and volunteers few. Organized "press gangs" swept through British seaports to secure sailors. At sea, captains could impress sailors from British merchant ships, as long as a bare minimum of hands were left behind to sail the vessel to port.

LANGRADGE A mixture of metal scrap, such as bolts, nails, and iron bars, sewn into a sausage of canvas and fired from a cannon. Cheap and effective, langradge was devastating when fired against masts, sails, rigging, and any sailor unlucky enough to get in the way.

LONG GUN. Another word for cannon, usually used to specifically differentiate a cannon from a carronade. A muzzle-loading large gun of long range carried as the main armament on frigates and ships of the line, from the dawn of naval gunnery until the latter half of the nineteenth century.

MAILBOX. A box or barrel (or any other handy waterproof container) set up in remote ports or deserted islands as an informal way for commanders to exchange letters. It was a very hit-or-miss system, better than nothing, though there was no way to ensure privacy.

MAN-OF-WAR. A warship of whatever size owned and operated by a legitimate government.

MERCHANTMAN. A privately owned ship used for the carrying of cargo and/or passengers.

ORDINARY. A ship not currently needed by its navy but still in too good a condition to sell or scrap was placed "in ordinary." The vessel was stripped of masts, rigging, guns, and stores and moored in an out-of-the-way spot in a port or shipyard. A handful of crewmen were left on board to do routine maintenance. Today such ships are "moth balled."

POUNDER. Before the advent of rifled artillery, the size of guns was described by the weight of the round shot fired, not by the diameter of the bore. A cannon that fired a shot weighing thirty-two pounds was said to be a thirty-two-pounder.

PRIVATEER. A privately owned armed vessel that operated in time of war against the enemy, principally against the enemy's merchant trade. The term *privateer* was derived from combining "private" and "volunteer." The activities of a privateer were made legal by a document called a "letter of marque and reprisal," issued by the government. Without this document, a privateer could be defined as a pirate and the entire crew hanged, if captured. America made great use of privateers during the Revolutionary War and the War of 1812 as a way of augmenting its small navy at little expense.

PRIZE. A captured warship or merchant vessel. Once a specially designated court verified that the prize had been legitimately captured, it could be sold and the proceeds divided among the victorious crew.

PROTECTION. To ward off possible impressment, many American sailors carried documents issued by United States magistrates and consuls to prove their true nationality. Such a document was called a protection. Many Royal Navy officers, in their zeal to impress any likely looking sailor, ignored these documents, claiming that they were bogus. In truth, many were.

QUARTER DECK. In a sailing ship, that portion of the uppermost deck aft of the mainmast. This is generally where the ship's wheel was located and where the officer of the deck stood his watch in order to direct the movements of the ship. This is also where the captain stationed himself during a battle.

REEF. When the wind increased significantly, a ship had to reduce the area of exposed sail or risk damage to masts and rigging. To do this the sails were reefed. Most large square sails were equipped with horizontal rows of short lengths of rope, called reef points. To take a reef in a sail, the sail was hauled part way up to its yard and the reef points tied together over the top of the yard. This action could reduce the amount of exposed sail by 25 to 75 percent, depending on which row of reef points was used.

RIGGING. The web of ropes and lines on a ship that supported the masts and controlled the sails.

SCHOONER. A vessel (usually of rather small size) with two or more masts rigged with fore and aft sails and handled by a very small crew.

SHIP OF THE LINE. A battleship in the age of sailing ships, it carried between fifty and more than one hundred guns.

SLOOP-OF-WAR. A warship carrying three masts yet slightly smaller than a frigate.

SPERMACETI. A white wax-like substance taken from the oil in the head of a sperm whale and used in making cosmetics, ointments, and candles.

SPRING. When at anchor, a sailing ship points into the wind like a weather vane. To turn the ship, a line was run from the capstan out through some opening near the stern and then made fast to the anchor line as near to the anchor as possible. This line was called a spring. By hauling in on the spring, the ship could be turned toward whatever side the spring tended in spite of the wind.

SUBSCRIPTION. A practice in the United States and some foreign countries in which private individuals (usually maritime traders) or local governments raised the money to build a warship that was then presented to the national government. Subscription was employed in the United States during the decade of the 1790s, when the American navy was being slowly rebuilt from scratch.

Salem Subscribers to Essex

Elias Hasket Derby	Merchant	$10,000
William Gray Jr.	Merchant	10,000
John Norris	Merchant	5,000
William Orne	Merchant	5,000
Ebenezer Beckford	Merchant	2,000
Samuel Gray	Merchant	2,000
Johnathan Neal	Shipmaster	2,000
Aaron Wait		
Jerathmiel Peirce	Merchants	2,000
Benjamin Pickman	Merchant	1,650
John Jenks	Dry Goods Shopkeeper	1,550
Richard Derby Jr.	Shipmaster	1,500
Joseph Peabody	Merchant	1,500
Benjamin Pickman Jr.	Merchant	1,500
Nathaniel West	Merchant	1,500
Jacob Ashton	Merchant	1,000
Ezekiel Derby	Merchant	1,000
John Derby	Merchant	1,000
George Dodge	Merchant	1,000
Richard Manning	Capitalist	1,000

Ichabod Nichols	Merchant	1,000
John Osgood	Merchant	1,000
Stephen Phillips	Shipmaster	1,000
William Prescott	Lawyer	1,000
Benjamin Goodhue	U.S. Senator	800
Edward Holyoke	Physician	800
Joshua Ward	Distiller	750
John Barr	Merchant	600
Stephen Webb	Shipmaster	600
Samuel Buffum		
John Howard	Sailmakers	550
Edward Allen Jr.	Shipmaster 500	
Joseph Cabot	Merchant	500
Benjamin Carpenter	Merchant	500
Clifford Crowninshield	Shipmaster	500
Israel Dodge	Distiller	500
Benjamin Hodges	Merchant	500
Daniel Jenks	Dry Goods Shopkeeper	500
James King	Bank Cashier	500
Abel Lawrence	Distiller	500
John Murphy	Shipmaster	500
Isaac Osgood	Gentleman	500
Thomas Perkins	Merchant	500
Joshua Richardson	Merchant	500
Thomas Sanders	Merchant	500
John Treadwell	Shop Owner	500
William Ward	Shipmaster	500
Joseph Waters	Merchant	460
Upton and Porter	Merchants	400
Elias Hasket Derby Jr.	Shipmaster	300
Joseph Hiller	Collector of the Port	300
William Luscomb	House and Ship Painter	300
Edmund Upton	Shipmaster	300
William Marston	West India Merchant	250
Nathan Peirce	Merchant	250
Benjamin West	Shipmaster	250

John Hathorne	Dry Goods Shopkeeper	200
Peter Lander	Shipmaster	200
Richard Manning Jr.	Blacksmith	200
John Pickering	Register of Deeds	200
Joseph Vincent	Ropemaker	200
Thomas Webb	Shipmaster	200
Samuel Archer	Hardware Merchant	100
Thomas Bancroft	Clerk of the Courts	100
Walter Bartlett	Auctioneer	100
John Beckett	Boatbuilder	100
Thomas Chipman	Shipmaster	100
John Daland	Storekeeper	100
Ephraim Emmerton	Merchant	100
Benjamin Felt	Pump and Blockmaker	100
Edward Killin	Shopkeeper	100
Edward Lang	Apothecary	100
Samuel McIntire	Carpenter	100
Joseph Mosely	Shipmaster	100
Joseph Newhall	Tinsmith	100
Page and Ropes	Ship Chandlers	100
Brackley Rose	Sugar Baker	100
Elijah Sanderson	Cabinetmaker	100
Jacob Sanderson	Cabinetmaker	100
Moses Townsend	Shipmaster	100
Samuel Very	Baker	100
Benjamin Webb Jr.	Shipmaster	100
Michael Webb	Grocer	100
Timothy Wellman Jr.	Shipmaster	100
William Appleton	Cabinetmaker	50
Nathaniel Batchelder	Shopkeeper	50
Enos Briggs	Shipbuilder	50
Samuel Brooks	Merchant	50
Thomas Cushing	Editor, *Salem Gazette*	50
James Gould	Gun Carriage Maker	50
Jonathan Mason	Merchant	50
John Morong	Trader	50

Henry Osborn	Storekeeper	50
David Patten	Shipmaster	50
Asa Peirce	Tailor	50
Samuel Ropes Jr.	Trader	50
Isaac Williams	Apothecary	50
Jonathan Lambert	Shipmaster	40
Jonathan Waldo	Trader	40
Joseph Osgood	Shipmaster	25
Asa Killam	Lumber Dealer	20
Edmund Gale	Shopkeeper	10

Acknowledgments

This book could not have been written without the assistance of a number of people. First and foremost, we thank Retired Naval Officer and Active Naval Historian Joseph McCleary, who provided essential assistance in helping two landlubbers get their sea legs as we cruised with *Essex* and her commanders and whose readings of the text provided us with many insights; Professor Christopher McKee at Grinnell College, who was extremely generous in sharing his calculations on David Porter's prize money, as well as his insights into the distribution of and rules governing prize money in general; the late Lt. William Bushby of Salem, Massachusetts, and the late Lieutenant Colonel M.E.S. Lawes of Sussex, England, who assisted with thorough research, as did Mr. Graham K. Salt, who scoured libraries and record offices in England for much valuable material. We are also indebted to our editor at Adams, Jere Calmes, for his unbridled enthusiasm (if Porter had only had him at Valparaiso!). Claudia Jew at the Mariners' Museum in Newport News, Virginia, provided timely aid with illustrations. Finally, we thank our friends and families for their help, patience, encouragement, and tolerance as we described for hours on end the pitfalls of carronades.

— FRANCES DIANE ROBOTTI &
JAMES VESCOVI

Index

NOTE: Bold page numbers indicate illustrations